17

The death and life of Private Jason Stuart Burt

born Tuesday, July 28, 1964
died Saturday, June 12, 1982

by Mark Higgitt

Published by Many Heroes
Copyright © Mark Higgitt 2015
All rights reserved
ISBN 978-0-9933003-2-5

CONTENTS

Foreword		4
Chapter 1	The uninvited guest	5
Chapter 2	Best friends	7
Chapter 3	Make or break	6
Chapter 4	Road to Brize Norton	17
Chapter 5	Leaps of faith	25
Chapter 6	Crows off to war	33
Pictures		49
Chapter 7	South	54
Chapter 8	Going in	67
Chapter 9	Breakout to Teal Inlet	81
Chapter 10	Advance to Longdon	88
Chapter 11	Longdon	109
Pictures		121
Chapter 12	Minor details	129
Chapter 13	The long goodbye	156
Chapter 14	Letting go	170
Chapter 15	Seventeen	190
Chapter 16	The fog of war	189
Pictures		200
Chapter 17	Epilogue	205
3 Para Mount Longdon Roll of Honour		210

Pictures: All are credited where the source is known

Front cover: The spot where Ian McKay fell on Longdon, with Joe Varney's portrait of Jason inset

FOREWORD

Jason Burt was frozen and frightened – and still around two months shy of his 18th birthday – the split-second he answered the call to 'Charge!' and ran, head on, at an Argentinian .50 cal machinegun post during the final days of the Falklands War.

At about 2am on Saturday, June 12, 1982.

An icy night of hell on the God-forsaken summit of Mount Longdon.

The other side of the world. Eight-thousand miles from home.

That's when, and where, he died.

At the age of 17.

Seventeen.

I happened on his story by chance. And the way it came to me made one thought unavoidable – that it was time to his story was told.

I just didn't expect it to take so long to tell.

CHAPTER 1

THE UNINVITED GUEST

When two Army officers turn up at your Petticoat Lane market stall, to tell you that your 17-year-old son has been killed in one of the bloodiest battles of modern times, and you ask how he died, it doesn't matter how hard the breaking of the news might be, it doesn't matter how badly bogged down the answer remains in admin and an 8,000-mile communication chain dragging from the wintry South Atlantic, the last thing you expect to hear is that such facts are "a minor detail".

When white flags are replaced by Union Flags in Port Stanley, a few days later, and the nation celebrates, and his face stares out from the pages of newspapers honouring his remarkable courage, you wonder why the Army still hasn't told you more.

When a national red-top puts his name in lights, leaking the word of an "inside source" that he's been recommended for a Victoria Cross, your broken hearts cling to the headline, to something slender that will allow to measure your devastating loss.

When his mates come home and tell the same story, that he's fallen storming a machinegun position with his platoon sergeant, you cling a little more.

And, when his closest pal visits, to commiserate, and tells you that's not how he fell….
well, what do you believe?
  Then, the headlines stop.
  His name and his deeds slip into the farthest recesses of the nation's consciousness.
  And the 'truth' you crave suddenly seems further away than ever.

War stories – real war stories – are like this.
  Put five men in the same room, bombard their senses for five minutes, and then ask them what's happened. Some details will tally, but you'll hear five different stories.
  Ask them again, five minutes later, and the ground will shift. The gaps between those

accounts will shrink or grow, imperceptibly or otherwise.

Ask them again, 20 years on, and which story will they tell then?

There is any number of possibilities.

The one that sight, sound, smell, touch and taste imprinted on their minds as things happened, until their brains reached overload?

Maybe the tale they first told, in the immediate aftermath of the battle, perhaps as the trauma of those five minutes subsided, perhaps as it raced towards a peak?

Or the one they've trimmed and smoothed over time, that makes things neat and understandable, that fits the facts as they believe them?

Or the one that spares feelings? Theirs. Yours. Your family's....

Seventeen. Only 17.

CHAPTER 2
BEST FRIENDS

Jason Stuart Burt was born on Tuesday, July 28, 1964, the first son of Syd, an imposingly built, jack-the-lad Jewish market trader whose days shuttled between Petticoat Lane, his favourite East End sauna, the pub, the bookies and home, and Terry, an Irish beauty with twinkling eyes that disguised a firm mind and the stoutest heart you'll ever encounter.

Spend more than a few minutes talking about young Jason with his family, and what takes shape before your eyes is a lad who was his mum's best friend but desperate not to be like his old man.

Unpick the memories of friends, and you could be talking about any youngster, anywhere, any time.

The penchant for designer tops, Lacoste motifs, Sunday football in the park, bunking off school to go fishing, stray cats, wrestling with his cousin Jackie, summer nights at Highams Park Youth Club, accident-prone, snooker, sneaky drinks, sneaky fags, his father's willful, bloody-minded streak, his mother's film-star looks, clandestine trips to watch his beloved Chelsea play at Stamford Bridge.... The list goes on.

Women like his Aunty Kay saw him as "one of those sons that you'd be proud of".

Neighbours like Jean Court recall a scrawny lad, "like an angel".

Girls like Linda Jennings wanted to hold his hand and look into his eyes.

Mates like Tony Layton just wanted to keep on having a laugh.

Then, one day, he walked into an Army Recruiting Office and took the Queen's Shilling.

Linda met him at school, when they were 14. She can't remember how they struck up their friendship. They were in the same year, but not the same class. Whatever, she remembers, they eventually became a kind of unofficial 'couple'.

"Girlfriend, boyfriend," she smiles. "I remember a couple of times going out with Mark Ayres and one of my friends, Karen Robinson.

"I lived right by the North Circular. All the other girls had their official boyfriends, but we were never an official couple. He was always popular with the girls, not because they all wanted to be his girlfriend. He was very gentle. He was lovely. If you went out, he'd tell you that you looked lovely and he'd open the door and stuff.

"He wasn't going to be a scholar," she laughs this time, and taps a small, blue bundle of letters on her lap. "I never knew what his ambitions were. Whenever we went out, we didn't want to talk about that sort of thing. He'd talk about football. Looking back now, when I think about children who are that age, I can't believe it. Looking at his letters, he never had the highest educational standards. But he coped with the interviews, so it was incredibly brave. Full stop."

The interviews. Ah. It's a day Syd and Terry never forgot.

Jason had wanted to be in the police, but he was too short. At 15, he was only a couple of inches over five feet two. To join the Met, you had to be much taller than that. So, out of the blue, a couple of months before he turned 16, he took himself off to that recruiting office for an interview to join the Parachute Regiment.

"I'll hear in about eight or nine weeks," he announced to his family that night. "As far as I know, I've passed everything."

He received a letter in the June, to the delight of his proud headmaster at George Monoux School. But not Syd and Terry. They were aghast.

"I always blamed myself," Syd admitted for years afterwards, whenever the opportunity to beat himself up arose. "I refused to sign for him and he turned round and said: 'If you don't....'"

Syd tore up the papers and threw them on the floor. But Jason had a spare set.

"I said 'What are you going to do?' He said 'If you don't sign, when I get to 18 I'll walk out of this door and you'll never see me again'."

"We'll say your brother knocked coffee over the papers," Terry clutched at a straw.

Syd snapped. Then he signed.

"Right, you skinny sod," he announced. "In three months, you'll come crawling back asking me to buy you out of the Army."

But he didn't.

CHAPTER 3

MAKE OR BREAK

From that day on, Jason never explained why he was joining the Army. Not to his family. Not to his friends.

On Tuesday, September 9, 1980, just 63 days after his sixteenth birthday, he made his way to Waterloo Station, alone, and headed for Aldershot.

Mark Eyles-Thomas was on the same train, but he didn't meet Jason until they'd settled in. Then again, there were lots of lads heading the same way. At Aldershot station, almost every passenger climbed out and lugged their suitcases to the exit, where they were met by a corporal bawling for any young man awaiting transport for Depot Para.

One by one, they gave their names and watched him thumb down his list, pausing only to observe the fashions and hairstyles before ordering them to "Get on the wagon outside".

At Browning Barracks, Depot the Parachute Regiment, they reported to another corporal who had his own list informing him which Junior Parachute Company platoon each new recruit was assigned to.

Jason was in 3 Platoon. So was Mark Eyles-Thomas. As they settled in, one potential point of contention was sorted. Mark was known by his family at home as Jason, his other name. He quickly ditched both, in favour of Tommy, to avoid confusion.

Home for the next few weeks of discovery would be the top floor of Queripel VC block, which also acted as their introduction to the importance of regimental history. Each block was named after a renowned Para soldier or a Victoria Cross holder. In his case, Capt Queripel had won his VC posthumously at Arnhem in 1944.

Each floor had six rooms. Each room had six beds on one side of a partition, and six the other. There was also the Platoon Office, an NCO's bunk, a store and the washroom.

Tommy recalls that the room was empty when he walked in. Each bed and locker was already marked with a surname. He nosed around and, in a corner by the window, saw 'Scrivens' written in chinagraph. He rubbed out the 'ens' and stretched out on his bed to wait for the others.

Ian Scrivens was the first to turn up, a 6ft skinhead wearing a bomber jacket, and drainpipe jeans cut to the top of his 10-hole black Docs, one of which had a bright yellow lace, and the other red. He looked at the locker with his name on it.

"My name's not Scriv," he told Tommy. "It's Scrivens."

When everyone had arrived, they were told to stand in the corridor. Then they met their guardians – four corporals (non-commissioned officers), one sergeant (Senior Non-Commissioned Officer) and a Lieutenant (Officer). The platoon was broken into four sections, each commanded by a corporal. The sergeant would oversee the corporals and the Lieutenant was in overall command.

The Platoon Commander was Lt Neil Young, a blond man whose educated voice and immaculate good looks underlined his action man charisma. Word was he'd been the young commander of a 2 Para platoon at Warrenpoint, in 1979, when the IRA had blown up a vehicle full of Paras. As medics arrived, a second bomb went off, killing 18 soldiers.

Cpl Tom Camp was 4 Section's commander, and the sergeant was Ossie Howells, a man whose reputation as one of the hardest men in 3 Para soon did the rounds.

"He had a weathered look," Tommy recalls. In the coming weeks, the recruits would become used to a demeanour that was nothing like the brutal stories told about him. He had an enticing calmness about him that made the lads want to know more and – crucially – want to be respected by him.

"It was obvious he was held in high regard by all of the other SNCOs and NCOs at Depot Para," Tommy told me.

The legend included holding the record for having the most fights when 3 Para were serving in Germany, and 'winning' them all. In one scrap, apparently, he'd been stabbed in his right arm, restricting his ability to salute officers by the drill movement. He adopted a version of the salute, and no one ever said anything to him about it.

Another of the NCOs was Spider Webb. He'd been blown up in the Warrenpoint massacre, in Northern Ireland. It left him with what Tommy described as a "grotesque" hand that looked like it belonged to someone else, a scar on his face, a false eye, and a habit of kicking into a raging fit around midnight, after an evening at the pub. NCOs had to come from other blocks to calm him down.

"He wanted to kill people. Now that was two doors away from you," Tom says. If nothing else, it taught them when to shut up and stay out of arm's reach.

If the new recruits hadn't realised before they stepped off the train that they were about to be immersed in that world, such tales must have set them thinking.

The first week was spent completing documentation, having the mandatory crew-cut and receiving uniform issue. Tommy also acquired his nickname. His full name is Mark Jason Eyles-Thomas, but he was known by his family as Jason. To avoid confusion with Jason Burt, he became known as Tommy. Just as quickly, they were taught how to wash, iron and wear all their kit. Anyone who failed to present himself in a manner acceptable to the inspecting NCO or Officer, each morning and afternoon, was severely punished.

There were regular helpings of physical training, but the immediate objective was for the corporals to teach the Platoon drill and ensure that the Platoon passed off the square. That was a big thing because, not only were they in competition with the other Platoons, the corporals had their own side bets going.

Satisfying the Company Sergeant Major – a Warrant Officer – and the Officer Commanding Junior Company – a Major – wasn't easy and led to many a beasting being handed out to the unco-ordinated, bet-losing offenders.

Eventually, though, they succeeded and were allowed to wear the regiment's maroon beret with a small, blue plastic backing behind the cap badge. It showed they were junior soldiers, still some months and many difficult days from being the real McCoy.

For some of the 16-year-olds, this was as far as they'd go. Para Reg wasn't for them. It meant they were soon down to four in a room – but Jason, Tommy, Neil and Scrivs remained.

Just before six every night, the duty NCO would escort Junior Company to the NAAFI to watch the TV news and keep abreast of world events. It was a pain in the neck. Apart from Mondays, that is, when it was an acceptable alternative to reporting to the gym for 'milling'.

Milling was the regiment's term for two individuals knocking seven shades out of each other for two minutes, under what was defined as a "controlled environment", though I'm not sure what the controls were. They'd have to demonstrate their ability to fight, with maximum aggression and a determined will to win, to the complete satisfaction of the Physical Training staff. Anyone who failed had to fight again, or face being branded a wimp who wasn't suitable for the regiment.

Jason and Neil were small lads, compared with some like Scrivs, but they quickly learned that milling was about what they had inside, not the exterior.

Jason fought every single Monday night. He had to. What they learned was how to find that primitive things inside that allowed them to bring on the red mist as if they were switching on a light.

It wasn't all as brutal, though. There was a vast amount of Adventure Training, including canoeing, climbing, abseiling, potholing, navigational exercises, sailing and hiking.

When Tommy harks back, it isn't long before he thinks of all the parents at home, worried about their sons but oblivious to the transformation that had taken place in Aldershot over those first few weeks.

Being around that violence all the time – the NCOs, every door being smashed open, aggression, aggression, aggression, from being woken up by a screaming command at five in the morning to climbing back in again – was obviously designed to take its toll.

"There's no way you'd want to piss these guys off," he said. "So, you've quickly got to get used to living with that."

Were there lines the NCOs wouldn't be prepared to cross?

"Yeah. There were lines, obviously…," he says, then laughs. "No, there weren't lines. They could do anything they wanted to you!

That often meant a recruit leaning with his back against the wall in a squatting position. You can only keep it up for so long. A full screw (corporal) would bet a mate that his section could beat theirs. The lads would be left squatting for ages, with the corporal patrolling the line, asking questions like 'Thomas, you're not going to let me down, are you?'

There was a purpose.

"You understand the aggression, and that the shouting is for one thing," Tommy says. "It's so that, when they say 'Red on, green on, go!' you'll jump out of the plane, it's going to be instant. You'll deal with it."

There'd come a time, once they were with their battalions, when the shouting would stop, when the lieutenants would be referred to as 'Boss!' But that wouldn't happen for a while and, when it did, only those who'd made it all the way would know the feeling of arrival and achievement.

Their mates. The reason they were taught to look after themselves, their feet, their weapon, ammunition, rations, water and so on wasn't general housekeeping. It was to make sure they'd be fully functional and able to provide an oppo with covering fire.

"If my feet are bad, you haven't got covering fire. I've let you down," Tommy explains it.

The other purpose was the principle of last man standing.

FRV is Para-speak for 'final rendezvous'. Throughout training, they'd have several RVs on the way to an objective, where kit and individuals would be checked and info passed around. The FRV is the last before the objective is undertaken.

If a reconnaissance met an ambush, and they had to 'bug out', they'd make their way back to the FRV and await the others. If no one else turned up, they'd go back through each RV, waiting a period of time for the other members. It didn't matter whether an officer was with them. The sharing of information meant that whoever reached the lines – possibly the newest Tom, on his own – the intelligence gathered would end up where it was needed.

If they ever came near forgetting it, the weekly regimental history lessons were a constant reminder. Tommy still tells the story today of Arnhem, where Paras extracted themselves from their positions, as and when they could, and found their orders posted on a church door. In essence, the message was 'make your way back to Blighty. See you back there'.

In the 80s, the Cold War, they were expecting to be dropped into Europe somewhere, probably behind enemy lines and on top of the actual objective. They weren't anticipating standing up and walking across miles of open land to get there, but making their way 'home', 200 miles away, was a different matter.

One of the books telling the story of Longdon, after the Falklands War, was called *Green-Eyed Boys*. It reflects the fact that, in common with many of their predecessors, some older members of the Regiment held Nazi Germany's elite SS troops in high regard, not for their political beliefs, but for their physical and mental prowess as warriors. Not everyone shared the view. Far from it. Tommy says the youngsters weren't in Aldershot long before they became aware of it, though he remains sceptical how big a part the culture of so-called 'green-eyed' violence played in Para life as he and Jason experienced it.

"What I'm saying is that, from Juniors, from Week 1, all it is is violence," he said. "Para Reg and the Army has changed dramatically, with everyone writing to their local MP. There was none of that when we was there. It was a hard regiment. The regimental history that we went through would always pick out the individuals who'd done this and done that. And you were the next batch waiting to do 'that'.

"Because you're young, you're all aspiring to be men. It's something you want to do. You worry about failing"

The 'green-eyed' culture, he says, played no part in what was yet to come on Longdon.

"The violence you're talking about, the majority of time, is fists, personal aggression. The violence at Longdon... it doesn't matter how many fists you've got, or how you throw them, it isn't going to stop the rounds."

Dear Linda....
November 5, 1980

By the way when you write back if it is alright could you please send a photo of yourself. By the way if you want I will send you a photo of me in uniform. I'll have to get a film for the camera first.
They asked me to go to Oxford University, but I turned it down. I still haven't made my mind up if I'm staying in. It gets harder every day. Do you know Andrew Holderness. Well his getting out before Christmas. They really muck you about. Lately we have had to stay in in the evenings for inspection. You get sick of it after a while....

Fitness and soldiering soon became the focus. To become fully-fledged Paras, they'd have to carry equipment, complete the mission and, if the situation called for it, be fit enough to walk home, under their own steam and initiative.

Their path to that level of fitness began with a gentle 'road walk and run'. Within weeks, they were doing it in webbing belt order, which means carrying the 35lbs of ammunition, food and water worn around the waist by a soldier going into battle. Runs grew till they hit the 10-miler that had to be completed within two hours, wearing boots, combat jacket and helmet, as well as carrying a 7.62 Self Loading Rifle, another 9lbs.

A Para's move on foot is known as 'tabbing', Tactical Advance to Battle, a combination of running and – when dictated by the terrain – walking extremely fast. Tabs were done daily and soon included, in addition to belt order, the bergens that housed all the essentials for surviving in the open.

In addition to 'tabbing', fitness periods would include the assault course, steeplechase, telegraph pole races, stretcher races, swimming and gruelling gymnasium sessions.

Fieldcraft, weaponry, survival techniques, first aid, marksmanship principles, communication equipment, theatres of warfare, unarmed combat and section/platoon attacks – their personal soldiering skills – were practised relentlessly.

Regular range days and live firing required each soldier to demonstrate his ability with all the platoon weapons. It was a formidable list.

There was his personal SLR, a semi-automatic rifle (range between 100-600m), the General Purpose Machine Gun (range up to 1800m in Sustained Fire Role), the Light Machine Gun, the Browning 9mm semi-automatic hand held pistol, the 9mm Sub Machine Gun, the 84mm Carl Gustav anti-tank weapon, the 66mm disposable anti-tank rocket launcher and hand grenades, all the things most parents wouldn't trust most 16-year-olds to touch.

Regimental history included where the regiment had fought, the battle honours it had won, the individuals who'd shown exceptional courage, the medals awarded and the lessons learned. At every turn, the regimental motto *Utrinque Paratus* (Ready for Anything) was reinforced. Other regiments and corps issued their berets in basic training because it was worthless – a 'crap hat'. Hence, to a Para, all other soldiers in the British Army who weren't Parachute Regiment were 'crap hats', or plain and simple 'hats'.

The coveted maroon beret, smock and wings had to be earned at different stages of training. They were never just issued.

If the recruits ever forgot just what levels of fitness and courage were required to be part of the elite fighting force, the high drop-out rate in Junior Parachute Company was a daily reminder. It made lads like Jason, Tommy, Scrivs, Baz and Grose feel special, a cut above the rest, even if most had days when they felt like quitting.

Dear Linda....
November 13, 1980

I was pleased to hear from you. You asked in your letter whether I went for a run on Saturday. Well I did, I went up the forts, got half way up there and run back at twice the speed because it

17: The death and life of Private Jason Burt

was to dark for me. After that I went down the dogs....
At this moment I don't to stay in the Army. Sometimes I think to myself what am I doing here. If I do get out I will be getting out after Christmas. Will you do me a favour and not tell anyone. As it goes, I don't know why I'm telling you. Maybe because I still like you a very lot.

By now, the lads were drinking and pulling partners. A night out quickly slipped into a familiar routine. They would stroll into the local disco as if they owned the place, knowing that Jase's swarthy movie star looks would have the female heads turning. After a quick recce of the talent, they'd agree who the lucky ladies were going to be and, whether they were accompanied or not, set about the 'mission'.

"Jase and I would ask them whether they wanted a drink or a dance," Tommy recalls "He'd do the talking and I'd take his lead. Should the boyfriend take umbrage, I'd also initiate the milling. Should it get out of hand, as it often did, Scrivs would step in and, from that moment, the thing would resemble a cowboy saloon bar."

One night in Ashburton, deepest Devon, almost the whole of Junior Para was fighting. Nights like it would be relayed to the NCOs, who'd egg them on. If the police were called, or it was reported to the Officer Commanding, they'd be bollocked – not for fighting, a prerequisite for a Para, but for being caught.

Whether they realised it or not, they were finding out about themselves and each other, the strengths and weaknesses, who could be relied upon, who needed help. And, as the recruits bonded, life in the block hit a high pitch and the characters emerged.

Motown fanatic Scrivs – a 6ft skinhead, hard as iron – would play Smokey Robinson's *Tears of a Clown* over and over, and prance around like Bambi.

Baz worshipped The Stranglers and was happy to give anyone within a two-mile radius a headache.

The Army's love of shortening things applied to surnames. Tommy's new nickname was shortened further to Tom. Neil's names were already short, so no one saw the need for change. There was nothing sinister about the fact that he was called simply 'Grose', Tommy says.

Dear Linda....
12 Jan, 1981

Weather is lovely. Wish you were here.... I found that this Xmas went really fast. Sorry I didn't take you out over Xmas.... I am coming down on Saturday. I might pop in and see you, then you can have a good laugh at my haircut. I have been in the Army now 5 months. Doesn't time fly when your having fun. The first week I was back I was really fed up and told my corporal that I wanted to get out but he said give it a bit longer but I think I will stay in now. I'm determined to now....

Did you make any new year resolutions. I couldn't think of any. I did make just one little one, that is to stick the Army.

Dear Linda....
Feb 81

We had the assault course yesterday and we had to climb up a net about 20 ft up and two people fell but they weren't badly hurt. I'm beginning to enjoy myself again now. Out of the 204 people that joined in September there are 61 of us left. Just think, at the end of October I would have done my 8 jumps. I don't think I'll look forward to my first jump, which is out of a balloon 800 feet....

A couple of my mates are going to Butlins in June to help out with the entertainment and sports. I was asked to go but you miss as lot of training. To tell the truth, I've done quite well because we had exams in weapons and I passed on all 3 weapons....

As the Juniors prepared to transfer to Recruit Company, only 60 or so of the 200 who'd stepped off the wagons on September 9 were left. Jase, Tommy, Scrivs and Grose were in the first 30 to walk across to Ridgway Block – named after a Para who'd sailed solo across the Atlantic – and joined 476 Platoon, along with 30 raw recruits from Civvie Street, in September, 1981. A week later, 477 Platoon did the same.

Dear Linda....
9th July, 1981

At the moment I am on guard. At the moment I'm trying to make it a long letter, if you promise to right a long letter in return. You wanted to know what recruit Company was. Well that is from the age of 16 to 17. When you are 17 you are then classed as an adult soldier....
I go on my final exercise as a junior on Saturday, which I won't enjoy because we are doing flotation, which is packing all your kit air tight and swim across the lake in full kit, this is at night as well. I should be coming home a week Saturday, so I'll probably pop in and see you....
I've now been in the Army 10 months exactly today. To tell you the truth, I never thought I'd stick it this long. Neither did a lot of people. My mum and dad said I'd be out after a month. But I proved them wrong. If I had the choice I would have never come in, but I'll definitely stick this regiment. If I don't I'll join the Royal Marines or the Militry Police....

CHAPTER 4

ROAD TO BRIZE NORTON

Jason was still only 16 when he and the other 60 or so survivors of Junior Para moved to Recruit Company, where they joined lads of 17 who were fresh from the streets, cul-de-sacs, towns and cities of the nation.

Those 60 young men had wrapped their minds and bodies round the violence of milling, the threat of beasting, the grinding hell of the assault course, and the seemingly endless reference to regimental history, and somehow emerged with their spirit, determination and – crucially – the satisfaction of their instructors in one piece.

If they'd seen them, Linda's letters revealed more than Syd and Terry Burt would perhaps have gleaned about his mind-set during that period.

Their officer was Lt. Young, the man who'd taken them through Junior Company. Their SNCO was a Sgt Bradshaw, a terrifying man who – according to Tommy – bawled at everyone, wore an SAS smock and appeared as if he'd just spent four years in the woods, living off the land.

"You all look too cocky, as if you could go straight to your battalions. How would you fancy that, Thomas?" Lt Young asked them outside the block before the transfer. There were one or two cocky replies. Tommy offered one.

"Not quite," he replied, and January 22, 1982, when Recruit Company officially ended for the survivors, suddenly seemed beyond the furthest horizon.

Then he made them remove the blue plastic Junior Para backings from their cap badges and swap them for green ones, denoting Recruit Company. They wouldn't lose these until Week 12, and then only if they completed P Company – pre-parachute selection – and all the tests of soldiering and weaponry that came before.

P Company's one of the hardest physical and mental tests in the Army. It's designed to take an individual beyond his limits. Jason, Tommy and the rest knew that anyone who fell short could either join Retraining Platoon, and face torture twice, transfer to a 'hat' regiment, or quit the Army totally.

For P Company survivors, the reward would be Brecon, three weeks of advanced tactical training. Those who passed would be allowed to wear their parachute smock and look forward to four weeks parachute training at Brize Norton. Then there'd be the small matter of eight successful jumps – one balloon and seven aircraft – before the fabled wings would be issued. The pictures on Jason's bedroom wall remain his mother's permanent record of the lads in training.

It was that first march across to Recruit Company that first left them feeling like real soldiers. And making it into Recruit Company was all about passing P Company, nothing else. That simple.

Dear Linda....
9/9/81

Thanks for your letter which I got today. Glad to hear you got your O-level in accounts or whatever. What day do you start college. By the way who are you going out with now. Have you been up the club lately. On the 18th of this month we go down to Brecon for a week. When we go there we have got two runs, one 16 miles and one 7 miles.
I should be home on Saturday, By the way, have you noticed I'm getting more words on a line. Have you thought about your holidays for next year. If I pass my training and get the battalion I want to go to, I go to N Ireland in May....
Sorry that it's a short letter. Bye for now.
Love Jason xx
PS It is now Monday, so I'll carry on with the letter. By the time it reaches you I would have been in Brecon a couple of days.
You looked so happy Saturday standing there working so hard. I've got one month left now before I take my tests to see if I pass out of the Depot. We do what you call P. Company which lasts 3 days. On the first day you have to go in the ring and fight for a minute and in the afternoon you do a 10-miler with 35 pound of weight in 1 hour 45 minutes. Then on the second day you do a 7 and a half stretcher race in 75 minutes and then you do the assault course steeple chase and a log race. By the way I had a good chat with your mum. I must go now. By the way I will put a photo in, I hope it doesn't frighten you to much.

They knew each week would be broken down into modules that had to be completed with a grade good enough for them to progress. The Junior Para lads had missed the first four weeks while the raw recruits learned about square-bashing and built their general fitness.

The drop-out rate among the new arrivals was very high. If more than 10 of them passed to join the Junior Para lads at the start of Week 5 – and the start of a month of soldiering and intensive physical training – it would be surprising.

Within days, Ridgway Block was full of backs covered with bergen burns, webbing sores and blistered feet. The burns and sores would be smothered with talcum powder and covered with a dressing. Blisters would be popped, powdered and dressed. No one wanted to miss a run, for fear of being back-squadded – made to repeat that passage of training – or worse still, binned to join the 170 or so youngsters who'd already headed home from Aldershot since September 1980, deemed to be lacking one or more vital ingredients.

The fearsome 'trainasium' is a legendary course designed to build confidence and test a recruit's head for heights. The lattice of scaffold and planks are littered with obstacles, illusion jumps, scramble nets and catwalks. Its pinnacle is a 20ft gap, 45 feet up, which is crossed by walking on two 'shuffle bars'. Each has staggered attachments, meaning the recruit has to lift his legs over, one by one. Halfway across, the recruit is stopped and asked his name, rank and number, then told to touch his toes, stand-up and continue. Fail the trainasium, fail P Company. Jason took it in his stride.

For Tommy and Grose, it was the first crisis point. Scrivs knew his two mates feared the test, so he talked them into returning to it one evening, to tackle the course. After several shouts of "I'm not ready yet", they edged across, urged on by Scrivs, and both managed to do it. They walked away, knowing the next time they'd be there would be during P Company, a week that arrived with startling speed.

On the Monday, Lt Young formed the platoon – hearts pounding, dressed in gym kit – outside the block, ready for the first test, milling. This was their moment to prove themselves worthy of the Regiment, he said. Then he read out Kipling's *If*.

IF you can keep your head when all about you
Are losing theirs and blaming it on you,
If you can trust yourself when all men doubt you,
But make allowance for their doubting too;
If you can wait and not be tired by waiting,
Or being lied about, don't deal in lies,
Or being hated, don't give way to hating,
And yet don't look too good, nor talk too wise:

If you can dream and not make dreams your master;
If you can think and not make thoughts your aim;
If you can meet with Triumph and Disaster
And treat those two impostors just the same;
If you can bear to hear the truth you've spoken
Twisted by knaves to make a trap for fools,
Or watch the things you gave your life to, broken,
And stoop and build 'em up with worn-out tools:

If you can make one heap of all your winnings
And risk it on one turn of pitch-and-toss,
And lose, and start again at your beginnings
And never breathe a word about your loss;
If you can force your heart and nerve and sinew
To serve your turn long after they are gone,
And so hold on when there is nothing in you
Except the Will which says to them: 'Hold on!'

If you can talk with crowds and keep your virtue,
Or walk with Kings – nor lose the common touch,
if neither foes nor loving friends can hurt you,
If all men count with you, but none too much;
If you can fill the unforgiving minute
With sixty seconds' worth of distance run,
Yours is the Earth and everything that's in it,
And – which is more – you'll be a Man, my son!

"By the time we were told to turn to our left and double to the gym, I was on cloud nine, ready to murder my milling opponent," Tommy recalls.

After a morning boxing, the afternoon brought the 10-mile Battle March, dressed in boots, denims, puttees, red PT vest and combat jacket, carrying a rifle and a bergen weighting 35lbs through woodlands, sandy banks, heathlands and hills with Long Valley as its masterpiece.

The ground there was cut deep by tanks tracks. In wet weather, the mud sapped the last ounce of energy from legs about to explode with lactic acid. In dry weather, the ruts were ready to break an ankle or two.

The course had to be completed in 1 hour 45 minutes for the maximum 10 points.

The clued-up lads knew this was no time or place to drop back from the front, so Tommy and Scrivs stayed in the lead until the startline reappeared. Instead of turning into camp, though, the lead PTI headed out for the training area ready to go round one more time.

Hearts sank, bergens instantly doubled in weight. Some lads had already dropped out. The PTI instructed the group to double and the runners dug as deep as they could for every ounce of strength they could muster, heart pounding, lungs ready to burst. As they turned into the wood, the PTI told them to sprint to the finish line.

After an evening digging trenches, scoffing a meal of Airborne Stew, and a night-navigation exercise over the 10-mile Battle March course in the freezing October rain, they were up at 0500hrs to fill the trenches before the Stretcher Race, a test that rehearsed the withdrawal of an injured comrade from the battlefield across rigorous terrain.

The stretchers were made of scaffold poles and steel sand tracks and weighed 180lbs. The race was over a 7.5-mile course between six teams of eight that were already depleted by the dropout rate. Two of each team would act as stretcher-reliefs and lug the weapons, while the others would carry the bone-bruising stretcher on their shoulders.

Within 200 yards, lads began dropping out. If your team lost two members, the survivors' hatred for the quitters grew with every excruciating step.

The test was about how individuals performed towards the overall team objective. Those who'd dropped out hadn't considered the consequences of their actions to the other team members or to the team's objective; but the remaining lads had persevered, when the odds were stacked against them. They'd done it the Airborne Way.

After they'd eaten, a hailstorm battered the catwalks, gaps and shuffling bars of the trainasium. The rehearsal Scrivs had nursed Tommy and Grose through paid off. Despite the psychological disaster of one recruit falling 30ft to the concrete base – without injury – everyone beat the course.

After lunch back at camp, the final event of the day was the Assault Course, a lap that had to be done three times in under seven-and-a-half minutes.

There were more timed tests on the Wednesday morning, starting with the Steeplechase, a two-mile cross-country run that had to be done in 18 minutes or less.

All that left was the Log Race, seven-man teams carrying a 200lb telegraph pole 'gun barrel' over a short, straight 1.5-mile course with a hill in the middle. It would last about 15 minutes.

The pain was intense from the moment they put their hands in the loop of the rope and took the weight of the log. Every step was murder.

The reward for the finishers was a march back to camp to await the results of P Company. Those who'd fallen by the wayside were told to put themselves and the logs on the wagons, their fate already sealed.

Dear Linda....
31 10 81

I told you on the phone the other night that I had past my tests. I am now in Wales in a place called Brecon. We are confined to camp for the first week. We are here for 3 weeks. The first week is all on the ranges then the second week is in the field for a week and the third week is another exercise but it is using helicopters which should be a laugh. And if you pass that I go to Brize Norton, which is in Oxfordshire, which is where we do our parachuting. So if I pass this course I should be jumping in 4 weeks.

There were 58 of us that took that course, there are 37 of us left....

The atmosphere in Ridgway Block was tense. None of the finishers had a clue whether they'd passed or not. As he sections sat on their beds, waiting for the section commanders and the results. Scrivs soon stood up and starting packing.

"What you doing," Tommy asked.

"If I've passed, I'm going to Brecon," Scrivs said. "If I've failed, I'm going to Retraining Platoon. Either way, I need to pack."

The minutes passed like hours as Lt Young discussed their performances with Sgt Bradshaw and the NCOs in the Platoon Office. Eventually, the door opened and the corporals went into their respective section rooms.

"Everyone here then?" Cpl Lewis asked as he closed the door behind him.

"Yes, Corporal," they replied.

He appeared relaxed and confident as he looked around.

"Anyone here thinks he could have done better?" he asked.

"Yes, Corporal." One lad stood up. Lewis looked at him.

"You'd better wait outside then."

The lad left the room and silence descended before Lewis broke into a smile.

"Congratulations, you're all going to Brecon," he said. "Get your kit packed. We leave in the morning."

The picture that charted Jason's achievement is also still on his bedroom wall.

"When you come up to see his room, you'll see where he done his training," Syd told me once. "He had to do a run with a pack on his back. He looked so skinny then. I thought Blimey! The pack's going to come off, his hat's going to fall over his eyes! He got through it and that amazed me. And that's when I began… I can't explain it to you. I respected him. I did."

Once Cpl Lewis had told the platoon who'd passed, and they'd run into each other's rooms to find out who else was heading onwards, it took 10 minutes to empty their lockers for the trip to Wales. The most important task, though, had been to remove the green backing to their cap badges.

If any of them thought three November weeks in the bleak Brecon Beacons meant the happiness continuing, they were mistaken. Relentless rain and snow were the order of every day. And the non-stop early mornings, the late nights and the sleep deprivation. Tasks like standing chest-deep in freezing streams, giving covering fire, added to the stress as they began to blend their individual fieldcraft, weaponry and tactical knowledge into effective personal and platoon fighting skills.

Recruits were assessed individually on combat ability and live firing happened every day. They had to double wherever they went in the 'battle camp', to the loo, to and from scoff, when retrieving weapons from the armoury. Everywhere.

When they were away from the camp, they also had to live off the land. Jason picked the phone up, one night, to tell his mum what that meant.

"You'll never believe what happened when we got here! The sergeant said 'We'll have dinner about seven o'clock. You'd better go and get it'."

They'd all looked at him and asked: "What d'you mean?"

"You see all those rabbits running around over there? You kill one of them, skin it, clean it, cook it for your dinner."

Many of the young lads couldn't do it, so the sergeant caught one himself and didn't share it. Jason picked the phone up again, a few days later. He'd given in.

"When you're hungry and wet," he told Terry, "you think 'Sod the rabbit'."

The grand finale was a three-day defensive exercise with the Platoon at the imaginary forward edge of a Battalion position, trenches dug and sentries posted. Reconnaissance patrols were sent into No Man's Land to gather information for fighting patrols to use. They also perfected the art of fighting, eating, drinking and relieving themselves while wearing a gas mask and an entire Nuclear, Biological and Chemical 'noddy suit'.

On the last day, the Gurkhas attacked the defensive trench position and the Platoon was required to carry out an exhausting, four-mile tactical withdrawal, known as a 'bug out'. The Gurkhas didn't make it easy. They pushed forward at every chance as the Platoon 'pepper-potted' backwards, section by section, providing covering fire for each other as they dropped back.

This went on for four gruelling miles or so. In every section of 10, the NCO would be on the radio, the two-man gun group would move back and give covering fire, then the other seven riflemen would pepper-pot back in twos and threes, one man providing the cover while his mate in front dropped back, then dropping back while his mucker provided the protection. Section by section, platoon by platoon they'd withdraw until they could pack their kit up and disappear.

A mile on, the wagons came into view halfway up a steep hill, a wonderful sight for the flagging recruits. It informally marked the end of the exercise. But, as they approached, the trucks drove off and the platoon's morale drained away.

Lt Young gave the order to continue tabbing back to camp, 10 miles away.

To reach this far, each lad had grown accustomed to the physical and mental grind of tabbing and running, the need to find a rhythm, to listen for the sound of their footsteps – one-two-three-four, one-two-three-four – and then let the automatic pilot kick in so that, after 'x' amount of time, he'd think 'Jesus, we're there – six miles', and he wouldn't be able to say what he'd been thinking, or whether they'd turned left or right to arrive there.

But this was tough. One lad packed up as the wagons pulled away. It was the final straw.

The rest soldiered on, dejected, struggling to find that mindless rhythm again. As they broke the top of the hill, the wagons were parked about 100 yards away, at the side of the road. Tommy's not sure what Jason was feeling at the time, but he wasn't fooled. He ignored them.

As they drew level with the vehicles, though, Lt Young stopped the Platoon and ordered them to unload their weapons and make them safe.

"Get in," he smiled. The exercise was over. Most of them fell asleep on the short journey home.

Back at camp, Lt Young and their respective section commanders gave them their gradings. Not many were worried about what they were. All they cared about was a pass. Jason, Tommy, Grose and Scrivs were among those who emerged weary but happy.

In Juniors, they'd had a blue plastic backing to their Para cap badge, denoting what part of training they were in. In Recruit Company, it was swapped for a green one. When they passed P Company, the green had been taken out and they'd been allowed to wear a normal combat jacket.

As a reward, for making it through Brecon, they were given their Para smock. All that remained were their wings.

That's where they were heading for next. Brize Norton, in Oxfordshire. Four weeks of parachute training – and the infamous Spotlight Club.

CHAPTER 5

LEAPS OF FAITH

The emblem above the double doors at No.1 Parachute Training School bore a parachute with crossed torches below and the motto that read 'Knowledge Dispels Fear'.

And the sign above the heads of the women who handled the chutes advised them to 'Remember a man's life depends on every parachute you pack'.

If the first notice appeared a little optimistic to the new recruits, as they filed in to start Course 885 at Brize Norton, the second reinforced what they already knew about the potential consequence of jumping.

If Tommy's thoughts can be taken as an indicator of what Jason and the rest of them were thinking – which is highly likely – from where they stood, none of them looked convinced by either, or by Sgt Bailey's reassurance that no one was expected to leap out of an aircraft until they'd understood the equipment and procedure for jumping. Until, in other words, fear had been dispelled.

However you might want to put another gloss on it, jumping out of something 800ft in the air is unnatural. That's the feeling Tommy recalls. I'm not sure when or where this grim, matter-of-fact thought began to take root, but this is how he looks at it now: "Should it go horribly wrong, it will present members of the Pioneer Corps with the choice of digging you out of the ground or throwing earth over you!"

The day had started with a surprise. The NCOs' attitudes had changed. They weren't recruits any more. They were colleagues and members of the Regiment. What a change. The sergeant might as well have been a housewife.

It took them a few days to make the adjustment, though. The sceptics had a field day when they were told a coach would collect them from the block at 0900. Morning parades were usually held at 0800, so this was a trap. At 0800, they all stood outside, waiting for the NCOs. No one appeared. At 0900, a green coach pulled up and took them on the half-mile drive to No.1 Parachute Training School. Half a mile? They could have tabbed it in three minutes!

Inside the hangar, parachute harnesses hung by steel wires from the ceiling, like oversized chandeliers. They would spend hours dangling, practising drills for all-round observation, landing in water, trees, colliding with other parachutists, twists in the rigging lines and numerous other possibilities.

Then they'd move to the ramps and practise the painful 'parachute roll' landing. There was also a mock-up where they'd rehearse boarding the aircraft, the 'airborne shuffle' to the door, with equipment strapped to a leg, and exiting the plane.

The last notable equipment was a platform in the rafters where the recruit would be strapped to a large fan. He'd then jump and his descent would be controlled by a combination of his weight and the spinning fan blades being slowed by the air.

Outside the hangar was the so-called 'knacker-cracker', a device that was supposed to simulate being tossed about by the slipstream of an aircraft. It lived up to the billing.

Week 1 was Synthetic Training (exiting the plane, air drills and landings), Week 2 was more of the same, culminating in the first aircraft jump, and Weeks 3 and 4 were set aside for them to complete the remaining six aircraft jumps. One of them would be at night, and others would be with equipment.

It soon dawned on Jason, Tommy, Grose and Scrivs that Brize was to paratroopers what Disneyland is to children. The dining halls were like restaurants. They had tablecloths, condiments and cutlery, and soft music playing in the background.

There were a number of counters where they could order a steak cooked to their taste or, if they fancied, a tossed salad with Italian or French dressing. Not that they appreciated the change in ambience.

"We were all too busy pinching the knives, forks, spoons and ketchup bottles to really appreciate the aesthetics of the place," Tommy admits. "When the chef asked me how I'd like my steak, I told him 'On my plate, mate'."

By the second week, the cutlery had disappeared. The ketchup stayed, but the facility to cook their own eggs didn't. In the spirit of adventure, they attempted to add to their field cooking skills, and all went well until one of them set fire to a curtain by the frying area.

No one was surprised. Someone's misguided actions eventually put paid to every good experience.

On Fridays and Saturdays, the Spotlight Club was the place to go. There wasn't much else to do in the village of Carterton, which surrounds the Brize airbase, so the local girls would congregate there, dressed up, looking for a suitable serviceman to attend to their needs. The lads – young, fit and often naïve – would oblige.

Tommy had long since grown used to the effect Jason had in places like the Spotlight. One particular night was no different.

For a petite, blonde 18-year-old trainee hairdresser and her friends, the Spotlight was the only place to go every Thursday and Saturday. That's why Claire Acock was with Rena

Scrivens and Linda Collett the night Jason walked in with Tommy, Scrivs and Co. Claire immediately knew what she was looking at.

"When you saw a Para, you knew he was a Para. It was this presence. This air that says 'I'm indestructible!'

"They all looked the same. They had the desert boots, they wore the jeans, the burgundy top," she told me. "They stood out.

"I remember seeing Jason in the club. Our eyes met and I just thought: 'God, he's gorgeous!' I'll always remember, he had long eyelashes for a man and rosy red lips. Oh yeah, he was gorgeous. He was lovely. He was such a nice character of a man.

"The Paras were laddish and a bit loud and mouthy. I don't know what he was like when he was with his friends but, when he was with me, he was a gentleman. He was lovely."

She resorted to the tried-and-tested.

"You always got your friend to go up and ask: 'Will you dance with my friend?' God, how awful! And you make a point of making eye contact."

Tommy remembers the moment too, if a little more sketchily. As often, they'd gone in to the Spotlight with Graham Collins, a lad from Tottenham, and Jason – " he had this bloody habit, like his dad" – had said 'I'll have a lager!' and headed straight for the fruit machine.

He was still at it when Claire plucked up the courage to wander up in her bright red dress and chat. For most of the lads, that would have been it. One chat, one night. But, while the weeks passed, they saw each other regularly.

Dear Linda….
30 11 81

Where suppose to jump tomorrow, but it's doubtful because of the weather. Today we had what you call air experience were we went up in a plane ready to jump with our chutes on, they opened the doors of the plane and one by one we had to go up to the door and stick our heads out. It was unbelievable. Can you imagine a plane travlling at 125mph 800 ft up and you sticking your head out of the door. Oh! By the way the reason I didn't phone was because I fell asleep about 6 and didn't wake up until 12 Sunday morning, so sorry about that…

When or if you see Kay, Karen and Meryl, wish them a happy Xmas for me. We were given the choice of our battalions the other day. I chose 2 Para, who go to Belize in April.

On Tuesday, December 1, 1981, a coach took the lads to the Dropping Zone, at Hullavington, in Wiltshire, for their first jump from the balloon.

The night before, they'd been down the Spotlight, deciding which mate they'd pick on. Drink, drink, drink. Tomorrow's what we do tomorrow.

Now they were drawing their parachutes, each bearing a unique number that was written on a log, with their name, providing the RAF with a record in the event of a malfunction. Then they were put, alphabetically, into fours and, group by group, they were called forward and stepped into a flimsy cage, slung beneath the balloon, watching ruefully as their instructor dropped a small metal bar across the opening to stop them falling out prematurely.

The cage jerked as the winch slowly lifted it 800ft up into the wind. Eventually, it stopped and, one by one, they were beckoned forward to hold the uprights either side of the exit.

Tommy doesn't recall where Jason was in the queue, but he was the third of his group to be called. It's a fair bet that the next few moments of their respective lives passed in much the same way.

"The instructor told me to look up and concentrate on the small red lanyard that hung from the main body of the balloon, 10 yards in front," Tommy recalls. "He reminded me of my air drills and told me to fold my arms across my reserve and step forward from the cage on the word 'Go!'" No going back.

"Go!"

The Standard Operational Procedure on exiting is to shout 'One thousand, two thousand, three thousand, check canopy!'

Tommy managed "One thousand, two thou...." before his guts hit his throat, rapidly followed by his testicles, and his eyes started streaming. In a flash, though, his brain re-engaged and he bellowed "Check canopy!" and looked up.

The beige canopy deployed, then closed for a scary moment before taking another breath and lowering him towards the ground as he went through his air drills – check air space, assess drift – and then settled to take in the experience.

The lads who'd completed their jump looked minute below him as the instructor on the ground yelled through a loud-hailer: "Feet and knees together, prepare for your landing, chin on chest, elbows in!"

Thirty seconds was all it lasted before the ground rushed up and he was on the floor.

"Your air drills were crap," the PJI yelled as he deflated his chute, but it didn't wipe the silly grin from his face.

One parachute jump is said to be equal to eight hours physical toil, so the joy lasted minutes back on the coach before they all crashed out.

Their first plane jump was set for Thursday, December 3, 1981, at Weston-on-the-Green. Brize was covered in snow, adding to the anticipation of Christmas, and providing the ammunition for fun. Scrivs, Jason, Grose and Tommy were passing the Officers' Mess on the way to scoff when they were ambushed.

17: The death and life of Private Jason Burt

The Officers had the advantage of surprise but, after the initial volley of snowballs and much guffawing, found themselves stranded. The 17-year-olds, on the other hand, did not. Within seconds, fresh from the freezing hills and streams of Brecon, they'd gone on the counter attack. The 'hats' scrambled for the safety of the foyer, but the four young Paras followed them in to complete the mission – only to be removed by the RAF orderly in charge of maintaining decorum within the Mess.

At about 1300, they were in action again, this time drawing their parachutes ready to board the plane. After a briefing, they went on to the runway to meet their Hercules C130 up close and personal. Minutes later, they were filing up the tail ramp into the fuselage and, soon after, the giant plane's noisy engines were lifting it off the ground.

While the instructors prepared for the drop, some of the lads tried to sleep. Before long, though, one side door was slid open and a refreshing gush of air ripped through, adding tenfold to the banging noise inside.

The 'drifter' was the first to jump, exiting the plane without steering his parachute to show the pilot the strength and wind direction. The dispatcher leaned from the door to make sure the 'drifter' was free of the aircraft, then the first stick of six heard the words.

"Stand Up! Hook up!"

The plane banked for its second approach to the dropping zone and, as soon as the instructor was happy everyone had hooked up correctly, he shouted.

"Check equipment!"

In succession, everyone checked their own equipment and then the person in front. After checking No. 6, No.5 turned to face the exit, slapped the back of the man's chute in front and shouted 'No.6 okay!' The chain reaction was triggered.

"No.5 okay!" – "No.4 okay!" – "No.3 okay!" – "No.2 okay!" – "No.1 okay!"

No.1 gave a thumb-up and the instructor yelled again.

"Action Stations!"

In unison, all six shuffled forward until No.1 was in the door. The aircraft steadied.

"Red On!" yelled the dispatcher, and No.1 took his arm from the door and folded it across his reserve.

"Green On – Go!" he ordered. "One, two, three, four, five, six!" he yelled in one-second intervals as he slapped each man's back and stepped into oblivion.

As the green light came on and each approached the door, all they concentrated on was a clean exit, an aggressive push from the step to ensure they didn't inspect the rivets all the way down the plane's tail.

In reality, most were sucked out and the first few seconds passed with their eyes shut. As they hurtled down at breakneck speed, each snapped back into drill – "One thousand, two thousand, three thousand, check canopy!" – and opened his eyes to find himself parallel to the ground, 1,000ft up, looking at the drop zone, assessing his drift, pulling down on his lift webs ready to be talked through landing by the ground staff.

Safely down, each gazed at the sky. The feeling of accomplishment and pride was overwhelming.

Back at camp, they were congratulated on completing their first aircraft jump and given a long weekend pass. They had to report for duty on Monday, December 7, 1981, ready to do it again. Two down, six to go.

The first jump on the Tuesday went without fear or hesitation, then they prepared for the second jump of the day, scheduled for 1800hrs, their first night jump. They were all at the hangar early, eager for the new experience. The inside of the Herc was lit red to aid night vision, a warm welcoming feeling for some that vanished when they left the plane and – after the mandatory 'one thousand, two thousand, three thousand' countdown – looked up to check his canopy.

For Tommy, that was a moment he'll never forget, because his main chute didn't deploy, and he had to pull his reserve, a moment that seared itself on his memory.

The Wednesday brought two more jumps, both with containers and bergens. Both went without a hitch, leaving the final jump set for Tuesday, December 15. This one would be in sticks of eight with equipment and, for the first time, from 800ft. If they brought themselves down safely, Tommy, Jason, Scrivs, Grose and all the other survivors of Juniors and Recruit Company knew the prize would be huge – their wings.

The jump went well and they were soon standing proudly on parade inside the hangar, awaiting the Officer Commanding (OC) No. 1 Parachute Training School. In true HM Forces fashion – Tommy laughs now, but tells the story in a tone of voice that suggests it wasn't funny at the time – the romance of the occasion soon gave second best to the stuffiness of the OC's official address.

"Once awarded your wings," he told them, "you are deemed to have accepted, as long as you are medically fit to do so, the obligation to serve with a parachute unit on operations, and to carry out parachute descents when ordered or required to do so. For this, parachute pay is awarded. Future failure or refusal to carry out a descent will result in disciplinary action being taken against you. This will almost certainly result in a trial by court martial and the withdrawal of the right to wear the qualified parachutist badge with wings. If you are not prepared to accept this obligation, you should say so now."

In short, 'if you take the cash, make sure you do the job'.

After a pause for effect, the OC was soon moving along the three ranks of shiny new Paras, shaking their right hands and placing a gleaming set of wings in their left. How proud they all were. All they wanted to do was leave out of the hangar and put them on.

After the parade was over, they spent their last night in the Spotlight Club. For most it was a time for final farewells and promises of "We'll meet again...." For most it was a pledge they'd never keep. Not for Jason and Claire.

Christmas was spent on Aldershot Rear Guard duties before New Year leave, then they were airborne again for Exercise Last Fence, a chance for the platoon to parachute into Hankley Common – a vast wild area near Farnham that still bears the evidence of D-Day preparations – as an operational unit with everything needed to carry out a mission.

They climbed on the wagons in camp and, 35 minutes later, they were in the air. No time for nerves. No fuss. Just do it.

On the flight to Surrey, Neil looked at Tommy. He'd taken to wearing the same thick red socks for every jump.

"I'm only here because of you," he shouted, which might have sounded like a word of thanks, until he added: "I f***ing hate parachuting!"

Tommy smiled back. "Airborne," he said.

The platoon's final party was booked for a couple of days before the Passing Out parade. For most, it went with a bang. The NCOs had arranged three strippers to entertain, and provided the girls with a bowl of fruit. I'm not sure what Jason thought, but Tommy regarded it as a pleasant welcoming gesture. He's never peeled a banana the same way since.

At 1015, a couple of days later – Friday, January 22, 1982 – proud families and friends gathered in the NAAFI. More than a year before, the Burts had waved off their 16-year-old, convinced he wasn't old enough to face what was coming, but knowing he'd go anyway, eventually. Now he was about to march past, a confident young man, physically equipped to take on the world and, in his own mind, invincible.

His mother, Terry, noticed that Jason's attitude changed the day he passed out. She'd arranged with friends to have a drink in a hotel to celebrate. Syd's brother and sister-in-law and son and daughter were joining them, but Ted and Lin had flu and, despite wanting to see his proud day, the weather was bitterly cold and they had to cry off.

It didn't sit well with Jason. He had a fiver for drinks in his hand when he came in to the bar and asked why they weren't there. Later on, Syd organised a drink at the hotel. But Jason refused to turn up in protest at Ted and Lin's non-appearance.

The Burts met Sgt Des Fuller that day. They already knew his name well. It would also return to their lives, five months later, in a way they'd never forget. For now, he loomed large as the man Jason had quoted to justify returning to training during a bout of shingles.

"Sgt Fuller said you can either be a man and a Para and continue, or be back-squadded," he'd told his mum. "I'm not being back-squadded."

The other thing on Jason's mind that day – as it was for all the lads – was where they were going next. At the parade, the Inspecting Officer, Major Tom Duffy, had offered them a few words of wisdom. Lt Young gave a final address to parents and told the boys they were free to go on leave, ready to report back in early February to be assigned battalions.

They'd already stated their first and second choices. Tommy's recollection is that all four of them – Jason, Tommy, Scrivs and Grose – had plumped for 3 Para. Jason's letter to Linda says otherwise, but the options weren't difficult to sift.

They'd been told already the lads who'd joined Recruit Company straight from Civvie Street were going to 1 Para, because the battalion was heading for Northern Ireland, and they had to be 18 to go there. None of the four wanted 1 Para – even though it had a sporty reputation – then sit in the block until they were 18. So that had left 2 Para and 3 Para.

As far as Tommy was concerned, 2 Para was about bull-shit and the parade ground. They were also based on the Lines. On the other hand, 3 Para was always out, doing what they regarded as "real soldiering". The lure and novelty of Salisbury Plain, a new area, new experiences. That's what they wanted, Tommy recalls. And one other thing – they just "wanted to get out of the Shot a bit".

For him, there was another incentive to head for Kandahar Barracks, in Tidworth, Wiltshire. His old Hoo schoolmate, Stu 'Doc' McAllister, was already there.

When they returned from leave, Lt Young told them where they'd be going. The three 17-year-olds who'd nursed each other through the horrors of Junior Regiment, the milling, the rock-climbing, the nights causing trouble in village discos, the weapons ranges, the sky-high trainasium, the Battle March, the Log Race, the freezing Brecon streams and the eight jumps were rewarded with what they wanted – 3 Para.

A few mornings later, the Platoon went their separate ways. The lads going to 2 Para were taken just up the road to Montgomery Lines. Those heading for 1 Para then watched as the wagon turned up from 3 Para and the rest climbed in and headed for Salisbury Plain. It was a new area and a new era. They were starting again, not as recruits, but as shiny, new and untested Crows. They wouldn't be accepted as Toms until the old hands 4 Platoon B Company 3 Para at Tidworth decided they'd earned the accolade.

CHAPTER 6

CROWS OFF TO WAR

Terry Burt was relieved her half-Irish lad wasn't heading for Northern Ireland, but she still worried when Jason joined 3 Para and set off for his new home in Wiltshire. They were no longer boys, but they weren't yet men either.

Whatever parental worries she and Syd harboured as he went, the milling, the assault courses, the trainasium, the stretcher races, the jump training and the ice-cold rivers of mid-Wales had forged in him an attitude and spirit that few of our children ever know. He was ready to take on the world!

In Tidworth, the question was this. Could the Crows hack it? Not a minute was wasted before 3 Para started finding out what kind of 17-year-olds they'd been sent. As soon as they stepped off the wagon, Jason, Scrivs, Grose, Tommy and the rest were ordered into PT kit and told to report to the gym. They hadn't been shown their accommodation or given a chance to unpack. No point. If they failed the induction physical tests, they'd be heading back to Depot as rejects.

After a severe beasting session and a break-neck run round the local training area, they were told to shower, change into working dress, and form up outside the gym.

Tony Barlow was already at Tidworth. The middle child of nine brought up in Manchester's tough Moston district, he'd joined up at 15. Comedian Bernard Manning spotted he had a talent that could be moulded and that he need to do something if he wasn't to head in the wrong direction, fast. That's why Tony found himself in front of a Recruiting Sergeant, and why the Army decided he was suited to Junior Para.

He'll never forget the day the Crows arrived at Kandahar Barracks. As they lined up for the parade, the lads from 5 Platoon soaked them with water from the first-floor balcony.

"They were like drowned rats," he laughed. "I remember Jason having to stand to attention as he got soaked. And he stood there, still standing to attention, still getting soaked. He didn't move and his beret fell over his head. It was funny. That was his first day at 3 Para."

It was another nervous wait until PTI Sgt Butler told them they'd all survived and could report to their Company Sergeant Majors. That's when John Weeks entered their lives.

Jason, Scrivs, Grose, Tommy and another 17-year-old – Steve Jelf – were sent to B Company. They waited outside his office, trying to pluck up the courage to knock on his door, not sure what to expect. Scrivs eventually did the deed.

"Come in!" someone shouted. They all froze.

"Come f***ing in!"

Scrivs led and they followed. The office was narrow with a desk, a phone, a chair and a filing cabinet. A large man was sitting with his back to them. They took up positions and stood silently. For a while, nothing happened. Then he swivelled and pointed to his swollen, purple eyes.

"If anyone wants to know, I got these playing rugby!"

No one said a thing as he looked them up and down, but Tommy admits one thought raced through his mind – *Jesus Christ! What have I let myself in for?*

"Right," Weeks smiled, finally. "Burt, Grose, Jelf and Scrivens. 4 Platoon. Thomas, 5."

Still no one moved or spoke.

"Lewis!" he bellowed. The door opened and there stood the Company clerk. "Show these lads to their rooms." Off Lewis walked, with the five in tow. For Jason, Neil, Steve Jelf and Ian, Lt. Andy Bickerdike, Ian McKay and Brian Milne were about to become an important part of their lives.

Their rooms were enormous, compared to the ones at the Depot. Each had five beds separated by odd bits of furniture, lockers, a table, chairs, armchairs strewn with clothes, and a large metal dustbin. The walls were papered with naked women and the floors were littered with rubbish.

Tales were rife of Crows being 'filled in' when they first arrived at battalion. They were regarded as cocky, the senior lads at Depot who'd left full of high spirits and too much 'bravado' from nights at Brize Norton.

In Tony Barlow's room, there were three empty top bunks waiting. Jason, Scrivs and Neil wandered in and started the next stage of their induction. In short, that meant being given "the shit end of the stick", as Tony describes it.

"You're Crows. You have to prove yourself," he says. "The way Paratroopers prove themselves is by getting pissed, having a fight, doing the most stupid thing you could do. Simple as. You wake up the next morning, you're in, you're on."

Over in 5 Platoon, after he'd unpacked, Tommy sat on his bed and waited in trepidation for his room-mates to arrive. It was hours before the door burst open and three of them walked in, looked at him, grunted, removed their belts and berets and crashed out. Tommy didn't say a word.

His old schoolmate 'Doc' McAllister was in 5 Platoon, but Tommy knew he couldn't just walk into any of the rooms looking for him, so scoff time was the best chance to find him.

He waited patiently until his watch said it was time to meet Jason, Scrivs, Grose and Jelf to go over to the scoff house together, and bumped straight into him.

Within minutes, Doc had told them a few of the B Company facts of life. Like CSM Weeks' eyes. Nothing to do with rugby. He'd been jumped by three Toms while zipped up in his 'doss bag' on the recent Oman trip for Exercise Rocky Lance. It had been four weeks of tactical training in the desert and the djebel, practicing harbour and patrol drills, actions on enemy contact, tabs carrying large amounts of equipment in their bergens and section, platoon and company level attacks.

"Nice to know that the 3 Para lads respect rank," Tommy said to Stu, quietly.

"Nothing to do with rank," he smiled. "If you get out of hand, the blokes don't forget it, doesn't matter who you are." Then he issued a warning. "Lads, Johnny Weeks is a right handful and can look after himself. Don't cross him!"

If they all felt the same sinking feeling inside as Tommy, it would be little wonder. Here they were, finally in battalion, at the mercy of the Toms, in the charge of what – to all intents and purposes – seemed to them to be a psychopathic CSM who had one, two or possibly three issues to tackle in the coming months. But that wasn't all.

"The boys in your room," Stu told Tommy. "Dominic Gray, Tony Kempster, Pete Hindmarsh and Lewis.... Nightmare. Just watch yourself tonight – and, until you're invited, don't go drinking down The Ram. You'll get killed!"

The room was empty when Tommy returned, so he turned the lights off and lay on top of his bed with all his clothes on, expecting the worst. He fell asleep until Kempster kicked the door open and sent the dustbin and its contents flying. The darkened room echoed with expletives. Tommy braced himself, but Kempster headed straight for bed, colliding with furniture on the way. Within seconds, he was snoring loudly.

Dom Gray followed, 10 minutes later. He kicked the door open and fell over the upturned dustbin. His chips went flying.

"F**k it!" he mumbled, but ploughed on through the black, ditching his clothes before crashing out. Two down, Tommy thought. But, by the time Hindmarsh and Lewis turned up, he was asleep himself.

Little happened in the first weeks as they learned about their new home and colleagues, but what did underlined the fact that they would be Crows until they'd proved themselves.

The camp was massive and mainly built of red bricks with concrete lintels and floors. The story went that the architect's plans for two Army camps had been mixed up. So, while the English design went up in India, the Indian building – two-storey blocks with large verandas, ironwork supporting their roofs, and high ceilings inside equipped with large ceiling fans – were left gracing Kandahar Barracks in Tidworth.

Most of the time was spent cleaning the kit and weapons used in the Oman excursion. There was the odd run, but that was about it. Life was relaxed. Morning parades were little more than a get-together when the CSM called the nominal role to make sure no one had done a runner. Then he'd hand the platoons back to their officers, who'd take it from there.

In Jason's room, Tony Barlow was already keeping an eye out for the new lads, remembering well what life had been like for him when he'd joined 3 Para. He watched how they behaved and recognised the signs.

"You have your webbing, you have your uniform all ironed and pressed. And you see these lads and they have theirs ironed and pressed and bulled. They have three pair of boots bulled. You have one. That's where you start to learn.

"I had a soft spot for all the young lads, 'cos I don't like bullying. I had a soft spot for Jason and Tom. Wherever I could, I looked after 'em."

It wasn't long, in fact, before Tom was with 4 Platoon. For reasons he never understood, he was moved from 5 Platoon and into a room with Grose and – enter another 3 Para legend – Pte Ron Duffy.

The Scot was regarded as the battalion lunatic, a loner known for keeping a black book in which he'd enter the names of anyone who'd either crossed or simply annoyed him, ready for the well-timed moment – when the individual was least expecting it, usually while sleeping – when he'd take revenge with whatever was to hand. It might be the heavy bumpers used to buff up the floors. It could be a wire coat hanger. Anything he could lay his hands on. But it didn't stop there.

Anything that wasn't a Scottish folk song was 'punk rock', and therefore detested. He hated chocolate and all who ate it. They were 'sweety bandits'. In Oman, the Platoon Officer had woken in his tent to find a 7.62 round on his chest, on top of his doss bag. No questions were asked. No one needed to.

Some said he'd also unhooked an officer, prior to a jump and after final equipment checks had been completed. It was only when the instructor was called forward to the cockpit that he noticed the strop hanging and hooked the officer back up. When Ron was asked for an explanation, he just smiled.

"He had the most brilliant, shining blue eyes that were the windows to a darker side – not that anyone stared at Ron," Tommy recalls. "But he was fine to Grose and me and even used to offer us a nip of his whisky to put in our tea."

It must have been around this time that Jason bumped into Duffy in the glasshouse. Four hours behind bars as a suitable 3 Para deterrent for going on parade in a uniform stained with a drop of blood.

All the rooms were filled with the sound of the latest chart music, except the one Tommy and Grose shared with the mad Scot. Theirs was like a library, silent and rarely visited. The two Crows simply didn't dare play any music in his earshot. Instead, they bought earphones for their stereos. In return, Ron never etched their names in his black book.

A couple of weeks after they'd arrived at 3 Para, the Regimental Sergeant Major, Lawrie Ashbridge, called the Battalion together and issued an unlikely request.

"Whoever's nicked the Royal Irish Rangers mascot, would they kindly return it!"

The parade was dismissed and, shortly after, the goat appeared on a lawn between the blocks. It wasn't complete, however. It lacked the splendid beard it had worn before its kidnap. And it had been sprayed in bright green – in recognition of the Rangers' regimental colours – and luminous orange, presumably in the interests of road safety. The Paras regarded the hairstyling and artwork as time well spent. But the Irish Rangers didn't. As a result, the Battalion was confined to camp for a short period.

In March, the Battalion was placed on Spearhead, at 24 hours notice to go anywhere in the world, meaning every Crow and Tom needed to have their full kit issue packed and ready to go. 'Anywhere in the world' normally meant Northern Ireland, so the Battalion was packed off to Hythe and Lydd – near Romney Marshes, in Kent – to prepare for it. It was the Crows' first taste of urban warfare training.

The next weeks were spent in a mock-up village, going out on four-man foot patrols, learning how to deal with the locals, and practising 'actions on', when the patrol came under fire. Each soldier wore a numbered bib allowing his movements to be tracked by cameras dotted between the houses, shops, discotheque and the green that made up the village.

To add to the realism, walls were daubed with anti-British slogans and dummies would yell suggestions like "Fuck off, Paras!" as they patrolled, to provoke a reaction. Others would tell them individually that they'd seen a man, dressed in black and carrying a weapon into the back of Number 12. They'd be expected to ignore the first and use the second to brief the Patrol Commander, verbatim, who'd decide whether to follow up the info or not.

The experience taught them personal patrolling skills. More importantly, it encouraged them not to take anything at face value or trust anyone. After each patrol, the section would sit in the debriefing room, watch the TV replay and pull their performance to pieces to learn from their mistakes, like spotting where a silhouette or weapon might betray their position to a sniper.

It was intensive, but extremely rewarding. If any of them doubted the purpose of it, all they had to do was study the pictures that lined the walls of the anteroom that led to the 'sangar' positions where they waited before taking their posts. In graphical black and white, they showed the victims of car bombs, shootings, explosions and the like. To underscore the ultimate price that could be paid, a mortuary tray and slab completed the scene.

Observation was a key skill. They'd sit for hours in an Observation Post in a mock attic, overlooking a number of streets with the order to look out for a number of individuals. Each member of the OP was responsible for recording any incidents of interest in a specific street and radio silence was only broken if one of the targets appeared.

In the province, the advantage would be with the terrorist. They could take one pot shot and run. Instinctively, if it happened – "Did anyone see where…?" "That house!" "Top left… Go!" – they'd have to race to where the shot had been fired, to try and grab the enemy before he disappeared for good. For those who hadn't been before, it was eye-opening.

The youngsters just sucked it in. It was a different from anything they'd experienced, and it made them think about soldiering on a personal level.

"It was totally the reverse of Brecon, where the arsehole's behind the rock and won't stop firing until you do." Tommy can laugh at the recollection… now.

On Saturday, March 20, Terry heard Jason's key in the door. He'd sent her a Mothering Sunday card, after explaining he wouldn't be able to make it back. When he walked in at about three, waving another card, she was thrilled.

"You've already sent me a card," you smiled.

He was back the next weekend, too. He was due to see Kerry on the Saturday, but met a mate on the market during the afternoon and decided to give her a miss in favour of a night out with his mates at a new club in Ilford.

He rang Kelly and claimed he had a bad cold. What he hadn't banked on was meeting her dad at a petrol station that night, but managed to talk his way out of it, something along the lines of "it wouldn't be fair to give Kerry a cold".

Syd drove him to the station on the Sunday, little realising the significance of the journey, of course. The thought occupying his mind was the start of three weeks training back in the Beacons, starting on the Monday.

As things turned out, they were back in Tidworth on the Friday.

Most of 3 Para would admit to thinking the Falklands were off Scotland. There was no point. They were going to war, whether they liked it or not.

At Tidworth, the briefings started in earnest. Whatever the history lesson might have informed them is lost in time, but it might easily have included that the first recorded landing was by Capt John Strong, in 1690, and that he named them after the Treasurer of the Navy.

In the years after, the French visited Les Iles Malouines, after St Malo, regularly. The name became Las Malvinas in Spanish after the French sold their claim on the Falklands to the Spanish crown in 1766.

17: The death and life of Private Jason Burt

Five years later, after negotiations to avoid war, Port Egmont – cleared of British settlers in 1766 – was restored to the British, even though the Spanish made it clear they hadn't yielded sovereignty. Three years later still, a plaque was left at Port Egmont as a token of British ownership. All this, however – as well as Argentina's split from Spain's authority in 1816, and its formal takeover of the islands in 1820 – would have passed most Paras by.

During the 60s, there'd been diplomatic hand-wringing and lobbying of the islanders and numerous acts of provocation.

In 1966, an Aerolineas Argentinas DC4 was hijacked by 20 Argentine nationalists, known as 'Condors', who forced the pilot to fly to Stanley and land on the racecourse. They took four Islanders hostage, handed out leaflets stating they'd arrived to take over the Islands on behalf of Argentina, and raised the Argentine flag.

The invasion didn't last long, though. The next day they gave up to a local priest and were put on an Argentine naval ship for the return home and a nominal prison sentence.

Later that year, a small detachment of Argentine Marines landed via the submarine Santiago del Estero and recced potential landing beaches near the capital, Port Stanley on East Falkland. A couple of years later, another Argentine aircraft crashed while attempting a landing to publicise Argentine demands.

By the early 1980s, the population of around 1,800 was administered by Governor Rex Hunt. More than half the residents lived in Stanley. For every man, woman and child among them, there were estimated to be 300 sheep supplying the wool and hides that provided the islands' main export.

More importantly, perhaps, they were far from Britain and of no pressing economic or military priority. There are some who believe this caused the Argentinian government's greatest misjudgment – in short, it was that the occupation of these islands would be treated by the British as a fait accompli.

Despite the reconnaissance of landing sites near Stanley, the 1982 invasion started on Friday, March 19, at an abandoned whaling station at Grytviken, on South Georgia, when Argentinian businessman Constantino Davidoff landed to salvage scrap metal on the fleet transport Bahia Buen Suceso, without British permission.

The Argentinian flag was hoisted near the work site. The British protested, and the political row escalated. Rex Hunt sent 22 Royal Marines to remove the workers, and Argentina sent 100 Marines to protect them. That quickly erupted into a gun-battle and the smaller British force was overpowered.

From there, events slid rapidly towards war. Britain protested in vain about the South Georgia landing. On Friday, March 26, British Intelligence reported that a number of Argentinian military vessels were at sea and, on Thursday, April 1, Rex Hunt received a top secret Foreign Office telegram. It read:

17: The death and life of Private Jason Burt

We have apparently reliable evidence that an Argentine task force could be assembling off Stanley at dawn tomorrow. You will wish to make your dispositions accordingly.

Hunt made a radio broadcast to tell islanders that the invasion was imminent, and it happened. At about six on the morning of Friday, April 2, the Argentinians attacked on a number of fronts with both helicopter and light armoured vehicles. They were faced by 40 Royal Marines of Naval Party 8901. The Marines were overwhelmed and surrendered at 9.30am. The invaders quickly reinforced their troops to about 10,000 and put a military governor in command.

Argentina didn't lose any time in making several changes to the culture of the Falkland Islands, and the islanders didn't waste many minutes following them. Port Stanley was renamed Puerto Argentino, Spanish became the official language and traffic was ordered to drive on the right. The islanders continued to drive on the left and set about remaining very British. If the Argentinians had hoped everyone would accept the occupation and move on, they were in for a shock.

Apart from the sudden change of plans, that day – April 2, 1982 – had been like almost any other at Kandahar Barracks. The men of B Company were busy winding down to a weekend leave or on duty after their reprieve from the wet and wild isolation of Brecon.

At 3.15am, Brigadier Julian Thompson, commander of 3 Commando Brigade, was phoned by his Royal Marines superior, Major General Jeremy Moore, and told to bring the brigade to 72 hours notice, immediately.

As the afternoon passed, United Kingdom Land Forces command decided to put 3 Para on standby.

By 5pm, UKLF HQ had called the battalion's second-in-command to see if they were ready to go. Seventy-five minutes later, commanding officer Lt Col Hew Pike gave the order for Exercise Fastball – to ready 3 Para for war.

It was the early evening before most of the guys heard. As soon as Pike made his move, British Rail were asked to put chalkboards at stations, telling them to return to Tidworth. By 7.30pm, telegrams were being sent out via Bristol GO, and those still in camp were told not to leave. Many acted on instinct – and made straight for The Drummer Boy pub.

Tommy seems to recall that he, Jason and 'Doc' McAllister had just climbed off the train at Waterloo when they saw the blackboards – "Members of 3 Para return to camp" – so they turned around. Well, Tommy and Jason did.

When they arrived back in Tidworth, the forecast of events board in the Sergeants' Mess explained why: '3 Para gone to war May, June, July: Sea cruise Falkland Islands'

They mustered in the Mess Hall and were told, in general terms, what was going on. Things progressed quickly from there. There were briefings with the whole platoon, using

17: The death and life of Private Jason Burt

tourist maps, and they had an intelligence briefing from somebody who'd had a holiday in the Falklands.

"It was very, very sketchy," Tommy admits.

Jason phoned home about seven that night.

"We've been brought back today. We're going out to the Falklands. Haven't you seen it on telly?"

Something about it had interrupted a favourite programme in the morning, but Terry hadn't taken a lot of notice.

"We're going there if the Argentines don't get of the islands," he added. "We're going to kick 'em off."

"When are you leaving?"

"We don't know. We're on stand-by."

The TV news was full of the story. Few of the British servicemen destined to head there would admit to knowing the exact location of the islands, beyond the fact that they were somewhere off the northern tip of Scotland. Terry were no different.

"I know you've never got any money," she told Jason when he phoned. "When you get there phone me up and tell me you've arrived safe, reverse the charges."

"What d'you mean, reverse the charge? You know where we're going? The Falklands."

"Yeah, Scotland."

"I know you're Irish!" He laughed. "You think I'm going to war and I'm going into a bar to phone? It's miles away!"

At 8.30pm, 3 Para's first campaign O Group – the means by which detailed operational orders are passed down the chain of command – of the campaign was starting at Kandahar Barracks. At short notice, Capt Giles Orpen-Smellie, the intelligence officer, gave a sketchy briefing on the islands from the few sources available. Second-in-command Maj Stratton considered the most likely options: an airborne assault, an air landing operation and an amphibious assault.

As the night wore on, 140 miles away in Plymouth, Brig Thompson's staff was working out how to move the brigade, lock, stock and barrel, to the Falklands, via Ascension Island.

At 0945 on Saturday, April 3, the 700 men of the battalion formed into a hollow square on the parade ground and Regimental Sergeant Major Lawrie Ashbridge – a veteran of Northern Ireland's undercover war – called them to attention. Then Hew Pike, a 38-year-old Sandhurst graduate, spoke. He didn't keep them long.

"Gents, just to let you know the full implications and developments. We will be going to Southampton on Wednesday or Thursday to embark on a ship yet to be named. We will then sail south. There will be a lot of running about and a lot of changes between now and then, so please be patient. You will have tomorrow off and then, by Monday the fifth, you and I will have a better idea of the coming events. Good day."

So, the battalion was definitely heading south. On the whole, Tommy remembers, the men were ecstatic. As far as the Crows were concerned at first, though, it didn't involve them. They were only 17 and wouldn't be going. Or so they thought.

Soon, however, it became apparent the battalion would be sailing at full strength.

"That was it," he recalls. "We were going too."

Doc McAllister had been dating one of the girls in the Women's Royal Army Corps, so Jason and Tommy joined them at a WRACs disco that night. During the evening, over the phone in the bar, Tommy asked Laura to marry him. She agreed, and he spent the rest of the night wishing he was at home with her.

Jason called his folks that Saturday morning, then again later. Terry went straight out and bought him some Good Luck cards, one from her, one from Syd, one from Jarvis and put a pound in each one. Jim sent one, too, and so did Terry's sister.

Jason called on the Sunday and Monday too, and again on the Tuesday, while Syd had gone to Sidney Glazier's to play cards.

Terry sat on the stairs with the phone to her ear as he kept throwing cash into the phonebox.

"Jason, are you feeling all right?" she said. "You'll use all your money."

"I don't know when I'll get another chat like this again."

The cards had amused him, though.

"You'll never guess," he laughed. "Sgt Fuller said 'Burt, it's your birthday, isn't it?'"

"No, it's not sir."

"It is! All these cards."

Jason didn't have a clue what they were, so he opened them while Fuller watched. Then the sergeant read some of them.

"Well, Burt's family has sent enough luck for the lot of us."

They weren't trusting everything to luck, of course. That day, Sgt McKay had persuaded the youngsters to take out life insurance, and accompanied Jason and Tommy to the office. He'd also overseen the youngsters as they filled out MoD Form 106 – their wills. Jason's was typically simple. It named Mrs Theresa Burt as his Executor and left all his Estate and Effects to Mr Sidney Burt. Then they put all their belongings in cardboard boxes. Jason laid his photos, his fishing rod and his provisional driving licence in his and then sealed it.

The term 'green-eyed boys' is one that's cast a massive shadow over the battalion since soon after the Falklands War ended. It refers to the soldiers of Nazi Germany's Second World War special forces, the Waffen SS. In 1982, many Paras were obsessed by the regiment, not for their beliefs or their blind following of Hitler – the black-cap SS were the epitome of that – but for their remarkable prowess and soldiering skills.

Mick 'Babycakes' Southall was one of the 17-year-olds who joined B Company with Jason. The atmosphere wasn't what he'd describe as welcoming when he joined 6 Platoon. Far from it.

The closest thing to a hand of friendship was the one that pointed him in the direction of a book called *Devil's Guard*. It was written in 1971, by George Robert Elford. It tells the story of SS soldier Hans Josef Wagemueller, who spent decades in continual combat, "unconditional warfare", as he called it.

After escaping from Allied forces, he fled abroad where he joined the French Foreign Legion, in which – he claimed – huge numbers of former-Nazis had been recruited to fight the Vietnamese. The German FFL soldiers formed their own units and had German commanders assigned to them.

The book explains how they found their SS tactics perfectly suited to the jungle war against the Communists. After the war, he retired to an Asian country where he related his memoirs to a writer. The result was a shocking book, in the true sense of the word. Its characters defend the Nazi beliefs and way of life. In the West, it was regarded as Communist propaganda, and the French denied that SS or Gestapo members were used in Indochina. Debate since has centred on whether the story's fact or fiction.

The answer doesn't matter. Back then, it was the Para bible.

"The people who didn't recognise that culture were the officers," Mick told me one Sunday morning, as we chatted among the travellers at Hilton Park Services, on the M6. "They didn't live in the barracks."

The so-called green-eyed boys, though, were obsessed with it. With death in particular. Mick's nickname, Babycakes, even came from a Vietnam book. The character he was named after was a mountain of a man.

"I was called it because I was so young," Mick laughed. "It was from a book called *Fields of Fire* (James Webb) which, again, I was told to read. I was told to read *Chicken Hawk* (Robert Mason). Every soldier had a copy of *Devil's Guard*."

I asked him the obvious question: "As a youngster, having gone through basic training, with all the demands placed on you, was that something you were expecting to walk into?"

The response didn't surprise me: "I was expecting a hard time and I got one. There was no getting away from it. Absolutely nothing came as a shock. It was the culture."

Very soon, the Battalion was holding intelligence briefings to keep the men informed of the latest events in the South Atlantic. Noticeboards plastered with information about the Islands lined the scoff hall. The first thing that dawned on most of them, the young Crows particularly, was just how far away the Falklands were.

Tommy was more concerned with how cold it looked. So he rang his mum and asked her, as a matter of urgency, to send him the high-legged Canadian Para boots he'd left in his room in Hoo on his last leave. She responded to the call as most mums would. She sent him a parcel containing a cake she'd baked, some other items of food and year's supply of sweets. But she forgot about the boots.

Warmth was on most people's minds. In fact, two things were at the top of the wishlist of most British infantry battalions. One was windproof clothing – high quality, tightly-woven camouflaged combat gear of the kind routinely worn by Special Forces and troops deployed to Arctic regions. They were difficult to obtain, but 300 sets arrived from the reserves held by Commando Logistics Regiment. Others were borrowed from the 1st Battalion the Prince of Wales Regiment's stores, the Army's Arctic warfare trained battalion, two miles away in Bulford. With each windproof came a quilted jacket and trousers, known as a Chairman Mao suit, which was designed to be worn under combat clothing.

The other wishlist item was a new communications system called Clansman, a robust and portable system that replaced the temperamental and unwieldy Larkspur system.

What didn't need to be said out loud was that, while being deployed as part of 3 Commando Brigade wasn't as good as the old Airborne Brigade, fighting alongside their Royal Marine arch-rivals was better than a 'hat' Brigade whose men hadn't survived such strenuous tests and didn't deserve even the grudging respect they afforded their Navy counterparts.

Behind the frantic activity at Tidworth was an atmosphere that dripped with excitement and tension. While the politicians either side of the Atlantic knuckled down to a long period of shuttle diplomacy, aimed at solving the crisis without another weapon being fired, 3 Para prepared for the minute it all kicked off.

The battalion's heavier support weapons were packed into containers for the 8,000-mile journey south, and the Toms and Crows zeroed their personal weapons at ranges on the Bulford road and at Perham Barracks, just outside Tidworth.

The three rifle companies – A, B and C – had already taken the opportunity to run through section, platoon and company attack drills so that they were thinking on the right lines if, at the end of it all, there was no chance to practice on terra firma.

They were commanded by Majors David Collett, Mike Argue and Martin Osborne. Collett and Argue had seen service with 22 SAS, while Osborne gained his commission in the Territorials, having been a *Leicester Mercury* journalist.

Each company had three platoons of around 30. They were commanded by a Lieutenant or Second Lieutenant with the assistance of a sergeant and formed into three sections of eight, and a small Platoon HQ. Each section was led by a corporal (full-screw) with a lance-corporal (lance-jack) as his second in command, and had a six-man rifle group, and a two-man GPMG team to provide firepower in attack or defence.

Support Company, commanded by SAS veteran Maj Peter Dennison, was composed of specialists using mortars, anti-tank weapons and the GPMG.

Each Tom had a 7.62mm self-loading rifle, devastating at 300m. He also knew how to make the best of the 9mm Sterling submachine gun that was usually carried by radio operators, and others who'd be hindered by a rifle's weight.

The GPMG – or gimpy – fired the same 7.62 round as the SLR but in bursts via a belt feed. It could find a target at 800m or, if tracer ammunition was used, 1100. It could wreck a brick wall, so it's not hard to imagine what it could do to a man.

The rifle group was led by the full-screw, with the lance-jack heading the GMPG pair. They'd support each other in manoeuvres until the final stages of a section assault when, in all likelihood, the riflemen would be operating in buddy-buddy pairs, covering each other and supported by the gimpy.

Their other weapons included the 66mm Light Anti-Tank weapon, a short-range high-explosive rocket launched from a disposable tube that could be devastating but was hard to aim and fire accurately without massive practice, and the L2A2 high-explosive grenade, creating a cloud of metal fragments that was lethal to anyone within five yards.

There was also the No 80 White Phosphorus 'Willie Peter' smoke grenade that had been banned by the Geneva Convention from being used as a weapon but which – whether illegal or not – could shower an enemy position with burning phosphorus that stuck to clothing and skin.

In addition to the section weapons, Maj Butler's D (Patrols) Company – broken into four-man patrols – deployed an 84mm Carl Gustav anti-tank rocket launcher. Formidable.

On Monday, April 5, the Battalion was informed it would travel to Ascension Island on the P&O cruise liner SS Canberra with various commando units from the Royal Marines. All their kit was packed, so the day was were spent sitting around speculating on the immediate future. Some of the concerns among the Toms were echoed in every corner of the camp. Others were left unspoken.

On Wednesday, April 7, word came from Battalion HQ that it would be moving to board Canberra at Southampton the next day. The P&O cruise liner was on its way back from Gibraltar. They'd embark on the Friday.

At some point, one evening, Jason travelled up to Brize to see Claire. The way he walked up to her and said "We're being sent to the Falklands" is still clear in her mind.

"He was concerned and I was trying to reassure him," she says. "I can remember thinking 'How much experience has he got to go to the Falklands? He's too young'. Jason was nervous about it. To this day I remember saying 'But you'll be all right. You'll be all right'. That's what sticks in my mind."

Her mates were in the Spotlight Club, but they decided to keep the evening quiet, and opted to sit in a friend's car, instead, cuddled up on the back seat.

"He was sat next to me. A muscle in his arm kept twitching and he showed me."

"Look!" he said, and they both laughed. Whenever the same happens to her, now, the same thought comes into her head – *Oh, you're just reminding me, are you? You're still about.*

Eventually, it was time to go. He climbed out of the car and wandered off towards the burger van by a side gate to the base.

"I can remember passing him on my left-hand side. I remember staring at him, right until I was out of view of him. I can remember getting his attention, banging on the window, just staring at him until I couldn't see him any more. That was the last time I saw him."

When B Company's fleet coaches arrived at Southampton dock, that mild April 8 back in 1982, there was a handful of girls standing waving banners saying "Go on the Paras" and "We love you". Tommy and Jason cringed. Everyone on the coach laughed and shouted at the girls to go home.

A few minutes later, the coaches stopped and the men climbed off and looked up at the white flanks of Canberra towering above them. It looked magnificent.

The ship was a hive of activity. In the two days since the ship had deposited her tourists at Gibraltar, the dockies had worked overtime to prepare the ship. Fuel intake pipes were being installed for refuelling at sea, two helicopter decks had replaced upper deck fittings and bulwarks, and standard Navy replenishment and communications kits had turned her from luxury cruise liner to a military landing ship.

The Battalion band played the Regimental March, *The Ride of the Valkyries*. They were guided to the Alice Springs Bar and sat around. Eventually, they were told their cabin numbers. And they weren't impressed. Officers of the Parachute Regiment and the Marines had been assigned A and B decks, Senior Non-Commissioned Officers were on C and D decks and the ranks were allocated cabins on F deck.

Tommy looked at Jason. Each knew what this meant. F Deck was deck above the waterline – the perfect striking height for an Exocet missile.

They were told to find their cabins, drop their kit and report back to the Alice Springs Bar. When they found F Deck, Jason and Tommy counted the cabin door numbers until they arrived at their billet and found themselves sharing with Taff Parry and Andy Stone, two old hands. Being the Crows, they were stuck with the bottom bunks.

The next few hours were spent in the bar, watching other members of the battalion and the Royal Marines board. As the hours ticked by, the dockside crowds grew with families and friends who'd come to see the Great White Whale off. Eventually, the order came to line the dockside railing and wave for the cameras. Jason found himself alongside a Marine with a photographer nearby. Soon, though, it became too crowded and the single men

17: The death and life of Private Jason Burt

were asked to step aside and let the married men say their goodbyes. Jase, Scrivs, Grose, Tommy and Steve Jelf hit the bar and tried to buy a drink.

"Sorry," the barman shook his head. "We can only serve non-alcoholic drinks until we set sail."

"F***ing good this is!" Jason complained, but the barman was unmoved.

By 7.30pm on Friday, April 9, the liner was loaded with 2,500 men of 3 Commando Brigade – 3 Para, 42 and 45 Commandos – and the Blues and Royals, better known as the Queen's Household Cavalry, but heading south as the Task Force's only armoured unit. With them were their logistical teams, as well as the media and their MoD minders.

Cabins accustomed to cosseting holidaymakers from resort to resort were crammed with fighting men who'd squashed in their bergens, kitbags, webbings and suitcases and weapons.

The Paras and the Royal Marines might have quietly respected each other's fighting skills in the face of the enemy but, away from the battlefield, their rivalry and resentment was obvious. Both bodies regarded themselves as the elite. The Paras told the Marines that, as it was the men of Naval Party 8901 who'd lost the Falklands in the first place, it was only natural they needed the Paras to win them back. The Marines countered with the taunt that only two things fell from the sky – birdshit and Paras.

On board at least one issue had been settled. P&O were worried that the men's DMS – direct moulded sole – boots would damage their decks. The military were determined their fighting men weren't going to be seen heading for war in trainers and desert boots. As a compromise, they agreed to board in boots and keep soft shoes close at hand.

But there were more practical concerns. Julian Thompson was worried six weeks at sea would take the fighting edge off his men. While Majors and above were allowed to keep a supply in their cabins, 3 Para's CO, Hew Pike, had ordered RSM Lawrie Ashbridge to restrict men to two cans of beer a day, the ration Northern Ireland veterans knew well. Undeterred, the ranks set about finding ways round the restrictions.

By 8pm, with men lining the decks as the Band of the Parachute Regiment played Wagner's *The Ride of the Valkyries* on the quayside, Canberra slipped her mooring and moved slowly down the Solent with buzzing Sea King helicopters ferrying stores to her and the container ship Elk in her wake, alongside the Royal Fleet Auxiliary ship Plumleaf.

Every watch on board was set to Zulu time, and that's where they'd stay, synchronised with the clocks in Northwood, Downing Street and a thousand other Para family mantelpieces around the country, so that 10am at home was always 1000Z on Canberra, whether it was Freetown, Ascension or the Falklands.

So, at 8pm – or 2000Z – the five 17-year-olds watched from the Alice Springs Bar windows as the lights of Southampton slipped slowly away into the night and the English Channel opened up before them.

The Burts switched on the television news that afternoon and the family watched the preparations gather pace. There was more on *The Nine O'Clock News*. This time, while Syd played on the Atari with Jarvis, Terry watched Canberra leave, on her own, with a growing unease. She'd told her sister of her fear that he'd lose an arm or a leg but, as the cameras followed the ship into the Solent, she'd started to believe he was sailing out of their lives.

The next day, as bold as brass, there he was in the national newspapers, leaning on Canberra's rail, lined up for the camera, smiling broadly. It still didn't alter her feeling.

17: The death and life of Private Jason Burt

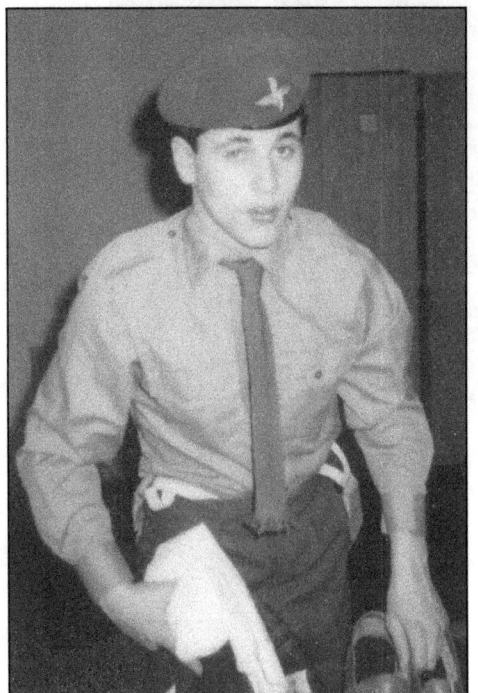
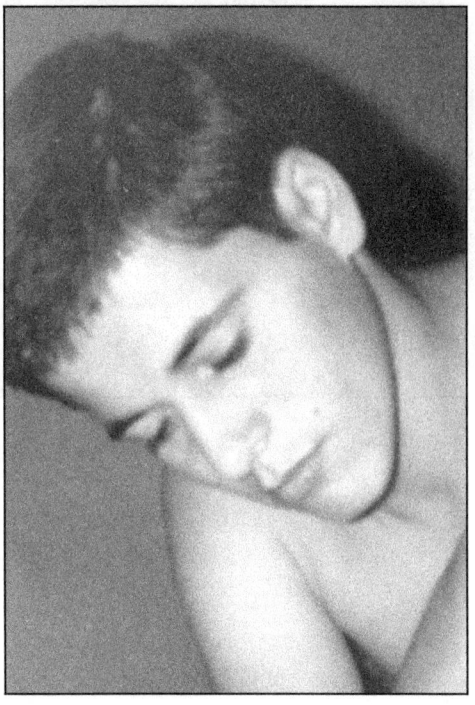

(Top) Jason at the ages of 11 and 16 and (above) while he was in Recruit Company

17: The death and life of Private Jason Burt

(Top, left to right) Scrivs, Neil and Tommy during the Recruit Company and Junior Para stages of training. (Below) 476 Platoon at Brize Norton during initial jump training. Jason Burt is on the left of the front row

Graham Collins' picture of a fellow 476 Platoon lad, maybe even Jason, leaving the balloon. This picture is courtesy of Tommy's website 'Sod that for a game of soldiers'

17: The death and life of Private Jason Burt

(Above) 476 Platoon line up for the camera after successfully completing the Brize Norton jump training course. Neil is on the far right of the back row, with Jason next to him. Tommy's seated eighth from the left in the middle row, while Scrivs is looking menacing second from the left on the front row

(Above) 476 Platoon march proudly on to the parade ground at their Passing Out ceremony

17: The death and life of Private Jason Burt

(Above) Proud dad and lad! Syd with Jason after the Passing Out parade at Aldershot

(Above) Jason smiles for the camera from Canberra's deck

CHAPTER 7

SOUTH

At the end of the security of childhood and before the security of second childhood we find the Paratrooper. Paratroopers are found everywhere, in the air, in bars, behind bars, in trouble, in Depot, on leave and in love.

Paratroopers come in assorted sizes, weights and states of sobriety, misery and confusion. Girls love them, mothers worry about them and the Government supports them and, somehow, they manage to get along.

A Paratrooper is laziness with a pack of cards, a millionaire without a bob, bravery with a grin, a protector of Great Britain and never without a copy of Mayfair in his pocket.

A Paratrooper is a composite. He is as sly as a fox, has the energy of a lion, the brains of a fool, the sincerity of a liar, the appetite of an elephant, the inspiration of a Casanova and the story of a hero.

The story of a hero, indeed.... So, the Burts had picked up a newspaper the morning after Canberra sailed – and there was Jason looking back out of the page at them. Of the 3,000 souls aboard, what were the chances that he'd be the one in the frame?

If there were other moments when the young lads were anxious about their prospects, when they stopped to think what might happen if the Argentinians refused to go, the split-second when the snapper's finger clicked the shutter didn't seem to be one. Neither did he give a hint at any misgivings when he phoned home from the ship the following Monday, four days out of Southampton and heading for Ascension Island.

Tommy was with him, munching on an apple.

"We're going to kick 'em off the island!" he told his mum, but – as most mothers would – she didn't pass the chance to offer some parental advice. In reality, it was less a suggestion than a plea to stay safe and come home in one piece.

"Keep yourselves to yourselves," she suggested. "Remember, you can't get on the wrong side of the older ones when you're going to war, Jason."

"We aren't Crows no more," he said. "We're Paras."

A few days later, a letter arrived.

17: The death and life of Private Jason Burt

"Mum, did you see us getting on the Canberra?" it read. "I can't tell you what we felt like. The whole streets were lined. The Para band played us on."

The nation was riding a roller-coaster. It peaked amid raw excitement as the preparations gathered pace, and dipped as quickly to stomach-churning apprehension in quieter moments when, without warning, we were visited by thoughts of what might be if the Argentinians didn't heed our warning that they couldn't walk into someone's back yard and take what they wanted. Britain didn't let that happen. Or the Paras.

The whole world's watching what we're doing. We're going to kick the Argies off the islands.

The night Jason said goodbye to Claire, they'd sat in the back seat and he told her he feared he wouldn't come back. What none of them knew was that he'd confided to his Nan his belief that, when you were born, God opened a book and wrote your last day on the final page.

Dear Linda....
12,4,82

Hope you are keeping well. At the moment we are just off Portugal, it is quite warm at the moment. We should be in the tropical climate by Wednesday. What have you been doing lately, your in your holidays at the moment aren't you?
At the moment I and feeling quite se sick. The cigarettes are only 25p a pack of 20. We are going to a small island off Africa. What have you been up to lately. Anyway I'm sorry it's short. I won't leave the address. Love, Jason xx

Dear Linda....
22,4,82

We passed the equator a couple of days ago. It was in the 80s. What's the weather like back there in Walthamstow. Not to cold I hope.
Have you been down the Dog & Duck or Rose & Crown.
The ship is getting on my nerves, up and down and side to side, 24 hours a day. Its like living on a rocking horse.... I've only got one complaint and that's the sun. Its to hot (ha ha). Did you see the farewell that we got on telly. Anyway I can't think of anything else to say....

Most of the time, the final page of the book was the furthest thing from Jason's mind. On the way down, he and Tom would write to Graham Collins, taking the Michael because 1 Para were stuck on ceremonial duty in Scotland, telling him how 2 and 3 Para would "sort this thing out".

They made him a card with 'Fighting 2 and 3' on it. He replied with an Action Man flag and an instruction that "when you get there, put this in Stanley". Jason and Tom didn't waste any time sending him a memento to tide him over until it was planted in the

Falklands' capital. They scrawled 'Fighting 2 and 3' on your Jason's backside, stuck Graham's flag between his cheeks, took a photo and sent it back to him.

"All the way down it was good," Tommy laughs when he tells the tale. "But we never thought it would happen."

Dear Linda....
27.4.82

We have now been on the ship for 3 weeks and I'm board stiff. It is very hot where we are. What's it like back there.
It now looks as if we are going in. Did you read in the papers or see on telly, that South Georgia has been retaken by the SAS. Got a letter of my mum telling me that she saw me doing PT when we stopped at a place called Sierra Leone in Africa. Are you going anywhere on holiday this year....

On Saturday, April 17, Canberra and her escorts paused at Freetown, Sierra Leone. That night, the pair sat on the upper deck with their feet on the rails, watching the Freetown lights twinkle, laughing about the stories they'd tell when they came home.

The pictures wouldn't appear on our screens for a few days, but the television cameras pointed at Canberra reflected the setting. Small boats chugged to and fro from shore to ship, a riot of colour and activity – the last time that a pause on the passage south would reflect tranquility rather than war.

Two days later, they were at Ascension Island. Within hours, despite the months and months of training for an airborne assault, they set about rehearsing an amphibious landing, still not convinced it would come to shooting.

Jason had found time – it doesn't seem to have been hard – to drop his folks a line describing the Freetown scene, the boats full of lovely young girls and fruit to match. They weren't allowed to sample either. The girls stayed in the boats, for obvious reasons, and so did the food, in case of food poisoning.

At Ascension Island, he wrote again:

"We had to run into water," he mentioned the landing practice. *"There were all kinds of stingy little fish in there... I've topped up my tan!"*

So it went on. Until 1550 on Sunday, May 2, when the Argentinian cruiser Belgrano was hit by two Mk 8 torpedoes fired the HMS Conqueror. Within ten minutes of being hit, Belgrano was listing. An hour later, she rolled and sank, taking around 350 souls with her and leaving another 650 or so in the freezing South Atlantic water, 30 miles outside the protective Total Exclusion Zone that Britain had thrown around the islands. The grainy pictures that emerged in the coming days told a story that didn't require words.

Two days later, a sea-skimming Exocet unleashed by an Argentinian naval Super Etendard ripped through HMS Sheffield's starboard flank and buried itself in the forward engine-room. The missile didn't explode, but the fires it sparked poured toxic fumes into the ship and 20 men died.

If the news of Belgrano had prompted the thought in most minds that this was it, that the diplomatic efforts to solve the crisis peacefully were doomed, the fate of the Sheffield was the moment when everyone knew for certain that war was unavoidable.

Tommy, at least, wasn't bothered.

"We're very insular in Para Reg. To be honest, if they get blown up on a boat, they get blown up on a boat. It doesn't really affect you in that way. The Belgrano and the *Gotcha!* type thing, I suppose, brings you a bit of bravado. But I wasn't that bothered. Some of our lessons were garroting people. So, being on a boat and being taken out by one missile? We were more bothered about the hand-to-hand combat. In fact, the air raid warning reds were a pain in the arse. We didn't take them seriously. The Navy lads shit themselves and run about, and we'd be *What the….*, but you couldn't relate to it. There was nothing to relate to it."

What did suddenly hit home for many of the Paras, though, was that they were in an alien environment. There was nowhere to run. It was something they didn't like.

"It conflicts with everything you've been taught," Tommy added. "Having a good distance between you, so that the sniper or the mortar round might not take the whole of the section, to 200 men on deck, crammed like this," he squeezes his shoulders. "There was a different mentality. They (the Royal Navy lads) knew what they were doing and how they were doing it. We were just being herded like cattle."

Belgrano was pivotal moment for the Burts. Syd looked at the front pages of *The Sun* and the *Daily Mirror* and said: "What have they done?" Millions of people were saying the same.

What had they done? It's a question that, even now, draws different answers from different people with perspectives on those harrowing events. Norman Tebbit was the Burts' MP. But, in all other respects, to them he was still just a face on the television and a name in the newspaper, as he was for millions. He would become part of their lives, but not for another eight weeks.

He wasn't in Mrs Thatcher's War Cabinet, at the very heart of the decision-making, but he was close enough to consider events with an eye scanning a political and military horizon that was wider than ours, and an ear tuned to conversations the like of which our families will never experience.

"The news was variable, wasn't it?" he considered, years later. "We had our worries, of course, because we had a fairly healthy respect for the Argentinian submarines. Pretty good quality submarines and, clearly, we didn't know if they were going to have a go at the convoys going down.

"If they'd sunk one of the major troop ships, like Canberra, it would have been a pretty serious blow. So, one worried about those things, especially about things that were not suitable to be made public about what was going on.

"There was nothing which, to me, was difficult about sinking the Belgrano. It was immensely sad because of all those young Argentinians that had died. But the responsibility for that lay very clearly with whoever sent it to sea, presumably not to fly flags of welcome as our fleet arrived at the Falklands, but to prevent us acting and try to destroy our fleet and our people. So our decision to sink it was straightforward. Enemy warships that wander around are going to be sunk. There were no worries about that."

Dear Linda....
5/5/82

Thanks for your letter. So Kay is going to University. Does that mean I'll see her on TV in University Challenge. Do you keep all my letters? We have know been on the ship 3 and a half weeks. I haven't had a decent might's sleep because the ship is going side to side. I haven't seen a female in 3 and a half weeks. That is bad news. I think I am forgetting what a girl looks like. I never joined the navy. Have you run over anybody yet? I still haven't got a clue how to drive. The weather is really hot. The water is virtually see-through.
Have you been doing much lately, have you ever been to that disco, I think its called elton's. Anyway I must go now. Lots of love, Jason xxx

Tommy and 'Doc' McAllister had grown up in each other's pockets in the village of Hoo, not far from Rochester. Their escapades make their childhood like a perfect preparation for the Paras. It was Doc who, like Tony Barlow, helped to make their arrival at 3 Para easier than it might have been. He still sensed the need to keep an eye on them during the passage south, which must have been tough, as he had his own misgivings.

"I thought we were going down there to scare them – then it would cease," he admits thinking until Sunday, May 2. "Then things started getting sunk. That's when it started getting real. I started questioning how ready I was to fight a war. The Marines did unarmed combat, practising it on deck. I thought 'we haven't done unarmed combat. How good are we going to be at this?'"

He was also seeing the preparations and the equipment they had and realised they lacked what they needed to do the job.

"They kept saying we was going to get this, we was going to get that, the right equipment, the high-leg boots...." he allows the sentence to trail. On the other hand, as he considered the circumstances, there were things that reassured him.

"As the days went on, we had more competitions against them (the Marines) and just kept winning. As we trained, I realised they weren't as fit as we were. I'd always thought we were equal to the Marines. But we were at a higher level of readiness than them."

At 1654 on Thursday, May 6 – six minutes to five in the afternoon, according to the clock on their mantelpiece – Canberra weighed anchor and set sail for the Falklands accompanied by the doomed HMS Ardent, her ever-present guard ship. For the next two weeks, their progress and course through the increasingly choppy, gloomy, grey seas and skies of the South Atlantic would be governed by the 16-knot top speed of the roll-on roll-off cargo ship Elk, carrying ammunition. And preparations gathered pace.

On Friday, May 7, as Britain widened the Total Exclusion Zone to Argentina's horizon, 12 miles off the coast, and when, in New York, United Nations Secretary General Javier Perez de Cuellar picked up the peace initiative dropped by Peru. Canberra was 252 nautical miles south-west of Ascension, and the big event on board was the call for volunteers to build up a blood bank. The donors would need 10 days to recuperate.

At 0330, with the tiny Ardent and the P&O cargo ship Elk as her constant companions, between six and 12 miles away, Canberra set off on a zig-zag course south. If the Argentinian Navy was going to venture out of port again, following the Belgrano sinking, zig-zagging across the South Atlantic would make it harder for the enemy to find them.

With each hour, the crystal-clear waters and sun of Ascension became an increasingly distant memory, That lump of rock in the middle of the ocean seemed further and further away. But not as far as home.

It was cold and rough and, if anyone on board was still trying to convince themselves that it wouldn't come to shooting, the first nine-and-a-half hours of Monday, May 10, would be a turning point. At 0220, while most of Britain slept, Ardent brought Canberra and Elk back to join the group led by the command ship HMS Fearless, around 1,000 nautical miles – 1,150 miles on land – north-west of Tristan da Cunha.

Using the stores ship Stromness as a guide, the three joined Intrepid, Norland, Atlantic Conveyor and Europic Ferry, and the escort warships HMS Antrim and HMS Argonaut, on a course of 190 at 17kts, about 19.5 mph. Forty minutes later, they changed tack to Co 213 and slowed to 15kts. Half-an-hour after that, the four-day zig-zag stopped.

Wednesday, May 12: After a day on which her Royal Navy 'chummy' ship Ardent demonstrated its Exocet missile systems alongside HMS Argonaut, a significant event occurred. At home, the QE2 embarked from Southampton with 5 Brigade – 3,000 men of 1st Battalion Welsh Guards, 2nd Battalion Scots Guards and the Gurkhas – on board. As with Canberra, 34 days before, the event was stage-managed for news-junkies at home and whoever cared to watch overseas. But its real significance was lost on most onlookers.

Eleven days before, an order had passed from London to HMS Fearless, instructing that the landing must happen between Tuesday, May 18, and Tuesday, May 25. If that order was to be met, the Amphibious Landing Force must be ashore for days before the back-up on QE2 arrived. In other words, the soldiers and sailors heading steadily south would have a long, hard task ahead. That day, Jason sat down and wrote again to Linda:

Dear Linda....
12,5,82

Thanks for your letter, glad you are well and haven't run anybody over yet. I have been to Lords once. I usually go up room up the tope. Its pretty good up there.
By the time you get this letter, we should be on the Falklands. How many letters have I written to you now, couple of thousand or is it more now.
The weather is getting pretty bad now, pretty windy anyway so its not to good here. One of the blokes sent off for a rubber doll and got it the other day, it's not bad looking either. When I do get home, I'm going straight down the Dog & Duck. I don't think I'll come out sober either. Anyway, I'm sorry its short but I've got to go now. Love, Jason xxx

A day later, after Sgt Ian McKay visited the lads in their cabin and made the suggestion, he sat down again and wrote to his family. It would drop through their letterbox weeks after his death, bundled with other items, in a creased envelope:

Tuesday nite, 13/5/82

Dear Mum, Dad and Jarvis,

I hope you don't have to get this letter. I thought I write it just in case. It is now D-3, which means we are going in in 3 days. There are so many things going through my mind. I will end it hear. I not very good at writing letters. I will miss you all very much and I love you all. Your loving son, Jason xxxxx

McKay treated 4 Platoon like his family. He visited them every night, went to every one of their cabins.
"You all right? Get some supper. Get showered, get some sleep, training in the morning."
He was looking for the same things that the officers and medics were looking for on all the other ships. Stress. The ones showing nerves who needed a quiet word, the ones who'd gone quiet, the ones who were un-naturally noisy and hyperactive.
At 2330 on Friday, May 14, as the lads on the troopship were hitting the pillow, north of East Falkland two Sea King 4 helicopters left HMS Hermes with 45 men of D Squadron SAS, heading for a Pucara airbase at Pebble Island, on the north coast of West Falkland.

The raid wasn't that loudly trumpeted, but it would be decisive. All 45 returned unscathed, but for a few scratches. Twenty-two of the men, however, would be dead within five days.

Half-an-hour after the Sea Kings took off, at 0000, Active Service was declared. Everyone at sea was now subject to service discipline, and covered by the Geneva Convention.

Preparations filled almost every waking hour the closer they steamed towards the islands, all of it geared to winning and surviving. Tommy recalls with some disgust – and, it has to be said, recounts with relish – a film they were made to watch, *Medics in Vietnam*. It was probably too gory even for an X certificate.

They were also told to brush up their survival skills – hiding compasses in boots – and tutored in something as macabre as the film they'd seen. They'd carry chains round their collars and D-rings through their zips to use as saws "and stuff". By "stuff", Tommy means a garrote. He remembers larking around with Jason as each, in turn, pretended to be the Argie and the other sneaked up from behind. Corporal Ned Kelly rebuked them for not taking the training seriously. That ticking-off is something Tommy's never forgotten.

Finally, their proper ID was handed in and they were given Prisoner of War ID cards instead.

Sunday, May 16: Anyone who braved the upper deck and studied the sky that morning will have seen grey clouds, low, no more than two or three thousand feet, and grey sea. The choppy conditions had pegged HMS Intrepid and HMS Fearless to 12kts, a speed that was fast enough to have brought this part of the Task Force back together with the dawn at 1100, around 600nm east north-east of Port Stanley, but slow enough to have missed their rendezvous with the remainder of the Amphibious Group soon after.

It wasn't until 1740 that it happened. Canberra was in the left-hand lane of three lines of ships when, out of the murk, one escort warship appeared. Then another. And another. Then the outline of something bigger. And something else. It's hard for anyone who wasn't there to understand what effect that sight would have had. To anyone watching, however, it seemed like most of the Operational Royal Navy was passing before them and into the grey beyond. Jason, Tommy, Ian, Neil and Co won't have known this but, to the Royal Navy boys, this was the moment they knew who was going to win.

Tuesday, May 18: On Canberra, there'd been much talk about whether converting the Whale's plush Stadium Room so publicly to an operating theatre would be good for morale. Whatever, as soon as it was rigged, its first visitors were Paras and Marines. In typical fashion, they wanted to walk through, eyeball the equipment and see the people behind it. They were reassured, I'm told.

With a couple of days to go before the landings started, the Amphibious Group went to

Action Stations twice before mid-day, fearing hostile aircraft were approaching. Both were false alarms, but the nerves were stretched further. No one had forgotten how the Sheffield had been hit. By coincidence, in the midst of it all, the Group had passed the BP tanker British Esk, heading north, carrying the destroyer's survivors.

Wednesday, May 19: The clocks and watches in the Task Force were all following what was known as Zulu time, meaning they were synchronised with home but four hours ahead of the clocks on the mantelpieces of Port Stanley.

As the minute hand slipped past midnight, Canberra and her escorts were 230nm east north-east of the Falkland Islands' capital. By 0445Z, they were in the Total Exclusion Zone and, if the activity on board was the same as on HMS Ardent, they were listening with fear and excitement as Air Raid Warning White moved rapidly to Yellow and Red. This time, the thud of boots running and hatches being slammed shut was for real. In Ardent's Ops Room, they were watching Sea Harriers heading north to intercept what looked like hostile aircraft. It was a false alarm.

Forty-five minutes later, Ardent detached to join the Atlantic Conveyor, which was carrying eight Sea Harriers, five Harriers, eight Wessex 5 helicopters and five Chinook warhorses on her improvised Flight Deck towards the Battle Group, towards HMS Invincible. The fate of that massive container ship would have a dramatic impact on what was to come for the Paras as they tabbed across East Falkland.

Almost six hours later, at 1115, the two ships rendezvoused and the giant Cunard vessel began to 'cross-deck' part of her precious cargo – in other words, transfer it from one ship to another. At the same time, the rest of the Battle Group began a frantic swapping of equipment and men.

On HMS Fearless, the Task Force commanders had calculated the likely casualties if an Argentinian Skyhawk or Dagger slipped past the Thin Grey Line of Royal Navy warships and took out a ship as big and white as Canberra.

The odds didn't look good so, to even them out, 40 and 45 Commando units – including 3 Para – were moved by landing craft to Fearless and her sister ship, Intrepid. It wasn't one of their favourite pastimes. For lads more used to arriving from the air, the thought of lurching around in a landing craft that resembled little more than a sea-going rubbish skip was alarming.

It wasn't easy for Marine, Para or sailor as men swathed in combat gear queued from the unromantic Promenade Deck, down D and E Deck stairs and corridors to the port E Deck Galley doors, waiting for the 'skip' to rise on the five-foot swell to the lip of the hatch… and to take their step of faith.

There was only one tense moment. Just after 1400, a Marine plunged into the cold South Atlantic, between the landing craft and the ship. Splashing desperately, he made it to safety before the waves hammered the craft back against Canberra's hull.

Miraculously, they were safely aboard Intrepid and one step closer to the Falklands.

The emergence of the Amphibious Group from the murky horizon, three days before, had been a breath-taking experience for those who'd seen it from the Bridges or handrails of their respective ships.

At 2215, shrouded in, shrouded in the black of a late autumn South Atlantic night, the re-shuffled Amphibious Group rendezvoused with the Battle Group.

The only people who caught it were the men in Ops Room of the Royal Navy ships. They watched their radar screens and saw the green blips as the other vessels steamed towards them. Thirty in all.

In HMS Ardent's Ops Room. Pete Brierley was following the track of a Sea King helicopter from HMS Hermes to HMS Intrepid, presumably transferring men. He was dog-tired after days at Defence Watches. His mind was beginning to see the pulsing screen as some kind of video game. In a blink, the 'contact' with the Sea King had gone.

He looked at another mate, a lad called Mick Newby. Both knew what had happened the moment the Sea King hit the water. Their immediate superior, Lt Tom Williams, looked at the screen. He knew more. He knew who the Sea King was carrying. The ship quickly offered assistance and joined the search for survivors, but there wasn't much she could do.

As rumours raced through the ship that a chopper had ditched, a picture emerged from the Tactical radio network echoing through the earphone headsets worn by the Ops Room guys. It gradually became apparent that the Sea King had been carrying 22 men of D Squadron 22 SAS who'd blown up six Pucara aircraft on Pebble Island four days before.

Col Pike had also assembled the battalion and its attached troops in the Meridian Lounge. Among others was this simple message. Don't delay the operation by stopping to help casualties until their individual objectives were secured.

Afterwards, with their watches now wound back an hour, the men had returned to their cabins with their thoughts and waited for the call to leave.

They included Sgt Ian McKay. A Para story that emerged in the years after the war – unverified – claims that he confided in CSM John Weeks that he didn't think he would survive the campaign. In general, though, among the understandable feelings of apprehension, the majority of men just wanted to get ashore. They didn't know whether the Argentinians would turn and run, or surrender, or stay and fight. But, after six weeks at sea, they were impatient to find out.

Clambering into the bobbing landing craft and, covered by Harriers from Hermes, ploughing through the rising swell to their new temporary home was a difficult task. They spent two uncomfortable hours in the open before making their entrance to Intrepid and watched in awe as the ship took on water and lowered itself to allow their LCU to sail direct into its hull. The rear doors shut behind and the water pumped out. All they had to do then was walk up the landing ramp to feel Intrepid's deckplates beneath their boots.

From there, though, things went downhill. Intrepid was brim full with soldiers and kit, as well as the usual ship's company. The grey metal corridors and passageways were unnaturally minute, and everywhere they went heads and knees were being knocked and kit was becoming stuck. There was nowhere to sleep either. While Jason and Grose found their own space, in the end, Scrivs and Tommy climbed deep through hatches and eventually found sleeping room in a cramped storeroom with two Battalion medics.

Tommy hated it. The crew walked round dressed in anti-flash gear, looking like something out of *Dr. Who*, hands, necks and chests covered and only a small gap for their eyes. Tommy studied the Intrepids and wondered what would happen to the troops, unprotected, if the ship were hit.

'Doc' McAllister didn't like either. Because he'd been in the Marine cadets, he knew a little bit about ships like Intrepid. His way of thinking was this.

"It's a good warship to go to war in because it has different compartments. It can take missiles and it won't sink. What happens instead is that they'll seal that compartment off and everyone in it will drown! When they issued us with flash gear, I couldn't stay down there. I'd rather take it on the deck than I would take it below. *I'm not staying down there. If you want to stay down there, stay down there!* That's what I did. I got up the top deck. The smells and the heat down there. The noise. You're just closed in."

That evening, as Scrivs and Tommy made their way to the storeroom from a briefing, a Naval officer grabbed them.

"You first-aid trained?" he asked. They nodded.

"Come with me."

In the galley, he told them a Sea King helicopter had plummeted into the sea cross-decking from Hermes to Intrepid. It had been carrying 30 SAS men.

Tommy wasn't ready for what greeted him. Spread out on tables and deck-tiles were the men who'd survived the crash. They were trying to remove their freezing, wet clothing and replace it with warm, dry blankets. Nearby lay the men who hadn't made it.

The medics worked frantically. The galley echoed with orders and requests for assistance and, within seconds, the Naval Officer, another naval rating, Scrivs and Tommy were carrying one survivor down the passage to the Captain's cabin.

As soon as they arrived, the semi-conscious trooper was lowered into a warm bath. He shook uncontrollably and his teeth rattled like castanets. Every time the soldier slipped into unconsciousness, he was woken and asked what his name was, what day it was.

All he'd do in reply was ask whether his mates had managed to escape the crash too. Over and over, he told them he'd gone back into the wreckage and managed to free two men from their seat belts. But the water had been too cold and he'd blacked out. Tommy looked at him and shook his head. They'd been briefed that a man would begin suffering hypothermia within 30 seconds of entering the south Atlantic. Within 90, he'd be unconscious. Some of these men had been in the water for 15 minutes.

Slowly, the warm water increased this man's blood circulation. The blue tinge to his skin when they'd first put him in the bath began to disappear, and so did his uncontrollable shivering. As soon as the officer was satisfied the trooper was going to live, he left Scrivs and Tommy alone to tend him.

One of his legs was strapped up and he told them he'd been on the Pebble Island Pucara raid when he'd slipped and torn ligaments. As he was the patrol's medic, he'd strapped his leg up and soldiered on. Then he looked up at Scrivs.

"Go back and find out how the others are, will you?" he asked. Scrivs looked at Tommy. Neither wanted to move or be the bearers of bad news.

"Someone will be along," they told him. "Just rest for now."

To their relief, within minutes the officer returned.

"Thanks," he said. "Go and get some rest."

They went back to the storeroom, but Tommy couldn't settle. His mind was spinning, about the crash, about the victims, and about what was coming up. Later, he learned that, of the 30 D Squadron men on the Sea King, only eight had survived. The 22 lost had included many from D Squadron 22 SAS, who'd wiped six Pucaras from the enemy's options on Pebble Island four days before.

Later still, among the gossip doing the rounds was that some of the Paras had sneaked on to the upper deck. Through the gloom, they'd seen the preparations continuing with Canberra, big and white, sticking out like a sore thumb. The carrier Invincible was at the rear of one of the two, close lines of ships. Also there was Norland, carrying 2 Para.

By dawn on Thursday, May 20, 11 hours later, the conditions had barely improved, if at all, as the Amphibious and Battle Groups changed their formation to defend themselves from an air attack. The previous day's hasty shift of men and machines from one ship to another had delayed the sending of the so-called Op Gen Mike signal to the commanding officers of the various Royal Navy and Army units. It gave final confirmation of who'd go where and why, outlining the amphibious assault, its timings, the whole plot.

The big picture was this. Reports had reached HMS Fearless of enemy on Fanning Head, but HMS Ardent would still lead the Task Force into Falkland Sound at midnight, then steam south to keep the enemy garrison at Goose Green distracted.

The Paras received the information they needed to know. It wasn't exactly a minute-by-minute schedule for the period from the approach to the AOA, the Amphibious Operating Area, and the initial assault. But it left little time for anything other than reading, sleeping, writing letters or going through another check of equipment.

Above all, it insisted, it might be necessary to change the timings, so they were told to "keep flexy". In other words, be ready for anything.

The Toms read the schedule. Between 2300Z and 0030Z Intrepid's NAAFI canteen would be open. By this time, though few outside the Bridge or Ops Room knew it, HMS Ardent would have sped through the 2.5-mile gap into Falkland Sound, past the enemy on Fanning Head, effectively a high-speed 'mine-sweeper' on its way to the gunline in Grantham Sound, the first direct move that marked the beginning of Operation Sutton.

At 0130Z all Intrepid's hands would go to action stations, ready for the assault ship's own move into Falkland Sound behind her escorts, HMS Antrim and HMS Yarmouth, with Fearless a mile astern.

Ten minutes after, leaving every bit of kit and weapons apart from lifejacket, survival suit and anti-flash protection, the "Embarked Force" would move to 2 Deck or above, a precautionary move that would minimise the number of men below the waterline in the event of an attack or mine-strike.

At 0210Z Intrepid's ballast parties would close up – lock her water-tight doors – to prepare for the operation of moving the troops ashore in their assortment of LCUs and smaller LCVPs – 3 Para's "rubbish skips".

At 0230Z, Intrepid was due to move into Falkland Sound. Ten minutes after, with the ballasting beginning, the troops would return to their messes to collect their equipment.

At 0330Z, half-an-hour after Intrepid was due to anchor, 3 Para would listen out for the pipes that called them to the Junior Ratings Dining Hall for a final meal. Z Company would go first, followed in turn by A Company, B Company, and C Company, with D and HQ Companies completing the flow.

Assault stations would be piped at 0600Z and, at 0630 B Company would assemble with the Z Company group in the cleared Dining Hall.

Another 45 minutes would pass before the Z Company men moved to the Tank Deck, then another 15 before B Company, finally, went to their landing craft positions. As Graham Colbeck describes in his book, *With 3 Para to the Falklands*, "it promised to be an arduous wait".

While they were taking all these timings in, Col Pike's voice echoed off the steel bulkheads around the ship from Intrepid's Main Broadcast speakers. He quoted the words spoken to the men of 6 Airborne Division by Brigadier Hill before the Normandy Landings in 1944.

"Don't be daunted if chaos reigns, because it undoubtedly will."

As Colbeck says: "This was it."

Before dawn, if everything went according to plan, they'd be standing on Falklands soil.

CHAPTER 8

GOING IN

The last hours and minutes were all about final preparations. The only items they'd left behind on Canberra were their bergens and sea kitbags. They were identified by a company colour and number that each man had painted on the back. They would be moved later. To a man, the Paras hoped nothing would stop that happening. The bergens contained their sleeping bags, spare clothing, rations and washing gear, as well as spare radio batteries.

For now, though, there was no point worrying about what they didn't have, just what they could take. Doc McAllister felt the checking and allocating of ammunition took hours. Everywhere, men were finding places to carry extra items – a grenade here, a magazine there – and asking themselves whether this pocket or that webbing would hold or rip.

Doc was typical. He had two 7.62 rounds and two 9mm rounds where there should have been batteries in his pen torch, in case he ran out of ammunition. He had razor blades hidden behind the DZ flash badge on his tunic, in case they had to escape and evade.

Finally, kitted up, he shuffled away up a corridor and met an SAS man coming the other way.

"What you got?" the man from Hereford asked, eyeing the attachments bloating Doc's slender frame. Doc told him.

"Yeah, that's good," SAS man replied. "I'm going now. I ain't got time to muck about. Give us it!"

He took everything off Doc. The young Para stood there and didn't argue. *Okay, fair enough*, he thought, and turned back to the galley to start again.

Last-minute snacks were available when the NAAFI Canteen opened for 90 minutes at 2300. By the time Hands to Action Stations was piped at the prescribed time, the clock had ticked past midnight into Friday, May 21, and HMS Ardent had led the amphibious force into Falkland Sound.

When they were handed the timings earlier in the day and they'd scanned an eye down

17: The death and life of Private Jason Burt

the lines, even the inexperienced lads knew the hardest part wouldn't be the sudden bursts of activity, or the need to stay 'flexy'. It would be the waiting.

With the sterile list of figures turning into ticks of the clock, half-an-hour after Ardent's high-speed dash past Fanning Head, the troops left their equipment and weapons, grabbed a lifejacket each, a survival suit and their anti-flash protection and moved to 2 Deck or above. The thinking was simple. If they were hit, they'd have a better chance of survival. Then they waited.

As they did, Intrepid's crew started closing up the ship ready for their own passage into Falkland Sound, at 0230Z. Ten minutes after that, the Navy lads began ballasting Intrepid so that the landing craft could embark their men and join the troops ashore. At the same time, Jason, Tom and Co returned to their Mess to pick up their kit and equipment.

Within 20 minutes, Intrepid had dropped anchor and the Navy's much-loved action snacks – a meal rustled up in minutes that would nourish them for hours – were issued in the Junior Ratings Dining Hall. 3 Para waited for their call.

At 0330Z, they proceeded to the JRDH. Jason and the rest of B Company were third in line behind Z Company and A Company. Once they'd eaten, they waited at Assault Stations. Three long hours later, they were called to move again, this time to their landing craft positions.

The landings were supposed to happen in darkness. 2 Para and 40 Commando would leave the car ferry Norland and HMS Fearless in the first of two waves and land on the beaches at 3.40am local time, 8.40am at home. 3 Para would follow them to the Tank deck at 0745Z and wait again. This time, to embark.

The wait was longer than they wanted or needed. A 2 Para Tom slipped stepping into the landing craft, breaking his leg as he was crushed between it and the flanks of the Norland. The consequence was significant. By the time the first wave neared the beach in San Carlos Bay, it was almost light.

At 0452, the second wave finally moved into position and, having put her Special Forces troops ashore, HMS Antrim began laying waste to the granite of Fanning Head. More than 250 shells – enough to flatten Windsor Castle – landed on the Argentinians' heads.

At 0530, little more than half-an-hour after the dust had settled, the Marines stormed in to see what 1,800 seconds of high-explosive could do and finish the job. Twelve Argentinians were dead. Nine were wounded. The rest had gone. It was anyone's guess what they'd reported back to Port Stanley before they ran, or died.

For the Falkland Islanders who hadn't already been woken by the distant 'crump-crump' of naval gunfire pounding Fanning Head, the waiting was almost over. As the Marines took Fanning Head, Intrepid's LCUs moved over to MV Norland to ferry 2 Para to their landing beaches at the southern end of San Carlos Water. From almost the outset, for all the

17: The death and life of Private Jason Burt

drills they'd gone through at Ascension, the lack of training began to tell, and the operation began to slip behind the clock.

At 0730, HMS Glamorgan began firing starshell from her 4.5-inch guns, illuminating the landscape with the light of 500,000 candles, then launching rounds of high explosive into the positions guarding the long bay of Choiseul Sound, on the south coast, the other side of Goose Green, doing what it could to convince the enemy that the rest of the Task Force wasn't far behind an SAS team that was attacking on the ground.

At exactly the same time, 2 Para went ashore at the southern end of San Carlos Water. Seconds after, 40 Commando landed at San Carlos Settlement, on the east.

The Argentinians at the settlement ought to have been around to offer a warm welcome and inflict serious damage. But, as the ramps went down, the beaches were quiet. Pausing only to report to Port Stanley that the British were landing, the enemy had fled to the east with the jeers of the locals – according to some accounts – ringing in their ears.

The delay meant another wait for 3 Para before the landing craft returned for the second wave. The tension was high. As they waited, thoughts of what he'd seen the night before filled Tommy's mind.

Eventually, B Company filed in to Intrepid's galley area, where CSM John Weeks hurried them all forward under the weight of their equipment and webbing. As they walked further down to embark on the landing craft, he offered a word here and there to the youngsters and handed them each two grenades to shove down the front of their smocks.

As they prepared to step in to the LCUs, they were also instructed to collect two mortar bombs to take ashore. They'd leave them on the beach, at a safe distance, for the mortar platoon to pick up later.

It added to the colossal weight they were already humping down the ramps. bergens were easily in excess of 50lbs. Webbing weighed more than 40lbs. With a loaded magazine of 20 rounds, their SLR personal weapon weighed 11lbs and the bandoleer of 200 rounds another 12lbs. The whole lot added around 100lbs to the luggage.

Tommy (around 11 stone) and Jason (a little less) glanced at the lads carrying the GMPG (24lbs) and the Carl Gustav (36lbs) and thanked their lucky stars it wasn't them.

They'd been told the landing should be unopposed, though the word 'should' hadn't instilled much confidence and news of 2 Para's arrival hadn't filtered back. Still, by now, many were itching to feel firm ground beneath their boots, even if none were looking forward to the Marine coxswain shouting: "Down ramp! Everyone out!"

Tom remembers the waiting lads and Navy guys quietly watch them go through.

"No great words or anything like that," he says now.

What did the Toms think about stepping on the battlefield with so many 17-year-olds? Would there have been doubt about how they'd handle it?

"I don't believe so," Tommy says. "There's an understanding in Para Reg that everyone has the ability to be there. You've had that grounding. Your full screw might have trained you in Depot and gone back to battalion and said 'I've got a couple of lads coming up... they're all right' or 'These are shit!' Like every walk of life, there'll be the odd one sticks out. But we weren't them. We were not them. We fit in. We were okay."

The only difference was that the old hands were more practised. They'd just done section attacks in Oman when Jason, Tom, Neil, Scrivs and Co joined.

"But, when it came to pepper-potting, we could all do it. We knew that the gun group had to go to high ground to give us covering fire.... It's not a two-month period before you're really accepted. With Para Reg, it takes six months to a year."

If one were needed, a sign that this was for real came when their ID cards were taken off them. As soldiers, they'd become accustomed to having them available all the time. Now they were handed replacements, green and brown, made of a composite material that wouldn't decompose in the ground.

Another brief moment of fright happened when a Para took his mortar round out of its plastic case and promptly dropped it on the floor. They had to be primed before they went off but, nevertheless, it was hard not to take a sharp breath.

Eventually, behind schedule, the LCUs returned from depositing 2 Para a few yards off their beach at the Southern End of San Carlos water, 3 Para were called forward to board the tiger-striped landing craft. For Doc McAllister, an LCU was a "little" boat with little benches down the middle.

"I wanted the big ones. The more troops you get on them, the more targets you've got. We'd got a little one. As soon as the ramp goes down, you've only got a few to fire at!"

As they shuffled towards it, Tommy saw one of the SAS troopers, hands deep in the pockets of his Arctic parka, staring into the distance. Tommy followed his gaze and, through the half-light, he could see land. The trooper looked around and gave the youngster an approving nod and wink, as if to say "You'll be alright son." You'll be all right, son. Tommy wished he'd be right.

As Tommy edged onward, the Sea King survivor recognised someone else behind and stretched out his hand.

"You're bloody freezing!" the Para joked.

"Tell me about it," the SAS trooper laughed back.

Tommy heard them exchange farewells and the obligatory "Look after yourself." Then they went their separate ways.

At around 0800 – 4am for the Falkland Islanders sleeping, mostly oblivious to events at San Carlos – 4 Platoon B Company 3 Para entered the LCU and, to a man, offered silent prayers that the landings would be unopposed, and that each would survive the day.

They also preferred to dwell on the fact that, while Marines could only arrive by boat, Paras could now do the same via an amphibious landing or by throwing themselves out of planes.

Section by section – Jason, Tommy, Scrivs, Grose, Cpl Brian Milne, Cpl Ned Kelly and the others – 4 Platoon were the first men of B Company to embark. Their LCU edged out of Intrepid's docking area and then sailed in circles, waiting for the other elements of B Company to emerge.

The LCU chugged away from Intrepid and into the Sound, then circled until the other landing craft joined it. The sea was rougher than at Ascension, and the LCU bobbed in time with the waves with everyone crouched low. As they chugged round, Canberra was conspicuous among the growing number of ships, a massive white target for any enemy jet that might, at any moment, race across the Sound. There was another silent prayer – that the Argentinians had fled Port San Carlos, and there wouldn't be a fiery D Day-style welcoming party facing the water as the ramp went down on the Sandy Bay beach.

In the distance, they could see the last remnants of the Fanning Head defenders being flushed out, tracer rounds from automatic gunfire cutting through the air, concentrating the firepower on one God-forsaken area. Everybody stared, then crouched lower.

After about 15 minutes, the circling stopped and the LCUs set course for Sandy Bay and 'Green Two Beach', 3 Para's designated landing spot. Tommy and Jason heard the crackle from the radio operator's direction and listened to the numerous messages being sent over the net. Among them came the news that there was a tent on the beach.

Tommy wondered what the hell it was doing there, then instinctively checked his weapon's sights, then his ammunition pouches to make sure everything was how it should be, then that the pouches were securely fastened, so that none of his precious magazines would drop into the water when the order came. Jason almost certainly did likewise.

They peered over the side of this over-sized rubbish skip and watched the other camouflaged LCUs crashing through the waves. Letting his mind run ahead, with a selfishness that was pricking guilty consciences in craft all around San Carlos Water, Tommy couldn't help feeling relieved that there were plenty of other targets to aim at, should there be an Argentinian welcoming party on the beach, after all.

Closer to the shore, their Marine coxswain used a white pole to test the depth of the water and the slope of the beach as the ramp went down. It was too deep. They moved another landing craft alongside.

"Prepare to beach!"

The call echoed off the metal sides of the LCU. It's straining diesel engine slowed to a throb and the men of 3 Para braced themselves for the moment the dropping ramp would open up their first view of the landing beach.

17: The death and life of Private Jason Burt

Dash, down, crawl, observe, sights, fire. The standard operational procedure for coming under fire was engrained in the mind of every Para packed in that skip as the ramp jerked into life and slowly, painfully dropped lower and lower. It took an eternity before the next command came.

"BEACH!"

Jason's eyes would have looked straight over the shoulders of the men in front. He wanted to see the foreground and the middle distance, to make sure the men who'd supplied the intelligence had been as good as their word. No Argentinians.

He raised his weapon to a makeshift firing position and stepped over the ramp into the sea, knee-high in the water, focussing on a spot just above the beach where he'd go to ground. To his right, other lads were up to their waists, wading the final few yards to touch the Falklands, mixing hops, skips and very small jumps ashore that would have been comical at Weston. But this beach was only about 40 feet wide, and covered in stones that made the race across it, laden like a packhorse, almost impossible.

He dropped his mortar rounds alongside Tommy's at the top of the beach, pumped his legs some more and ran on before hitting the soggy, boggy ground to take stock.

"Marvellous," Tommy winced. For the locals, it was 6am. To men with soaking feet, it was 1100Z. As the days and events unfolded, the wade through the water would have huge repercussions. For now, it was simply a nuisance.

As they gathered their thoughts, they could hear gunfire from their right and were told it was the SAS attacking an observation post. At least no one was shooting at them, yet.

The order to move off was given, and Jason's section joined the Platoon and Company formation advancing up a dirt track towards the Port San Carlos Settlement. As they tabbed forwards, word passed down the staggered file formation that the 40-odd Argentinians they'd been expecting to greet them had fled on seeing 2 Para go ashore. Instead of a fight, it meant they could head for Windy Gap.

As A Company moved in to the settlement itself, and C Company headed to a large group of nearby hills called Settlement Rock, news came that an Army Gazelle helicopter had been shot down by the fleeing Argentinians. Word spread that the crew had been shot in the water while trying to swim to shore. A patrol was sent from B Company to find the helicopter pilots. They found them both, dead.

Before they began their four-mile uphill walk to Windy Gap, an exposed knob of land above the settlement, the order came to 'buddy off'. Jason was paired with Cpl Brian Milne, an old hand who'd helped to make his arrival in B Company as smooth as possible. Tony Barlow was told he'd be with Sgt Ian McKay. Tommy remembers clearly the sinking feeling when his 'buddy' was identified. He looked at Jason, Scrivs and Grose. They were laughing.

"I thought *Oh, f***ing hell!*" It was Ron Duffy, the intolerant, mad Scot with a deep desire for everything to be as he liked it, and a black book to record the names of those who didn't see things the same way.

The Company then broke down into platoon and section formations for the hard uphill slog through bracken, fern and bog. With the absence of trees and rocks robbing them of cover from enemy fire Cpl Brian Milne, the section's commander, put them in arrowhead formation with the gun group high to the left. Within minutes of the tab starting, they were back on the wet ground and cursing.

"Air Raid Warning Red!"

In seconds, Argentinian aircraft had come and gone, screaming overhead towards the ships in San Carlos Water. The sky lit up. Missiles and naval gunfire diced the air from all directions but, while Tommy lay there feeling vulnerable and useless against the attack, Milne decided he'd seen enough and ordered the section forward. Time and again the air raid warnings were barked out, so many that, in the end, the last few were ignored.

Once they arrived at Windy Gap, they too began to dig in to their front-line defensive positions and, as the beach-head was established below, waited for the counter-attack. It seemed inconceivable that the enemy would not mount at least some sort of harassing attack. The Paras, after all, would have hit the Argentinians hard and quickly if the roles had been reversed.

The trenches weren't dug randomly. There was precision and purpose in where they were put. From either end of a six-foot trench they gave themselves arcs of fire. The man of the left of Trench 1 had arcs of fire to the left and the right. His buddy on the right had an arc that met the arc from the left of Trench 2. With no overlap, the line of trenches created one massive defensive area through which the enemy would have to come in a head-on attack.

Milne sited the trench he was sharing with Jason overlooking Cameron's Ridge, across Port San Carlos Water, with the 'Knob' – a reference point on the map – to their front.

The trench would be in three parts. The first, the centre, was for their firing positions, dug about chest high. The two either side of it would be their individual sleeping areas, not dug as deep as the main trench but still managing to look like a grave, to Tommy's eyes. They'd overlap the sleeping areas with string mesh held in place by foot-long metal spikes rammed into the soggy Falklands soil and stretch a waterproof cover across. On that 'ceiling' they'd spread a thick layer of soil to offer 'protection' against air attack and then add the finishing touch, a covering of camouflage flora picked from the surrounding area.

Tommy and Ron had only dug four feet down when the trench floor filled with water. Tommy could have cried. He was already dripping from the constant dive for cover from the air raids. But not Duffy. He happily went on digging for Britain.

Once the trench had taken shape, they set about putting up the sticks that would stop their weapons going past the end of the arc of fire during the hours of darkness, a precaution against shooting each other.

Then they completed their range cards, a sketch of the land in front with reference points and ranges to help them concentrate fire towards the enemy at a pre-determined spot. For them, for instance, 300 metres would be The Knob. It was a basic system, but very effective.

In some areas, the ground was easier to work than in others, but in all it wasn't long before all the deepening trenches filled ankle-deep with water. Some of the guys gathered rocks from the surrounding area to provide protective walls.

Doc McAllister and his 5 Platoon mates found themselves on a part of the line where it was harder to dig quickly. To add to the problem, the Argentinians chose the moment to launch their riposte, from the air, heading for the Thin Grey Line of Navy ships in San Carlos Water. The Toms grabbed their rifles took pot shots at the incoming Pucaras.

"Then we knew we were actually in it," Tommy says.

Some of the planes were so close the lads felt they could almost reach out and touch the pilots. Doc, understandably, was only interested in making that distance as far as possible.

"We'd only dug about two foot and we was getting these Pucaras coming in," he laughs.

Salvation came in the shape of a 9 Squadron Royal Engineer who ventured past. He was in possession of some P4 explosive and a tamping tube.

"You having problems?" he asked Doc.

"Can't get down."

"Got a ration pack?"

"Yeah."

"Gis a ration pack and I'll dig your trench."

He tamped his big metal tube down into the ground as far as he could, pulled a detonator cord from a pocket, then some P4, tamped it down… and promptly blew a big hole right where Doc and his oppo wanted it.

Cool. That'll do, Doc thought.

Not long after the trenches were completed, Doc was doing a stag – a lookout duty, scanning the horizon in the direction from which the Argentinians would most likely come – when he heard the sound of a motorbike approaching. He turned to look and saw that the rider was wearing a blue PTI's top and carrying a sniper's rifle.

The soldier stopped, said "Two to us!" and rode on again.

The Paras put two and two together – literally – and decided the SAS had just avenged the Gazelle crew who'd been shot.

Ron either liked you or he didn't and there was nothing you could do to change that. That's how Tommy starts reflecting on being in the same trench as Ron Duffy. Although the gruff Scot clearly liked him and Jason, Tommy still regarded him as "a nutter. He really was not balanced". It didn't take long for Tommy's worst fears to materialise.

To start with, Duffy wasn't happy with the name Cameron's Ridge. Whether or not Tommy wanted to know, he was going to find out.

"The Camerons, like the Macdonalds, cannay be trusted," he declared. Tommy recalls them settling on naming it Scottish Ridge.

Not long after, they were on stag, peering towards Scottish Ridge with Ron on lookout, the sights of his rifle set on 300 metres and his eye glued to the weapon.

"Are you looking through your sights?" he quizzed Tommy.

"Yes, Ron."

Tommy knew everyone else would be on stag would have having a crafty cigarette. Not Ron. As far as he was concerned, they were now in charge of the battalion.

"If they come over the ridge, we'll expend all our ammunition, then fix bayonets and charge them," he growled.

"Yeah, okay Ron," Tommy heard himself reply, even though the voice inside his head was saying *Yeah, right, I'll run down there with me bayonet on while everyone else is hammering it in here.*

But Tommy freely admits that he'd have found that day and the coming 20 much, much harder to face without him.

"Ron was this kind of bloke. You'd tab 15 miles, freezing cold, soaking wet, and every time we stopped for ten minutes rest he'd say 'Right, get you boots off, take your socks off, wring them out, swap them over your feet'.

"I wanted to say 'Piss off! Leave me alone!', but you'd go 'Okay, Ron. Yeah' because, once you were in that book...."

So Tommy would take his socks off, wring them out and swap them over.

"Honestly, it was like having new trainers on. I was so much the better for it and so many of the other lads didn't do it."

Jason was one of those who didn't.

After returning the surrounding area to its natural state, the afternoon was spent taking a grandstand view of the Argentinian aircraft, sun glinting off their wings, banking and running towards the ships in San Carlos Bay. They watched the Navy send up a wall of anti-aircraft fire. It was awesome but unnerving. The planes came and went long before the roar of engines turned the sky to thunder.

Back at The Settlement, though, tragedy had struck. A and C Companies were patrolling their own map areas, moving within the confines of particular grid references to stop one patrol running into another. But something had gone badly wrong near the beach-head when a section from A Company reported contact with the 'enemy' and requested artillery support. It wasn't the enemy, it was C Company. They fired back on A Company, who'd made the mistake of giving their own position as the artillery target. The so-called blue-on-blue 'friendly-fire' tragedy lasted 62 minutes and left eight men seriously wounded.

At dusk that afternoon, B Company began a ritual that would continue through to Longdon by 'standing-to' for an hour, prepared for attack. At dawn, they'd do the same. Before that, however, they'd experience their first long, 14-hour night dealing with whatever the early winter could throw at them.

Down the line, men wore long johns and a long-sleeved vest covered by lightweight green trousers and – though they weren't widely liked – an Army KF shirt to keep the icy wind at bay. On top, they'd pull an Army jumper and their camouflaged windproof smock and trousers. Sometimes they'd wear a quilted jacket beneath the smock and quilted trousers. And, if they had them, two pairs of Arctic socks. Many took to wearing their standard 'headover' balaclava round their necks, but their helmets – with their cherished maroon berets tucked inside – were usually replaced by an Arctic cap.

2 Para and the Marines had been issued with closed-cell sleeping mats, to insulate them from the cold ground, but 3 Para weren't. They were left in their 'doss bags'. To a soldier in the field, his doss bag's a lifeline. It provides the warmth and comfort that, in turn, provides a night of peaceful rest. In Tommy's case, it didn't.

Once the zip on his 'green maggot' broke that first night, that was it. However hard he tried to cover himself in the four hours he had to sleep, the wind found a gap and kept him chilled. As the night progressed, he and Duffy took their turn on a two-hour stag duty, watching and listening for signs of unusual activity to the front of the section position. Ron had already ensured that the sights on Tommy weapon were set to the battle setting of 300m. Then for two, long hours, he stared down them. Nothing happened.

Saturday, May 22: Col Pike visited 3 Para and moved one of the platoons further south down the slope to a new position that gave the company more depth.

The three B Company platoons had dug in on what had been designated the reverse slope, which assumed the north slope was the forward slope and closer to the enemy. The Milan posts were set up to cover any attack from any direction except the northern slope, upon which they were sited, which was regarded as the forward slope and, therefore, closer to the enemy. This area was covered by D Company patrols, who were active well in advance of the main battalion positions, and routine patrols from the rifle companies, like the ones that had ended with the blue-on-blue shortly after the landings.

Pike also brought the first intelligence briefing since the landing. The NCOs filtered the news down, and it was encouraging. A number of enemy aircraft had been shot down, with very little damage caused to the aircraft and ships of the Task Force. At the end, Sgt Ian McKay ventured that, if the number of enemy aircraft shot down was correct, the Argies were already out of their light turbo-prop Pucara fighter-bombers.

They waited for more air activity that day, but none came. What the troops establishing the San Carlos beachhead didn't know, grateful though they were, was that bad weather on the Argentinian mainland had locked the airbases down.

Sunday, May 23: The next day, the bombing raids began again. From their south-facing trenches, they watched as Daggers speared towards the fleet on such contour-hugging bombing runs through Port San Carlos Valley that, once again, they felt they could almost touch them. Daggers and Pucaras. The intelligence reports obviously weren't worth a jot.

If that didn't exactly make them smile, neither did the fact that, a few yards to the rear of B Company's trenches, the Royal Artillery had set up their Rapier guided anti-aircraft missile launcher. A prime target for any pilot.

"Thanks a bunch," Tommy thought. First bayonet charges. Then Pucaras. Now this. More attention. Still, he mused, if the enemy did appear over Scottish Ridge, and found Ron and him in mid-charge, at least they'd have a little extra firepower to call on. Frustratingly, however, when the next stomach-turning roar of an enemy plane cut through the air, there was a lot of shouting and rushing around and the Rapier system refused to fire. To make up for it, they fired their own weapons at the low-flying machines, like some real-life arcade game, until the order came through the stop wasting ammunition.

A while later, more bad news came. HMS Ardent, the frigate that had escorted them on Canberra from Ascension, then led the Amphibious force into Falkland Sound two days before and bombarded Goose Green to keep the enemy's heads down, had been sunk with the loss of 22. To the Toms who'd had a glimpse of Navy life below decks on Intrepid, it was a sobering moment. But Ardent wasn't the only setback.

That night, a large, bright orange flash lit the sky to the south-west. Jason and Tommy shot out of their trenches to watch. They wouldn't find out for a few days, but it was the Ardent's sister ship, HMS Antelope. An unexploded 1,000lb bomb had detonated, killing the disposal man trying to defuse. Soon after, consumed by fire, her main Seacat and torpedo magazines erupted. She sank the day after.

Monday, May 24: The beautiful weather was as beguiling as it was welcome. The Argentinians were back in the air for the second day running, this time looking for blood around Windy Gap as well as out in the Sound. Two Daggers attacked the Battalion positions. The order went out again that small arms fire was no longer to be used against the enemy aircraft but, for the most part, it was ignored.

Tommy and Ron were the obvious exceptions, as they were still working on Ron's plan to expend all their ammunition against the enemy before running at them with bayonets fixed. On the other side of the Sussex Mountains, to the south, 2 Para were preparing to raid Goose Green, but B Company were still sitting tight, conducting patrols to the east of the Battalion area and hoping that – if the gossip was right – the Rapier system would be working the day afterwards.

Tuesday, May 25: Another good day, if windy. Uneventful on the ground, except for one Mirage attack. The Rapier fired but missed. Feet wet, trench foot increasingly likely to be a problem. Word came in some corners of the 3 Para positions that 2 Para wouldn't be attacking Goose Green just yet.

Brigadier Julian Thompson's plan was to lift the brigade in a series of night moves towards Port Stanley using helicopter support in the shape of the four Chinooks and six Wessexes heading for the islands on board the container ship Atlantic Conveyor.

On the evening of Tuesday, May 25, though, came news no one wanted. An Exocet had sunk the ship. Twelve men dead. One Chinook had been saved. Just one.

It left Thompson and his fellow commanders trying to work out how the plan to hit Stanley could be completed. The Atlantic Conveyor loss meant only one company could be moved at night. It would be possible, but risky. The troops moved forward would be open to counter-attack, without support, while the long-distance shuttle continued. In the event, Thompson decided it was best to await the arrival of 5 Brigade.

Wednesday, May 26; Col Pike visited B Company to tell them they'd be doing just that before cracking on. It didn't go down well. For some, the idea of waiting for Guards and Gurkhas added insult to injury. Whatever the love lost between Paras and the Marines, they each recognised each other's fighting prowess and would have settled for going into battle side by side.

Far from waiting, though, Mrs Thatcher and her military advisors had other ideas. They feared that Al Haig's continuing efforts to broker a diplomatic settlement – despite America's statement of full support for the British – would prevent the islands returning to their rightful possession. London told Thompson to get on with it.

The obvious solution for a quick success was to resurrect the plan to hit the garrison at Goose Green and Darwin, the plan involving Col H Jones's 2 Para that had been aborted on the Monday when bad weather stopped support artillery being moved into position.

While Jones prepared, the COs of 45 Commando and 3 Para were given their orders. The Marines were to head for Douglas settlement, Hew Pike's men were going to Teal Inlet, half-way to Port Stanley. On foot.

That night, Jason, Tommy, Scrivs, Grose and Ron strode away from Windy Gap with the rest of their section – led by Cpl Brian Milne – on patrol to clear the ground to the east. A few miles out, as the temperature dropped and the wind picked up, they came across an old farmhouse with sheep pens and several other outbuildings.

Milne laid the section up short of the buildings and they patiently observed the area, looking for signs of movement that could mean enemy troops. None could be seen, so Milne decided to take a closer look. He called Tommy and one other – Tommy can't remember who – and briefed them to take out one of the first small outbuildings.

They were to move close as possible to the outbuilding undetected. If they detected any Argies there, Tommy would lob his grenades inside, then follow his oppo in and clear up.

As the section crawled nearer, their hearts pounded in their chest. Tommy recalls hearing every thump echoing in his ears. But the raid never happened. Just before the pair of them set off, Milne decided the barn was empty and called it off.

Tommy felt relieved but untested. After another period of observation and listening, they all nervously entered the barn. No one was inside, but there were signs that it had been used to house sheep and they were amazed how warm it was, sheltered from the icy wind. Milne told the section to have a hot drink before they set off back to the Company position.

They hadn't gone far on the return journey before they heard the familiar thud-thud-thud of twin rotor-blades. Jason instinctively turned as several Chinook choppers rumbled overhead. The radio quickly informed them they weren't friendly. It would transpire later that they were heading for Goose Green, carrying reinforcements, tipped off by what the Paras were told was a British newspaper story that 2 Para were ready to strike. There'd be moments to come when the Toms would wish the loud-mouthed journalist could be made to pick up a weapon and face the same fate awaiting H Jones' men. The word 'betrayal' was uttered by the most angry of the Paras.

Thursday, May 27: They were gathered at an intelligence briefing. Top of the list was Atlantic Conveyor. The ship had been sunk laden with the Chinooks that were meant to leap-frog them forward quickly and capture large slices of No Man's Land.

If that wasn't bad enough, the container ship had also been carrying their Arctic boots and other essential Arctic clothing. It meant they'd be tabbing to Teal Inlet, 30-odd miles away, where B Company would lead the Battalion advance against the Argentinians.

The Marines had opted to 'yomp' west, carrying all their gear, as was their tradition. The Paras resorted to type as well.

"We'll be tabbing in light order," Sgt McKay informed his 4 Platoon Toms. "Your bergens will be airlifted in once we've secured the settlement. If Para Regiment remains true to form, we'll probably end up tabbing all the way to Port Stanley!"

Tommy says his heart sank, so we have to assume that Jason's heart did the same. Not that any of them could do anything about it, even if they'd wanted to. Seventeen or 27, Tom or Crow, this was what they'd signed up for.

Thirty miles to Teal Inlet was bad enough, but Port Stanley was more than 80 miles away. They were seriously compromised. The Falklands is a cold and wet place where the wind chill factor can drop to minus 70. That fact had buttressed Mrs Thatcher's determination to draw a line under the search for a diplomatic solution before the three-week weather window for a counter-invasion had passed.

Their bergens carried all the essential items of spare clothing they'd need to stay warm and dry. But, with a 30-mile march ahead, no one wanted to wear too much. The uncomfortable sweat of the slog would soak their clothes. On the other hand, wearing too little would be risky. Every time they stopped, the wind would cool them down and exposure might set in. Saying goodbye to their doss bags was painful. A warm night's rest was going to be a thing of the past.

At around 1430Z, just after dark, they turned their backs on their bergens and set off in a long, semi-tactical snake for Teal Inlet. In the gloom, 45 Commando marched out of Port San Carlos too, heading for Douglas.

CHAPTER 9

BREAKOUT TO TEAL INLET

The men of B Company who started snaking from Windy Gap towards the horizon at around 1430Z on Thursday, May 27, had been trained to cope with what was to come on that body-breaking tab across East Falkland towards Mount Longdon. But, if most of the rest of us live to be 100, we'll never know or understand how that was possible.

B Company's initial pace was furious and the Marines were soon out of sight as the Battalion stretched back in an 'S' formation as far as the eye could see.

The snake could be demoralising if you were at the back, but being at the front had the opposite effect. Within 90 minutes, however, the pace dropped. The ground was too difficult. If it wasn't walking uphill, it was walking down. If it wasn't wading through knee-high streams, it was hauling boots from boggy marsh. Before long, trousers, boots, puttees and socks were soaking wet and the Toms were complaining of blisters.

Every hour, they'd stop for a 15-minute break and Ron Duffy would immediately be on Tommy's case, reminding him of the advice he'd growled earlier.

"Socks off, wring 'em out and swap 'em from foot to foot."

The result was uplifting. He felt a thousand times better.

The tab was endless, though, and so was the rain. At times, they'd find themselves in double-file formation. As darkness fell, Tommy looked right and saw 5 Platoon coming up alongside. For several minutes, he scanned the gloom, hoping with every squelching step to pick out Doc McAllister, to see the walk he'd watched since childhood, hoping for a brief moment of morale-boosting chat, respite from the relentless grind.

When he finally saw the shape he recognised, it was hunched, face down in a wasted effort to cheat the wind and rain. It's the sight of the Arctic hat that sticks with Tommy. When the headgear was issued on Intrepid, they'd howled. A hat was for 'hats'. This one was quilted and camouflaged. Most laughably, its woollen flaps pulled over the ears and tied under the chin. Everyone knew a Para didn't cover his ears. A Tom with his ears covered couldn't hear, and that put him and his mates at risk. Stu's flaps were down. Tommy was shocked.

"How you doing mate?" he murmured as Stu neared. Stu looked in his direction.

"F**k this," he groaned. "I've had enough."

Tommy didn't know what to say. The wind and rain was never-ending. The terrain was tough. The streams were freezing. His feet were killing him. But he was a Crow and Stu was a Tom. He was still very proud, very indoctrinated, very 'here-we-go', so he'd been trying to tab with his head up. They were Paras. Things like that never bothered them. Did they?

Stu tabbed off as 5 Platoon moved to the head of the snake, and Tommy was left with his thoughts again. All around him, wind-driven rain ripped like sandpaper across their faces. Webbing was digging in to their hips and backs. Feet squelched with every step. Boots rubbed through soaking socks. For the 17-year-olds, the tough skin of P Company was being softened by the constant wet, giving less and less protection to the soft, blood-filled layers beneath. They were cold. Cold to the bone.

In the blink of an eye, the tab had become unbearable. But there'd be hours more tabbing before respite came.

Eventually, they halted in a bog at the junction of two wire fences. Two fences meeting wouldn't normally amount to much. In the Falklands, though, it was an occasion for the map-maker to celebrate and put pen to paper. They were given the order to rest for a couple of hours and change into warm clothing.

Warm clothing?

As he removed his wet gloves to undo his wet puttees and laces, Tommy's hands shook. *What is the point*, he thought. *I'm going to wring out my socks, put my boots back on and step straight back in the water!*

The sight that greeted him as he peeled his first sock off was greeting men all around. The sole of his foot was swollen, white and water-logged. He was ordered to jam the foot under the mad Scotsman's armpit. So he did and, after a few minutes, he felt heat, a tingling sensation that turned into a jab of pain as blood started flowing.

He felt better until first light, when the order came to stand again in the freezing, ankle-deep water and continue the tab. The groans told their own story. After 15 hours of tabbing, exhaustion was obvious everywhere.

For Private Tony 'Frog' Barlow, an incident on the approach to Teal Inlet illustrates the physical and mental torture of the tab, Jason's determination not to give up, and the brotherly concern that still, at times, makes him feel guilty.

"Major Argue got us lost, big time," Tony curses still. "We're talking five, six hours here. No sleep. No food. Marching through the night, not having a clue where we are. We've marched in circles and we're soaked and freezing cold.

"We were having a rest and Jason came back down this hill. His trousers were down by his arse. He was soaking wet and he just didn't want to go on any more."

Tony went straight to him. He knew Jason and the other Crows were young. They hadn't had time to go on exercise with the Battalion. If they had, they'd have known what it was like to tab with wet feet, and they'd have learned how to cope.

"What you doing?" he called to Jason. "Come here. Get changed, while we've got a break."

Tony handed his dry pants and dry socks over, took Jason's off him and did what Ron would have done, put the wet clothing by his own skin so that his body heat could dry it.

"I got him perked up, got him a brew and got him back. He'd just had one of those moments. We used to call it 'a moment'. You just want to jack. Once he'd got his dry gear on and had a brew, a bit of sleep, he was as bright as a button." Like the other hardened men around him.

He knew jacking wasn't the answer: "If you jack, you lose the respect of the lads. But you don't jack. Everybody notices. They know he's on the verge of jacking. You don't go through it on your own. The guy was a paratrooper. He wasn't going to jack. He was a young lad, he had his cup of tea...."

"It's like I say to Tracy.... Sometimes, I blame myself. If I'd have let him jack then, he could have still been alive."

They'd slogged for 15 hours, but there were hours more to come, up hills, down hills, through bogs and marsh, bent double, hobbling like old men on a rainy day.

Eventually, they came to a wide, deep river and, one by one, the agony increased. On the other side, as they prepared to clean their weapons and ammunition, B Company's OC, Major Mike Argue, told them to rest. They were ahead of schedule, so they'd pause for three hours or so.

It was 1500Z, around 24 hours since they'd left Windy Gap. The promised three-hour respite lasted two hours before word came that they were moving off to catch the last of the light and pick up the back-breaking pace on the final leg to Teal Inlet. The plan then was to set up an ambush outside the settlement.

Those last eight miles were merciless, but soon they were ready to take up positions in the ambush area. They lay there for hours, waiting, thankful that the rain had finally stopped, but cursing the freezing temperatures, the frost, and – without warning – the snow that began to fall.

When Major Argue eventually decided it was time to enter the settlement, Sgt Ian McKay rounded up 4 Platoon as his back-up. They followed him to the biggest house in the settlement and knocked the front door.

Jason, Scrivs, Tommy, Grose, Brian Milne, Duffy and the others were huddled behind McKay, weapons at the ready, as a woman opened the door and peered round.

"Who is it?" she asked.

"Major Argue, B Company, 3rd Battalion Parachute Regiment," he told her formally.

"There's no one here," she said, and tried to close the door.

"You don't understand," he stuttered. "We're from Her Majesty's Forces – British Army. We've come to liberate you!"

"Oh, in that case, you'd better come in."

The door opened and Argue entered, followed by the whole of 4 Platoon. They were shown in to a large front room with a huge table at one end. At the other, armchairs were spread round the large, open fire, the main source of light. The platoon's eyes were drawn to the homely flames.

Argue gathered Sgt McKay and the other NCOs around the family, and the lady apologised for her abrupt welcome. She was embarrassed. Only hours before, the Argentinians had left with some Land Rovers. She'd thought 4 Platoon's knock on the door was the return of the invaders, and she didn't want to talk to them.

She set about making pots of strong, sweet tea, which she took out to the Paras with a huge selection of homemade cakes. For the first time since setting foot on the island, Tommy felt a gratitude for the sacrifices being made and forgot about the hardships. She rearranged the furniture so a few could dry their wet clothing and boots by the fire. Then she left the room and reappeared with a pile of towels.

Without a second thought for the blokes digging trenches outside, they stripped and watched steam rise. As the hours passed, it dawned on them that Argue was going to let them stay, and many of them dozed off.

Before first light, though, he told them to dress and take up defensive positions outside. Jason reached down to the hearth, picked up his boots and realised they were rock hard. He tried to wedge his feet in but couldn't. They were too swollen.

Tommy had done the same. He looked around in panic, fearing what the NCOs would say, and saw he wasn't alone. After several painful attempts, he crammed one foot home, then the other. Walking, though, was almost impossible.

A thin coating of snow greeted part of 4 Platoon as the thin sun rose over the inlet on Saturday, May 29, and revealed a collection of small huts and trees. They formed up and waited to be told where to take up their defensive positions. What they heard was Major Argue's anger, aimed at the men who were still unable to put their boots on and would stay behind.

"Get a grip," he shouted. "You've got a job to do."

After clearing the snow, it took most of a back-breaking morning to dig a trench in the frozen ground. As they toiled, the Milan sections arrived via Sea King from Windy Gap. Later, the sole Chinook to escape the Atlantic Conveyor sinking landed near the Settlement manager's house and swapped its load of ammo and stores for an Argentinian who'd demanded the keys to a vehicle, at gunpoint. He'd intended to make his escape from the approaching British, but hadn't banked on the locals disabling the getaway vehicle.

Stu McAllister's mood hadn't improved with the hours of rest. His frozen feet were still the centre of a horrible burning sensation, like a prickly heat. He reflected on what he'd said to Tommy during the tab. He would never have made his school friend's spirits plunge on purpose, but they'd shared their thoughts since childhood. No bull. Tell each other how it was.

There was no prospect of it improving, either. Every time anyone asked a question about kit, the answer was the same – "It was on the Atlantic Conveyor".

Late morning, Col Pike and Regimental Sergeant Major Lawrie Ashbridge made their rounds with news of 2 Para's success at Goose Green the day before. They also revealed the price. Eighteen men were dead, including Col H Jones.

Worse still, two 2 Para men had been shot dead carrying a white flag to take the surrender. The euphoria at their sister battalion's victory quickly turned to anger. Pride and tradition had been upheld, but their blood boiled and many thought back to the media stories that had announced the battalion's original plans to attack Goose Green.

That evening, trench by trench, they were allowed to have a cuppa and a warm in the house. Duffy, true to form, declined the offer, so Tommy walked there with L/Cpl Tony Evans, the section's second-in-command.

The front room was filled with people Tommy didn't recognise. As they sat, staring into the flames, four men came in, dressed in black. Their equipment was also black, and they carried ropes over their shoulders.

"SBS," Evans whispered.

The two Paras stayed in the house all night, chatting with the SBS boys, and left prior to stand-to at first light. Other than Ron, no one was any the wiser.

After stand-to, Major Argue mustered the Company in front of the house and called them a dejected rabble. He was appalled at the number who'd quit the tab with foot problems.

"It's time to wake up and smell the coffee," he warned. "Let's get on with the job in hand."

Then he told them what 'the job' entailed.

Brig Thompson had flown in with orders for 3 Para to tab to Estancia House, 25 miles away and within striking distance of the mountains guarding Stanley. But Argue's worst mistake was mentioning coffee. The lads were more interested in the fact that someone might have a brew on to take much else in.

"Get your kit packed and get a f*****g grip," he yelled. "You're Parachute Regiment and this is what we do!"

As they prepared to set off for Estancia, Jason saw the battalion Medical Officer. The MO examined his feet and shook his head. They were too bad for Jason to go. The news filtered through to Tommy's position. Trench foot, immersion foot and frostbite were all mentioned. He went to see Jason.

"At least I'll get a lift," he joked. Tommy felt for him, until he heard that the Mortar Platoon had commandeered a tractor and trailer to hump their base-plates and mortar tubes east, and that Jason would – indeed – be going along for the ride.

"Lucky bastard," Tommy thought, and walked away.

As the snake departed, this time escorted by Scimitar and Scorpion light tanks of the Blues and Royals, one of the locals stood at the edge of the settlement and, in turn, offered a hand and a few words of appreciation to everyone who passed.

"Thanks for what you're doing, and good luck."

Conditions had been tough since they'd stepped off the landing craft, but now they began to deteriorate. It was wet and cold as B Company led again, guided by Terry Peck, a 44-year-old bobby and member of the Falkland Islands Legislative Council whose determination to stick one up the invaders was evident in the pace he set. When the Argentinians invaded, he'd fled to the hills and gathered intelligence in preparation for the British arrival.

At one point, they heard "Yippee!" and turned to see Duffy chest-deep in water. They just laughed. He climbed out, shook himself off and carried on. Inspiring, but bonkers.

It was painful going, broken only by a two-hour rest and snack before last light, at a bridge over a ravine near Lower Malo House. After another two or three-hour slog until midnight, they stopped and bashered up. The tallest of Stanley's mountain ring, Mount Kent, was in front of them. The SAS and 42 Commando would be dealing with any hostile forces there in the days to come.

They were told to avoid unnecessary movement, as they were now within range of enemy artillery. They stayed till the following afternoon, still without their bergens and warm kit. Everyone was exhausted and, like rations, tempers were short. For many, without doss bags, so was sleep.

Monday, May 31, dawned with at least the illusion of warmth. They stayed there until around 1600Z when the snake formed again and they set off for Estancia. It was only a few miles away. The trouble was that the single-track path between Teal Inlet and their destination had dozens of little paths running off it.

"I've got to say, there were points on the march when I thought *When we're back, I'm getting out. This is shit!*" Tommy laughs now.

17: The death and life of Private Jason Burt

It was Duffy who kept him going through the endless grind, and the frequent occasions when the snake would double back on itself because the map-reader had made a wrong call, again.

Eventually, they saw a small collection of buildings in the distance and were told to lie up until dusk, while patrols were sent forward for signs of the enemy. Another couple of hours passed while they huddled together again, shivering, sticking to the ground, before the order came to move. They'd arrived at Estancia.

CHAPTER 10

ADVANCE TO LONGDON

So far as Jason Burt's family's concerned, B Company's arrival at Estancia on Monday, May 31, marks a point of no return, the place after which unanswered questions would lurk at every turn for more than 30 years, the start of events they'd run and re-run in their minds, on each occasion wondering how different life might have been.

What if he'd taken a step this way at some stage, not that?

What if a quick word with Tommy, or Scrivs, or Brian Milne, had delayed him a second?

What if he'd stayed at Teal Inlet to nurse his rotting feet?

What if he'd followed that nagging thought of quitting Junior Para and trying the Military Police instead?

What if, what if, what if.

Estancia was where he might have been taken out of the proceedings. Instead, it's where he faced the same misgivings as almost everyone else, and pointed himself in a different direction – ultimately to his death.

The Company was forced to lie up and wait for dusk as patrols were sent forward to search the settlement for signs of the enemy. They huddled together again, shivering, for two hours, sticking to the ground, before the order came to move.

There wasn't much to the settlement. In essence, it was Estancia House, the home of Tony and Ailsa Heathman and their baby daughter. Ailsa's parents had lived there too, until the Argentinians turned up and shipped them to Fox Bay as prisoners. It had a barn and four or five outbuildings and a stream that ran into the inlet. It stood slightly to the west of the ring of mountains surrounding Stanley, whose lights twinkled 15 miles away.

3 Para was the first unit to arrive. They quickly put the buildings to good use and occupied defensive lie-ups in the hills around the settlement. Not far south-west, without a fight, D Squadron 22 SAS had already taken control of the commanding heights of the 1,504ft Mount Kent, the tallest of the mountain ring. They were joined by a company of 42 Commando and elements of Brigadier Julian Thompson's tactical HQ.

Back at Estancia, one of the locals hung a sheep's carcass up and, in seconds, the Paras had helped themselves. RSM Lawrie Ashbridge angrily reminded his men that, although they were fighting a campaign, discipline had to be maintained.

Tommy remembers the Medical Officer saying "start getting the blokes to come to me". He set up surgery in the main house, ready to inspect feet, half-a-dozen at a time. Some drifted over, but it was obvious that not everyone would bother him.

"You didn't want to take your boots off, because you knew if you did you wouldn't get them on again," Doc McAllister recalls. "Your feet were warm in the warm water in your boots. If you took them off, they'd go cold. Everyone's extremities, your toes... you'd get this horrible burning sensation. So I tried not to take my boots off if I possibly could."

In short, no one wanted to be seen in the Regimental Aid Post complaining about something that wasn't a wound. Jason and Tommy feared the MO would take one look at their feet and decide they were too bad to continue. Tommy hid in an outbuilding. He wasn't the only one to seek sanctuary there. Jason also made himself scarce.

Inevitably, a distinct lack of attendees prompted to the MO to set off on rounds from his makeshift practice. One by one, they were ordered to remove their boots and socks.

Tommy queued in trepidation as the MO neared.

"Your feet are bad," he told him. "You need to rest."

Tommy knows now that it was a big decision for the MO to make. How many men could he afford to take out of the firefight to come before the Company was too short of men to take Longdon? For the moment, Tommy didn't even think about that question. He was gutted. He'd tabbed all that way. Now, in a blink, someone had decided he was unfit to continue. He felt he'd let everyone in the Platoon down, and that he'd be branded a waste of rations.

He didn't see Jason in the queue. The next time their paths crossed, he learned Jason had somehow avoided the same fate.

"I'm carrying on," Jason told him. To this day, he believes Jason probably found a better hiding place. He knew how bad his feet had been at Teal Inlet, how he'd been forced to ride on a trailer to Estancia.

It might have been the fear of failure, the result of all that milling in Junior Para. It might have been the fact that he'd been able to have a brew, grab something to eat, take shelter from the wind, in his doss bag, maybe in a shed, and felt for a moment as if he were in Paradise. It might simply have been that he wanted to be there.

Whatever, Tommy says, "it was Jason's decision to carry on. Whether he got himself out of having his feet checked, by going to the latrine or something out of the way, I really don't know, because his feet were bad".

Tuesday, June 1: Five days after leaving Windy Gap, 10 days before the eventual advance to Longdon, A Company moved through in the early hours and, a few hours later, Tommy and the others branded unfit to tab watched as B Company moved out to the southern slopes of Mount Vernet and C Company left to occupy the main part of the same hill. Meanwhile, the Blues and Royals said goodbye and went south to join 5 Brigade, who were due to land at Bluff Cove, on the south coast. That would be their own date with fate.

The dull thud-thud-thud of chopper blades was a sweet sound, soon after, as Sea Kings flew in and unloaded the battalion's bergens, stacking them in company rows, each identified by their coloured patches. Everyone left behind set about changing their clothing and socks, before tucking in to a much-needed hot meal.

As Tommy watched his mates disappear from view, the Battalion Quartermaster started shouting at him.

"What the f*** are you doing standing around?" he yelled. "Get yourself shaved!"

Tommy wanted to tell him to go and screw himself. The officer ignored his insolent glare and turned his attention to some other lads standing by the newly dug latrine.

It wasn't long, though, before Tommy was back with Jason and the others. He walked to his bergen and found a British Forces Post Office letter – a bluey – on his doss bag. A letter from home was what he needed, so he sat down and opened it.

It was from Laura, telling him what had been happening at home, how she was helping to save a children's playgroup from closure. She'd enclosed a cutting with a picture of a sponsored walk. It showed a group of women, in St. Trinian's uniforms, displaying their wares. A crowd of men and boys, mouths open, were clearly enjoying the moment.

Tommy looked around him. Men in various states of dress and health were hobbling in front of him, putting on brave faces. The wind drove rain against the tin sides of the outbuilding and through its leaky roof. Heavy Para footsteps had already turned the front entrance into a quagmire.

He packed his kit and went over to the MO and informed him he'd be making his way up the mountain to join the Platoon. Then he lugged the bergen on to his back, screwed up Laura's letter, dropped it in the latrine, and set off.

About an hour-and-a-half later, Neil Grose looked up from his position and saw Tommy trudging towards him, in a state. Tommy ignored his happy greeting and ripped his head off – then apologised.

"You're okay, Tom. You can buy me something for my birthday. Coming to my party?"

Tommy looked at him and laughed at the absurdity. There they were, in the middle of nowhere, on top of a mountain, wet through and exhausted, joking about Grose's eighteenth birthday on Friday, June 11.

The section had found a disused peat pit to set up their bashers. Its high wall gave excellent cover from the wind. As he approached, Jason called out.

"Over here, Tom!"

As he walked over, Cpl Brian Milne asked how he was doing. Tommy quickly reported what had happened with the Quartermaster and RSM.

"You're better off up here, away from all that bullshit," Milne said. "Get your basher set up and into your doss bag. We could be here a while."

Tommy mimics a Scottish accent when he recalls Ron Duffy's welcome, a few seconds later.

"How's yer feet, laddie?" He seemed respectful that Tommy had chosen to be with the Platoon at the front line.

"They're okay, Ron," Tommy said. But Duffy knew he was lying and gave him a nip of whisky. They'd been on the Islands two weeks, yet the Scot's hip flask had never run out. It was one of 3 Para's great mysteries.

Wednesday, June 2: Six days after leaving Windy Gap, nine days before the advance to Longdon, the dawn was misty and didn't improve. As the rain and wind drove across the mountain, they tucked into their Arctic rations. Each pack was intended to last 24 hours and came with hexamine solid fuel blocks for the tiny metal cooker each man carried. They were simple and efficient.

Rumours of an attack on Longdon, the low feature overlooking Stanley from the northwest, were rife by this point. No one was sure when – but they felt certain it was coming. In fact, before 3 Para had arrived at Estancia, Col Hew Pike knew that would be their task.

Friday, June 11, wasn't originally meant to be the day they advanced to battle on Mount Longdon. Two other deadlines were set and scrapped before they finally left Estancia for good. This day – Thursday, June 3 – was the first.

Believing their rapid tab from Port San Carlos had given them critical momentum towards Stanley, Col Pike gave the order for 3 Para to "advance to contact" against Longdon. That meant the rifle companies would move forward until they came upon enemy positions, engage them and capture them.

After days waiting and moving, it was music to most ears. Traditionally, the three rifle companies would advance in battle formation, with one company forward and two side-by-side to the rear. The leading platoon would have one of its eight-man sections, commanded by a corporal, in advance. The whole unit would be supported by machine guns, anti-tank weapons and mortars. And any Argentinian positions would be dealt with as the moment required.

Although there was no mention, the men assumed there might also be artillery support, and perhaps even Naval Gunfire Support and Harrier air cover. Extra anti-tank missiles had been sledged up to Estancia House by tractor.

Except for those who'd joined since – including the 17-year-olds – they'd practised a battalion advance to contact in Canada in 1981, with live ammo. This time, though, there was a disadvantage. 3 Commando Brigade was ahead of its support artillery, meaning 3 Para would have to depend on themselves.

Eventually, they moved out and the lead units took their position at the head of the advance. They were over a low hill, out of sight of Estancia House, and heading for mist-shrouded Longdon, when Brig Thompson flew in and spoke to Col Pike. Within minutes the attack was called off.

Instead of a daylight attack, without support, on an uncertain strength of enemy, they were to return to their defensive positions to plan. The rumour mill sprang to life.

Thompson was furious with Pike for advancing under his own steam. The Brigadier had wanted a Brigade assault involving several units with several objectives hit at the same time. However, no other unit was battle-ready or as far forward as 3 Para. Pike hadn't wanted to wait. But Thompson was having none of it. So back they tabbed to their bashers, fuming that they'd been halted because "the Marines, carrying everything including the kitchen sink, couldn't keep up".

The plan in the mind of Gen Jeremy Moore – Commander Land Forces, who'd arrived on QE2 with 5 Brigade – was to attack in five days time, as the night of Tuesday, June 8, became the early hours of Wednesday, June 9.

Between Mounts Estancia, Vernet and Kent, and the Argentinian-held peaks of Longdon, Tumbledown and Two Sisters, there was a No Man's Land. It had to be patrolled to stop the enemy launching operations of their own before the assault on Longdon began. Among the British patrols that crept into the area for a shuftee by night was D Company. But they didn't just probe No Man's Land. They looked at Longdon itself.

Pte Dickie Absolon, Cpl Jerry Phillips and Sgt John Pettinger spent hours crawling among the enemy, gathering intelligence about numbers and weapons. With each visit, the picture grew until, eventually, it seemed that between 300 and 500 troops were there, equipped with anti-personnel mines, radar, mortars, 106mm rifles, .50 calibre machineguns and enough ammo and food to see out a long siege.

For the ordinary Toms in the rifle companies, life became an endurance test. All they could do was dig in, stay hidden from view, shelter from the sleet and the snow, look at Mount Longdon and think of the battle they knew was coming.

Shortly after stand-down that Thursday, a British-made Argentinian Canberra bomber dropped a stick of bombs 500 yards from B Company's anti-tank sections at Estancia House. The target might have been the house, or a group of Sea Kings stationed for the night at the foot of Mount Estancia but, although the ground shook, no damage was done.

By this time, including the friendly-fire injuries back at Port San Carlos, the battalion had lost around 40 men. Most men, though, had made it and worked out their own way to prevent the cold and wet from keeping them out of the battle.

17: The death and life of Private Jason Burt

The farm had a pile of freshly-cut peat and the men closest to it trudged back and forth regularly to keep warm. For the rifle companies in their forward defensive positions, though, comforts were almost non-existent, so they worked out a rota that allowed them to enjoy the Spartan pleasures of the barn at Estancia as a rest area.

Saturday, June 5: Nine days after leaving Windy Gap, six days before the tab to Longdon.... In Walthamstow, bathed by warm days and sultry, cloudless nights, Terry Burt went to bed every night hearing Jason whispering "Mum, my feet are killing me!"

"Jason's feet are in a right old state," she told everyone that week.

She'd taken to leaving the radio on all night long. Jean, next door, remembers how it became part of the background hum of night sounds that month.

Sunday, June 6: Ten days after leaving Windy Gap, five days before the advance to Longdon, a pattern had emerged at Estancia. The mornings weren't bad, but the rain and wind was unrelenting later. But at least mail arrived. Perhaps it was this day that Jason opened the letter from his mum suggesting that, if there was any sign of danger, he should run.

Terry regrets it to this day. She worried that it affected him. It didn't. By this time, he was as chirpy as could be expected. Apart from the mail delivery, the only event of note that Sunday had been D Company's contact with enemy Special Forces, near the Murrell Bridge. After an intense firefight, the Paras withdrew without casualty.

Tuesday, June 8: Twelve days after leaving Windy Gap, three days before the eventual advance to Longdon, there was more mail, another pleasant start to the day, and more freezing rain to follow.

More daytime patrols were also undertaken to pass the time waiting for the Marines. At one point, 4 Platoon arrived at Murrell Bridge. Tony Barlow and Tommy both recall it well.

They were starving when they arrived at Murrell Bridge and crossed the river. They hadn't seen "proper food" for 48 hours. They knew it was some kind of a mission, but not what. Sgt McKay told them to dig in.

Tony and Steve 'No-Neck' Playle were the furthest forward, ready to set up home, when the lack of food triggered something unplanned. At least, that's how Tony explains it.

"We were starving. We used to have a thing called Diddly-D. It was heather. We called it Diddly-D. Every time we came across it, we'd grab it and stick it in our sleeping bags. It kept your feet warm."

It's unclear whether it was Tony or No-Neck who set eyes on one particular clump of Diddly-D first. To a degree, it's academic, because they were both quickly on the sodden ground, punching lumps out of each other.

"Over Diddly-D! He said it was his, and I said it was mine."

Ian McKay quickly broke the fight up.

"Right, you two," he yelled. "Basher together."

The message was clear. Live together or die together. They started digging.

After the defensive positions were complete, the rest of the Platoon relaxed to enjoy an unusual bout of dry weather and observe the area. Two Sisters was less than a mile away to the right, with the start of a man-made road that stretched into Stanley in front of them. It was a good feeling.

In the night, Tony was on stag – a watch duty – when a D Company patrol appeared. Sgt John Pettinger was at the head of the group. Tony stopped him.

"Advance and be recognised."

Pettinger identified himself and they came through.

"There's thousands over that hill!" he told Tony, then asked him what they were doing there. The ridge in question, from what Tony remembers, was a hundred yards away.

"Don't know," he answered.

Wednesday, June 9: The next morning, they'd put their first brew on when they heard Support Company firing at the Argentinians over the hill. They hadn't been able to have a cuppa after dusk the night before, because the glow from the Primus would have been as good as a big neon arrow to the Argentinian spotters.

Tony put their last porridge oats in the brew and was stopped in his tracks by the scream of more shells, this time very definitely heading their way.

"All hell broke loose," Tony says. "Bombs were coming. Mortars were coming."

The rest of the platoon had dropped back over the bridge.

"I just heard Louie Lewis shouting 'Get out!'."

"I'm not leaving me brew," he told No-Neck. "No way am I leaving me brew!"

He didn't have a choice, though. They cleared out.

During the early afternoon, through their telescopic rifle sights, they watched Argentinians queuing for scoff on Two Sisters and called in a fire mission. Disappointingly, the artillery was moving positions, and the enemy was outside their own mortar's range. A Blues and Royals Scimitar light tank provided them with an alternative.

"They're in range," the Scimitar commander said.

They all put an eye to their sights. In seconds, they were watching Argies run as the shells rained down. The chaos was highly amusing for a few minutes, until they heard the distant crump of guns and, moments later, the front of their positions were ripped up too.

The Blues commander decided he'd seen enough, battened his hatch and retreated towards Estancia. It didn't take Lt Andy Bickerdike long to give the order to 'bug out' and, in a flash, their kit was being packed.

17: The death and life of Private Jason Burt

One section was forward and to the left in a cluster of rocks, airing kit. They saw Scrivs and a couple of others scrambling to gather their kit while shells landed all around. They wouldn't find it funny until later. For now, they knew they'd been lucky.

While all this was happening, moving 5 Brigade into position ready to join the battle had hit logistical problems, so the operation was postponed for three days. Now, instead, they'd form up on the Thursday – June 10 – and hope to have the mountain by daybreak on Friday, June 11.

It wasn't long before those plans were consigned to the latrine too. That Wednesday, bad news reached the battalion. At around 1.15pm local time, the day before – 1715Z, or 5.15pm on the clocks back home in Britain – the landing ships Sir Galahad and Sir Tristram had been hit in Bluff Cove while waiting to put Welsh Guards ashore. Both had caught fire immediately. Fifty men were dead or missing, 57 were wounded.

The choppers earmarked to fly the Paras to the edge of their start point were diverted to fly casualties to the field hospital nicknamed 'The Red and Green Life Machine', in Ajax Bay. So the operation was put back another 24 hours. Now 3 Para's assault on Longdon and Wireless Ridge, 45 Commando's attack on Two Sisters and Tumbledown, and 42 Commando's attack on Mount Harriet would take place as Friday, June 11 – Neil Grose's 18th birthday – became Saturday, June 12.

Late that Wednesday morning, HQ 3 Commando Brigade issued an order summoning all commanding officers to what's called an O Group the following day at Brigade HQ. In other words, a briefing.

Thursday, June 10: At first light on the Thursday morning, 14 days after leaving Windy Gap, four Pucara appeared out of nowhere and strafed the forward rifle company positions on Mounts Vernet and Estancia. No one was hurt.

A little later, Col Pike paid a visit with BBC reporter Robert Fox and fellow journalist Max Hastings – later editor of the *London Evening Standard* – and two Sea Harriers flew past in the clear and sunny sky, spearing low and fast over Estancia House towards Port Stanley.

While the rifle companies went through their routines, at 1630Z the commanding officers gathered at the O Group and were told what was expected of 3 Commando Brigade – including 3 Para – in the imminent operation to take the crucial high ground north-west of Stanley. It was this:

- 42 Commando were to attack Mount Harriet and be ready to move on to Mount William.
- 45 Commando were to capture Two Sisters, then head for Tumbledown.

- 3 Para were to take Mount Longdon, then Wireless Ridge, if they were able.

Although the Argentinians might have expected some kind of reconnaissance operation by the British, it's unlikely they ever saw the shadowy figures that had moved in and around them, studying their positions, their strength and their equipment, over the previous 10 days.

As for an attack, they'd have been expecting something to happen, and soon. The artillery and mortar bombardment aimed at them from the south and south-west should have been a big clue as to which direction the attack would come from.

Mind you, from the day of the landings in San Carlos Water, they should already have known, given the very public news about which British units had come ashore and were heading east across the islands. In other words, the main British assault would not be the almost direct attack they'd expected on Stanley from the south and south-east – the one they'd prepared for by deploying six infantry battalions, two artillery regiments and an air defence regiment around the capital.

History suggests the penny hadn't dropped, however. No units had been moved to the mountainous western defences that Jason and the lads were preparing to assault. The only Argentinian reserve available was a single infantry company, believed to be made up largely of conscripts.

While all that might have been the case about the Argentinian strength, the information discussed at the O Group meeting of British commanders that Thursday still wasn't clear. This is what they thought they were facing.

British intelligence believed the mountain was occupied by 800 men of the 7th Infantry Regiment (RI7), in three companies. In fact, although RI7 did control Longdon, it had only one company. It was B Company, largely fledgling conscripts from the capital, Buenos Aires. They were supported by a detachment of engineers and five .50 calibre machineguns from an independent Marine heavy machinegun company.

It was the clever positioning of these 0.50 machineguns – each able to take an aircraft out of the sky – that would make the coming battle so atrociously costly, and heighten the heroism of every Para on the mountain that night.

If the British didn't know precisely how strong the enemy defence was in numbers and battle-readiness, they at least had a much better picture of where the main weapons were located. The Argentinians had been on the mountain, digging in, preparing their defences, almost since arriving on the islands on Tuesday, April 13. Sgt John Pettinger had tip-toed into the heart of the enemy several times and sketched where the main trenches lay. This is what 3 Para knew:

- The bulk of the defenders were around the high western summit and a central

'bowl' created by the rocky rim.
- They'd rammed peat and grass into cracks in the rocky face of their sangars.
- It meant that what looked like part of the landscape were, in fact, well-established defensive positions.
- Those positions had a grandstand view of the approach.
- As a result, the positions would be hard to overcome... as long as the Argentinians knew the British were coming.

As long as the Argentinians knew the British were coming?

The plan taking shape in Col Pike's mind was to make sure they didn't. Although it's not for us to say whether he was right, his decision was to have massive consequences. These are the things Jason and his 3 Para pals knew of Longdon:

- It wasn't a big mountain, but its isolated position meant it dominated a huge area.
- On its south-east side, it overlooked the Moody Brook Barracks that the Marines had abandoned in April.
- It was a ridge, running east to west, about 1,200 yards long and perhaps 200 wide.
- Its top and sides were littered with enormous rocky slabs that faced north, creating channels, gullies and caves – a gift to anyone defending it.
- Its highest point – 782 feet – was at its western end.
- Its second, lower summit was at the eastern end.
- To the south-west was the mountain called Two Sisters, 45 Commando's target.
- Directly south was Tumbledown, which would now be hit by the Scots Guards. Both rose higher than 2,000ft and were within range of most infantry support weapons.

Pike's logic was that a silent advance on the mountain would allow the Paras to appear almost toe-to-toe with the Argentinians before anyone opened fire. He hoped for a quick victory, with minimal casualties. For that to happen, surprise was the key. That meant that laying waste to the battlefield with a relentless artillery and naval bombardment for hours before was out of the question. It would merely tell the Argentinians that someone was about to come knocking.

That Thursday, Jason wrote his last two blueys. This one didn't arrive home until the end of June. It carries the voice of a son who'd won the battle of mind over matter.

Hi Mum + Dad,

Hope things are ok, it's not here. Apart from the rain and cold, we have marched about 50 miles in the last week. I missed about 15 miles of it because I have 8 blisters and also called trench foot. Anyway, I'm in my sleeping bag at the moment, speaking to Tom. I haven't had a wash for 2

17: The death and life of Private Jason Burt

weeks now, and its great to think your not behind me telling me to wash behind my ears. That's the best thing about this, no washing.

Tom said to tell dad to send him some sandwiches and to tell him his a tyte bastard. And that he is going to treat him to a drink. We are now waiting for the Marines to catch up. We were told by the brigadier to slow down because we are going too fast for the Marines. They can't keep upso they are getting helicopters everywhere and they still can't keep up. Any I must go now, lots of love, Jason xxxxx

The same day, possibly, he dropped a line to Linda Jennings. The postmark when it dropped on o her doormat was June 28.

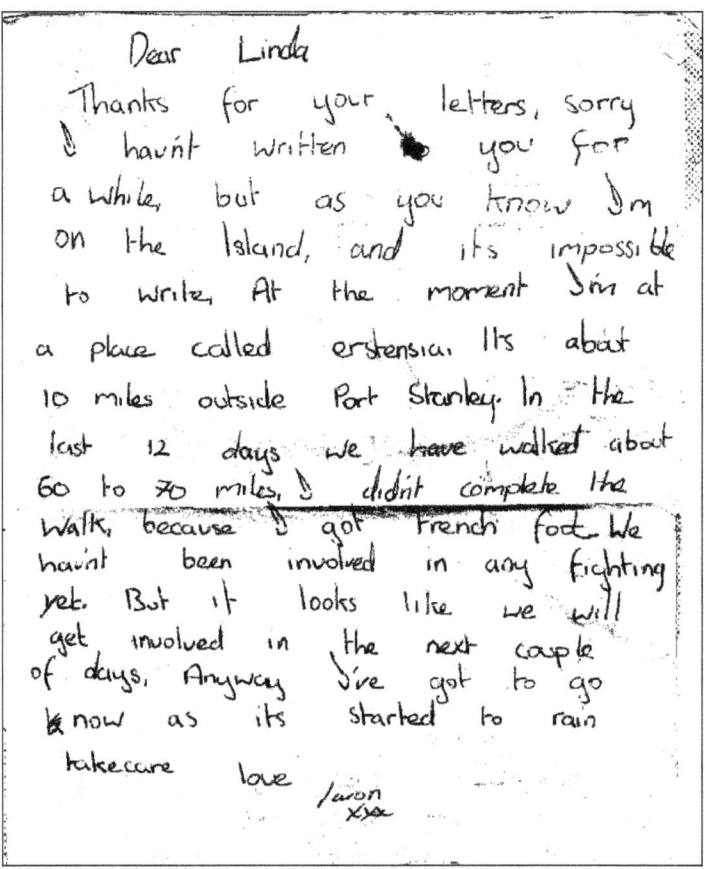

So did Terry's letter upset Jason?

"No, he never got upset at any letters," Tony Barlow insists. "He was just chuffed that he got them.

"He knew his mum meant well when she said 'Run!' He wasn't going to run. You've got to remember this Airborne spirit. Whether you're bedded in or not, it's a spirit that's with you for life, and you'll die for your mate. It's a spirit that you can't take away. It's something I can't describe.

"Twenty years on, I still grieve for Jason. Grosey, thinking of him kills me.

"I'll never forget what they done for me. I know 100 per cent, no matter how naïve Jason was, or scared, if I was injured, Jase would have come and got me, not matter what. Scrivs. Grosey. They'd have come and got me. I know that."

Friday, June 11: The next afternoon, Jason was with the rest of 4 Platoon, squelching in the peaty basher at the forward edge of Estancia, when the conversation turned to the big leave they'd have when all this was over.

As they spoke, with their little cooking stoves battling against the elements, they sat in their doss bags, checking their equipment and ammunition, and cleaned their weapons.

Brian Milne, Geoff Logan and Taff Wynn Jones were with them, doing nothing because there was nothing to do. Jason was talking about "when we get home, we're going to be heroes, stacks of money and we're going to have whoopee!"

The chatter drifted on the wind as they were mustered for their orders to be read.

The Battalion Battle Plan had been filtered down from Col Pike. He'd told his Company Commanders. They'd gone separate ways and gathered their Platoon Commanders to do the same. They, in turn, detailed the objective to their sergeants and NCOs. And they stood in front of their men – in small groups, so as not to present a big target to any opportunist enemy pilot marauding nearby – and completed the cascade.

Cpl Brian Milne brought 4 Platoon together and revealed what would be required of them. The Battalion would attack Longdon that night.

They all listened intently as he went over and over the Platoon's objective, where it fitted in to the Company's mission, and how that would achieve the Battalion Battle Plan. This is what he told them:

- 3 Para would advance from a startline codenamed Free Kick, which was a stream running south-north just over half-a-mile from the foot of Longdon.
- A Company would be forward on the left of the formation – the north – with B Company on the right, guided by members of Patrol Company.
- A Company would advance to the north of Longdon, to the left of B Company, clearing the ground until it could occupy a spur of high ground codenamed Wing Forward. Once there, they'd be able to advance to Wireless Ridge.
- B Company would assault Longdon towards its summit, codenamed Fly Half.
- They'd then continue along the ridge to Longdon's lower second peak, on the leading edge of the mountain facing Stanley. This had been codenamed Full Back.
- C Company – codenamed 'Lucky Bastards' by the blokes in B Company – would be held in reserve and deployed as deemed appropriate.

A few thoughtful glances might have been exchanged, but the men concentrated hard as the plan to secure Fly Half and Full Back was laid out before them.

- 4 Platoon had two objectives.
- Part One. It would advance through open ground and clear a path to the northern slopes of Longdon, then move south to a central area to Fly Half, the halfway point.
- Part Two. It would join 5 Platoon there and head for Full Back, the second peak.

5 Platoon's route to Fly Half would take them south of 4 Platoon and north of the central ridge. While they went, 6 Platoon would advance to the summit and secure Fly Half. Job done, it would hand on to 4 and 5, who'd head for Full Back.

The Mortar Platoon were to set up a mortar line at the startline, while a mixture of GPMG machinegun teams and Milan launchers would support wherever needed.

In addition to their own support weapons, 3 Battalion would have back-up available from six 105mm light guns of 79 (Kirkee) Battery of 29 Commando Regiment, with more batteries nearby ready to join the fray.

To the north of the islands the Type 21 frigate HMS Avenger would be ready for the call for fire from its 4.5-inch gun. The Navy boys would be guided by a Special Forces observer hiding in a position overlooking the enemy defences.

Col Pike's decision to hit Longdon through the front door, head on to the enemy's main defences, was relatively simple as well as controversial. So what led him to settle on it as a way to take Longdon? Let's consider it by asking a few more questions:

- To begin with, why couldn't the British simply give Longdon a wide berth and tab round the outside, out of range? Well, intelligence had told him that the Argentinian positions on Wireless Ridge, to the east, were strong enough to stop that happening. What's more, if they tried it, they'd have needed to cross several thousand yards of open ground to the south that were mined.
- So, could a head-on attack have been planned differently? Possibly, possibly not. British Army thinking in such a situation is that a head-on assault on an enemy position that's so well prepared requires outnumbering the enemy by three to one. In short, a battalion attacks a company, or a company attacks a platoon. In 3 Para's case, that numerical advantage didn't exist.
- Could the lack of numbers have been made up by using overwhelming artillery or air support? The theory is good, but the reality was different. In 3 Para's case, they had neither one nor the other.

It's hard not to see Col Pike's dilemma. He had to avoid the frontal attack turning into a turkey-shoot. His way of achieving that was to depend upon surprise. That meant a silent approach under cover of darkness. And it had to happen without raining shells down on

17: The death and life of Private Jason Burt

the heads of the Argentinians defending Longdon before the Paras went in.

Doing that would simply tell the enemy that, as soon as the shelling stopped, a battalion of Britain's most elite troops were about to appear from the smoke, the snow and the dark.

In the cold light of day, the plan was open to doubt. Although D Company's patrols had probed the Argentinian defences thoroughly and with apparent ease, they hadn't been able to complete a minefield recce. So no one could say with certainty that the route chosen for the approach to Longdon wasn't mined. Nor could anyone know whether the Argentinians had set up any other devices to detect an approach by the British.

Long before Cpl Milne explained it to Jason and the others, it had already failed to impress B Company's Officer Commanding, Major Mike Argue, and his Company Sergeant Major, John Weeks.

At the O Group meeting, Weeks had apparently asked if the enemy positions were going to be "stonked" before they went in. He was told they weren't.

In the minds of some was the thought that 29 Commando Regiment had been hitting Longdon with artillery fire for nine days. Would the Argentinians have known the difference between that and a barrage that came before an attack?

B Company's Major Argue spoke with his A Company counterpart, Major David Collett, after the O Group and admitted being anxious. Collett urged him to push Col Pike to change the plan. But it stayed the same. Argue left the O Group briefing to work out exactly how and when B Company would put their part of the plan into action. He must have realised his men had the hardest task.

Longdon was physically large to take with just one company. And, even if the enemy failed to offer much resistance, clearing the positions after the fight-through was a tall order.

If CSM John Weeks was concerned about his colonel's original orders, though, he was just as troubled by what Major Argue came up with as a way to achieve the objective. In short, he didn't have much faith in this, the plan that Cpl Milne had outlined to his boys:

- The three platoons would advance in line abreast, with no reserve platoon to reinforce any success they might achieve – or rescue any disasters.
- 4 Platoon would then clear the north side of Longdon.
- 5 Platoon would advance along the central ridge.
- And 6 Platoon would sweep along the southern side of the mountain.

From where Weeks saw it, B Company was being split dangerously. Sgt Des Fuller, who knew Jason well from his Junior Para days, was a spare sergeant in B Company HQ. He agreed with Weeks. They believed 6 Platoon would be cut off from the others by a shoulder in the hill, robbing the platoons of the ability to easily support each other.

As Milne went on, Tom's concern was a little different.

"We were going over this clearing, 5 Platoon were going over the top, 6 Platoon were going this way. Surely at some point there's a conflict in the line of fire," he still reasons. But those were the orders.

"You take notes, you understand totally what you're doing. And that's the end of it. There's only one place it can be questioned. That's when an OC has made his plan. He may call the O Group forward and say 'These are the possibilities, anyone got any thoughts?' But that was Plan A and there was no diverting from Plan A."

In the early evening, Major Argue gathered B Company and walked with them to a vantage point, looking east.

"That's where we'll be this evening," he pointed to Longdon, though none of them knew yet that he, too, had huge doubts about Col Pike's plan.

Then he swung in the direction of Stanley, in the distance. One hundred or more pairs of eyes followed his finger. "And that, gentlemen," he said, with as much conviction as he could muster, "is where we're ultimately going."

I can't imagine how difficult it must have been for him, to convey confidence and determination, while apparently having so little faith in the plan.

Many men then gazed back at Longdon. It looked like any other mountain. Huge, grey and un-welcoming.

Argue continued, reminding them what support the battalion would provide – the Mortar Platoon, the Milan detachments of the Anti-Tank Platoon, the Machine Gun Platoon, and snipers from Patrol Company. They'd also be able to depend on the Royal Artillery and the Royal Navy's gunships. And casualties would be evacuated immediately by chopper to the hospital ship Uganda, fewer than 20 minutes away at sea.

From the intelligence gleaned from D Company's patrols, Major Argue assured them there were no landmines. In all, it was anticipated there'd be approximately a battalion-worth of Argentinians – around 1,000 men – dug in on Longdon. Their morale was expected to be low and their resistance weak.

Around the circle, men looked at each other. Jason glanced sideways. Neil and Scrivs were undoubtedly looking for signs that others were thinking the same. Tommy could see Stu with 5 Platoon and wondered what he was thinking. As Tommy turned back, he caught Argue's last words.

"May your God go with you."

He stared at his Company commander in disbelief.

What the hell did he say that for? he thought, unaware of his OC's true feelings, but beginning to suspect something close to the truth. *He must know people are going to die tonight. He knows things that we don't....*

Tommy looked to Longdon, once more, and then back at Major Argue. As he turned to join the others drifting back to their positions to kit-up, he caught Baz Barrett's eye. They'd been mates since that first train ride to Aldershot. They'd shared moments of fear before, but few like this. They both raised their eyebrows. But this wasn't the time to speak, so Tommy turned away and said a prayer as he walked to join Jason and the others.

But there were no complaints, he explains. Instead, "you get the bravado coming out. You can whinge to your best buddy, but you don't whinge out in front of everybody because it's derogatory to the whole morale".

Soon after the briefing, Jason, Scrivs and Tommy wandered over to the basher Neil was sharing with another 17-year-old, Steve Jelf. They wished him a happy 18th birthday and shared a beer. Neil had already asked Brian Milne to make him a "birthday present brew" and, as they drank, they swapped stories of the march from hell.

Except for Jason, whose feet had been a mess at Teal, everyone had tabbed the distance. They'd answered every question. Their determination was beyond doubt, even if their fitness had been hammered, and they were proud of what they'd done. They knew there was more to come. When it was over, they'd celebrate Grose's coming of age properly.

Tommy reckons it was Neil's best day since the landing. The others shared the feeling. It was good for the 17-year-olds to be together because, though they were all in 4 Platoon, they were in different sections and the tabbing and tactical situation had often left them unable to speak. In fact, it was probably the first time they'd chatted since Canberra.

That afternoon Tommy and Jason were lying in their bashers when Cpl Milne walked up and handed out blueys for everyone to write home. Tommy didn't need to. He'd done that at Estancia and was concerned that, with the battle nearing, he might say something to worry his Mum. Writing to his Dad didn't cross his mind, so he handed Jason his bluey. That blank letter would cause Syd Burt consternation for years to come.

The last-but-one letter they received from Jason was this:

Hi Mum + Dad + Jarvis

Just a short note to let you know I'm ok. We have marched 75 miles in the last week. We are about 8 miles outside Stanley it has rained every other day and my –ucking feet –ucking sting. It is very cold. Anyway, must go love Jason xxx

Was this scribbled on the sheet of paper Tommy had given him and handed in? Or, having already written that day, did he slip the blank sheet into his battledress pocket as a spare, ready to pen something later, in the wake of the battle? Or did he start to jot something, maybe an 'in the event of my death' letter – as Tommy describes it – then put it away?

One thing appears certain. he wouldn't have gone into battle with anything other than a blank or a 'goodbye' in his pocket.

"That, to me, would be the most logical explanation," Tommy explains. "You're taught it's a tool to be interrogated with. Professionalism is that you don't take anything on to the battlefield. If you leave a cigarette butt, whether it's been smoked right to the end... Roll-ups? Can't get tailor-mades any more. There's all kind of things that tell about morale. It tells you about the support, the logistics."

At some point, Brian Milne or Taff Wynne-Jones walked round, collecting the letters. The padre also wandered among his flock, handing spare socks out.

"He come and bored us for half-an-hour," Doc McAllister explains. He asked him a question.

"How can you be a good Christian and go and kill people?"

"We're like the Crusaders," Derek the Cleric replied. "We're on the right side. Just like the British Army in the Second World War. They believe in their God, we believe in our God. But we've got God on our side."

"I wasn't a good Christian," Doc laughs. "I didn't discover religion until we started to get artillery."

It was around this time that they all heard Christ mentioned, not just Doc. In his two years as B Company's Company Sergeant-Major, John Weeks had bolstered a reputation – according to Tommy, Doc and Tony – for solving most moments of crisis by force of will or fists. In that period, he'd grown close to many of his senior ranks. He had a feeling that there were more "on that bloody hill" than the 70 guys standing in front of him. So it must have been especially difficult to have to prepare them for what was about to happen.

"Some of you won't come off this mountain," he told them. "Expect hand-to-hand fighting from trench to trench. It will be very, very slow.

"And, believe you me, you can't visualise what it's going to be like, because it's going to be so slow and you're going to have things happen that you've never had before when we've been practising.

"You're going to have live things coming at you and exploding around you and it's going to confuse you. But you will do well. Now, if you have any thoughts, or if any of you believe in Christ, here's the time to sit down and have a little talk to Him. It's not stupid because I'm certainly going away now to have a little prayer."

A few minutes later, I believe, he spoke to the senior ranks.

"I don't expect anything less than what I'm going to do," he added. "If you don't see me do it, you do it."

As they made final preparations for the three-hour advance to the start line, the sunshine and almost clear sky promised one thing, a cold night.

With the light fading, men talked in small groups. In some corners, there was a calm and cheerful atmosphere, surprising though that might sound. Everyone seemed confident, despite the predicted odds.

The older guys, I understand, took confidence from their experience and training and a strong belief that they were superior to the enemy. The youngsters could only take confidence in their training and the wise heads around them.

As they moved out, Jason caught Mick Southall's eye, one of the 17-year-olds who'd joined up together, a close friend of Neil. Jason smiled at the Chester lad. Mick smiled back.

The five-and-a-half mile advance began at nightfall, around 4.30pm local time, 2030Z on watches in the battalion snake, 8.30pm by the clock on the Burts' mantelpiece. The plan was to complete the tab to Longdon in three hours and cross the start line – Free Kick – at midnight, as Neil's 18th birthday ended.

The supposedly leisurely pace was to assist the Support Company Platoons whose Milans missiles, mortar tubes, base-plates, machineguns and tripods were being dragged on pallets part of the way from Mount Vernet to the flanks of Longdon by islanders using Land-Rovers and tractors.

Daily Express photographer Tom Smith and Reuters correspondent Les Dowd were with the support team, and news was soon filtering through that the SAS had seen enemy positions being reinforced on Longdon that afternoon.

The three greatest concerns during the advance were the possibility of the extended, single-file line of B Company men bumping into an Argentinian patrol; the risk of stumbling into an unmarked minefield; and the chance that they'd be spotted by enemy forward observers, who'd call in artillery support long before they reached the start line.

As it turned out, they were held up, but not by the enemy.

The tab was hard going. As they trudged off Mount Estancia and on to the lower levels, Longdon looked daunting against the skyline. Within a mile or two, many of them were dripping with sweat and drenched from the boggy ground.

Most were carrying well over 100lbs – the common load made up of two 84mm rounds for the Carl Gustav launchers, three individual 66mm rockets, six fragmentation grenades, three phosphorus grenades, 400 rounds of linked 7.62mm ammunition for the GPMGs, as well as their rifle, bayonet, magazines and bullets topped off by new-issue Para helmets.

As the darkness closed in, the agony of their swollen, decaying feet was masked by thoughts of the hours to come. I can tell you what some of them were thinking.

Neil had had a premonition that he'd be shot in the chest. They all carried waterproof dressings to seal a sucking wound, where the lung's been punctured and air's being dragged in.

"I've got the dressing in me top pocket. You know how to put the seal on, don't you?" he asked them, time and again.

For Private Dom Gray – like many – the fear wasn't of going into battle or dying, but of mutilation. He has said so in one of the many Longdon books. I know it's an accurate quote, because Tommy's lad's named after Dom.

"A soldier going into battle knows there are no more ifs and buts," Dom reflects. "It's the end of the line. The ultimate challenge. There's no point whinging, because that's why he's there. It's do or die, as simple as that. Losing an arm, a leg or my eyesight was what I dreaded. I'd made my mind up that, if I lost part of my body, I'd top myself on the spot if I could."

As they tabbed towards the start line in follow-the-leader fashion, Tommy found himself wondering if he was going to die that night. Whether it would be quick and painless. Whether he'd be able to cope with a drawn-out death.

With every step forward, he hated the very things that would fill the Burts' lives and minds for the next three decades. The thought of dying before his eighteenth. The fact he wasn't old enough to vote for the Government that had sent him there. The fact that he wasn't old enough to see an X film, or to have bought a last drink legally before they'd left home, eight long weeks before.

He wondered how his Mum and his sister Jo would go on after hearing news of his death, and whether they'd leave him in a place he felt nothing but contempt for.

His head raced and fear touched his shoulder. He missed them. For the first time, he felt as young as the 17-year-olds 8,000 miles away, splashing Brut aftershave on, their blood racing on the promise of a Friday night pint and, maybe, a fumble to take them into Saturday, June 12.

Just ahead, Jason was lost in his thoughts too. Somewhere in the gloom, Scrivs, Neil and the others were alone with theirs. Mick Southall was among them, in the 6 Platoon line.

"I felt confident in my own ability and training," he says. "But, as for experience, I didn't have any and felt quite scared."

He recalls thinking *There won't be any Argentinians on Longdon… they'll have seen us coming and legged it*. Mind you, he admits thinking the opposite too. If the mountain was so big and important, and full of the enemy, one of them was bound to see the advance. In that case, you could forget surprising them by appearing out of the darkness, in silence.

"I have to be honest. I felt quite alone as the Crow in my section. Even though I'd been with these guys for two months, I still didn't feel comfortable with some of them. I seem to remember Taff Edwards, my section 2i/c, asking me if I was okay, and Gaz Juliff, another Tom about 20, and a couple of others. But, in general, it seemed to be a case of the odd wink and a nod in my direction, as opposed to a full-blown conversation. They weren't being nasty or cruel. It was just the way things were done in 3 Para in 1982, and I knew that."

17: The death and life of Private Jason Burt

He also knew that, if the enemy hadn't legged it, the older Toms would look after him as much as he'd look after them. All he could do, then, was place his confidence – and his life – in the hands of his platoon, the battalion and the bosses.

"They were paratroopers, for God's sake! And so was I. So I just cracked on like everyone else."

Free Kick was situated where Furze Bush Pass meets a stream that runs south-north. But, before they arrived, they had the Murrell River to cross. Assuming the bridge to be mined, the sappers of 9 Parachute Squadron Royal Engineers had improvised a crossing for B Company by placing planks from bank to bank, then laying Texas Homecare-stickered ladders on top. It was the right idea, but the wrong way round.

In the pitch black and the light snow, as sodden boots tried to tread between the rungs, the plank beneath bowed and became unsteady. The B Company snake soon ground to a halt. Those who'd crossed had to wait on the far bank for the others to join them. The delay did nothing to ease fears.

After crossing, there were more problems. While the heavier equipment was being ferried part way by Trudi Morrison's civvie team, Support Company's fire-support teams were flown by Wessex helicopter from Estancia House to the reverse slope of a hill near A Company's position. From there they were meant to march parallel to B Company. But the two ran into each other, leaving 6 Platoon and half of 5 Platoon heading in the wrong direction. By the time John Weeks had rounded them up, valuable time had been lost.

At around the same time, with a strange quiet cast over the darkness, they passed some of the lads from Support and Patrol Companies. Several of them were in tears, because it was the rifle companies going in first. One lad from Patrol Company, Gary Body-Smith, kissed Dom Gray on the cheek.

"Mind how you go, Dom," he said. He was crying.

On the other side of the stream, just before the start line, CMS Weeks passed the order to split up into their fighting order and fan out in an extended line.

At home, it was another balmy night. As Jason lined up beside Cpl Milne, Terry was glued to the radio, waiting for any news, unaware that – in a couple of hours – an icy chill would invade their bedroom, then their entire lives.

Within a few minutes, 8000 miles away, the cold wind and the sleet and snow began to bite. It was 13 or 14 degrees below zero. As Jason crouched, waiting for the rest of the section and platoon to join the formation, they all knew there was no turning back. Come what may, very soon, they'd have to summon everything they had and face the ultimate test. Longdon was only a few hundred yards away, its rough outline and highest peaks – the objectives Full Back and Wing Half – silhouetted in the darkness.

Shortly before the signal to move, CSM Weeks walked down the line. No chat. The time for talk had passed. From now on, they knew the rule was 'fend for yourself'.

"Come on now," Weeks said as he passed Tony Barlow, "we've got to get this done."

That was it.

CHAPTER 11

LONGDON

The heart and heat of a battle isn't the place where detail is recorded in the way the Burts needed it to be – methodically, consistently and with forensic precision.

Some veterans are what you might consider fortunate. For them, the memories are fleeting. In conversation, they select moments from a million sights, sounds, smells and sensations that either mauled or slipped, un-noticed past their senses.

What others remember are intimate moments of all kinds that took them, in a blink of an eye or the turn of a head, from crazy, inexplicable laughter to abject horror. The events recorded by their eyes, ears, nose, mouths, hands and feet are lodged deep in their minds, often on a hair-trigger, primed to go off at some unknown point, at the slightest motion or word or smell.

Little wonder most just want to leave such demons undisturbed.

I've sat between men who fought an arm's length from one another and I know they've traded blows and insults in pub conversations, years after, because each believes their version of what happened is the correct one.

For some, the story of the battle is the version they've stuck to since the first telling, in the immediate aftermath of survival. The story isn't necessarily accurate, but it'll do. It's consistent. It doesn't require them to dig too deep in order to tell it again. And again. And again.

That's why finding the right man at the right time to provide the Burts with the key to Jason's story – how he would shortly die on Mount Longdon, and where he would fall – would prove to be the biggest obstacle to Syd and Terry Burt finding the 'minor detail' they craved. Their truth. Their cue to let go.

Finally, the whispered order to move came. After swapping final glances and the odd word of encouragement, at 0015Z – 10 minutes late – Brian Milne led his section over the tape. Within seconds, men were spread out in both directions, advancing in extended line across the open tufty ground, silent curses rippling down the line. Why hadn't someone bombed the crap out of the mountain for a couple of days? The Argies knew they'd be coming, sooner or later, anyway. A huge crater would have been far better than what loomed.

Doc McAllister watched 4 Platoon and Sgt Pettinger's patrol group go, then moved too, 10 steps from a 5 Platoon mate either side, on their way to rocky cover, thinking *I want to get up and get in front. I don't want to die on my own.*

After a few minutes, the order was passed to break down into staggered-file section formations. Milne was to the front right of 1 Section, with Pte Ron Duffy to his right and Jason directly behind. Tommy was in Jason's boot-steps, eyes fixed on the valley. It seemed to stretch as far he could see.

Low ground.

Open.

Bathed by the yellow moon.

Cloudless.

Strangely beautiful.

About 100 yards from where Sgt Pettinger's recce had seen the first Argentinian bunkers.

Maybe they wouldn't have to fight their way in.

Maybe they could breach the defences. In silence. Maybe.

The mine blast that blew Milne's foot to pieces echoed around the mountainsides. Then they heard the corporal's voice as they'd never heard it before.

Then all hell broke loose.

Green enemy machinegun tracer rounds filled the air at head height, criss-crossing, sending B Company running for the first cover they could find. Flares lit the sky as Jason and Tommy went to ground and the shocking reality dawned. The whole section was trapped in a minefield.

In Para Reg you understand that, however long it takes, you will achieve your objective. They don't necessarily kid you that you'll be there at the end, because there are lectures where they say the life expectancy in certain situations is about six hours. Until then, the mentality is *Just keep throwing it at me!*

But Tommy had never dreamt it would be like this, and it's safe to think that Jason was the same.

Cpl Milne's screams had been replaced by the horrendous groans of a man in pain, and shock was setting in. For a few, brief seconds the Toms and Crows spread themselves on the freezing, wet grass, gathering their wits. It was only a matter of time before the Argentinians had them in their sights. Shaking, Jason twisted in Tommy's direction and shouted.

"I'm going to him!"

He crawled, the first heroic deed Tommy saw that night.

No one else moved. They watched as he closed the short gap, every inch across the elephant grass as good as a spin of the barrel in a game of Russian roulette.

He reached his injured section leader, one of the men who'd been a father figure, and fumbled for his morphine syrette.

Break the phial....

Get it out....

Little syringe in....

Push it forward like a toothpaste tube....

Jason shook until Tommy arrived on his shoulder and saw he was in shock.

"Get this f***ing thing in to me!" Milne yelled. Jason was trying to push the needle through his tattered windproofs.

"It hasn't worked," Jason said. "I'm giving him mine."

Tommy looked at him. The morphine syrette round a soldier's neck is his own. He didn't say a word. Then Pte Ron Duffy crawled over.

"I think he's lost part of his leg," Jason whispered, shaking.

"Okay, don't tell anyone else what you've seen," the Scot told them. "I'll deal with it."

From the fringes of the minefield, the three men heard Sgt Ian McKay's voice with the rest of the platoon at the foot of the mountain, urging them on, anxious to pull the section through the minefield towards the enemy gunfire.

Tommy looked at Jason then stood up, stared across the deadly ground, and tried to walk. But his legs wouldn't move.

He tried again. Nothing.

A few yards away, Pte Tony Barlow was the same, feeling cowardly and frightened. A pub fight? They'd both be in without a blink. Here? Paralysed.

Tommy prayed for the strength to take a step, just one, to begin with. Nothing happened.

Then he thought *If I want to see Mum and Jo again....* and, suddenly, he was off, his weapon shaking in his hand, knowing each step could be his last, walking faster and faster.

"Slow down, Tom!" someone bawled from behind, and he realised they were using his footprints. He didn't want to, but he gave in, edging forward as enemy fire poured down, death creeping closer until Jason and the rest of the section couldn't continue the slow creep any longer, and they dispersed in all directions, seeking cover wherever they could.

From 5 Platoon's high vantage point on the rocky ridge above, deafening gunfire couldn't muffle a sound that Doc McAllister would hear for years. As Tommy hit the ground somewhere below, Doc was on a slight up-slope, trying to make himself invisible, hugging the ground as rounds zipped inches above his head, Milne's scream was like something Doc had only heard once before, when Tommy had shot a rabbit on the golf course back in Hoo, when they were kids. Except Milne's screams were constant.

While the lead sections of 5 Platoon found themselves confronted by a huddle of pup tents in an Argentine position close to Fly Half, their first objective, Tommy strained his eyes to pick out a foxhole below. There were none.

While 5 Platoon pumped bullets into the flimsy canvas shapes, and kept low as enemy fire flew from the darkness, all Tommy could make out were the boulders, pitch black crags and rock faces they'd have to climb through to reach Fly Half, up above. That was where the torrent of fire was coming from.

Slightly ahead, to his right, he could see men in an old peat pit. It was Jeff Logan and Taff Wynn-Jones.

Logan looked like a hard nut. He had a skinhead cut and a big nose. When the lads first went to battalion, he made it obvious that they were the Crows, and he was the old sweat. Sweats didn't talk to the youngsters. At first, they didn't even know if they should go in the room when there was a section briefing. Logan was that school.

Now Tommy could see him in a place of safety. He flinched as bullets meant for him hissed past. *I can't bloody ask them.* They were Toms. *Jesus Christ! I'm out in the f***ing open!* He glanced across again. Logan. Skinhead. Big nose. A sweat. A Crow dare not presume to join them. But as he stared, he saw a gesture.

"Get over here!" Logan yelled. Tommy ran.

"What the f**k were you doing out there?" the section machine gunner asked. He'd never uttered a word to Tommy before. Wynne-Jones said nothing.

"I didn't think there was room," Tommy lied, shaking.

Lt Jon Shaw's 6 Platoon had been luckier. Their progress on the southern edge of the mountain had been relatively easy from Free Kick. But the sound of Milne losing his foot changed that.

A radio message from Major Mike Argue's company mortar fire controller confirmed what they'd suspected and they made rapid progress up the hill, passing empty sangars, bunkers and tents. They grenaded some as they went, to be on the safe side.

As they neared the top of Fly Half, they still hadn't made contact with the enemy, but their luck didn't hold out.

They'd missed a bunker that hid seven Argentinians. They opened fire, and so did other enemy positions along the ridge. Within seconds, several men went down. The platoon medic, Pte Mark Dodsworth, was called forward to tend L/Cpl David Scott and Pte Tony Greenwood, two men from HQ Company who'd made up the numbers. But they were both dead.

A massive explosion topped the deafening thunder of noise, throwing up a huge plume of white smoke as a 66mm anti-tank missile ripped into one of the Argentinian sangars, clearing the ground for 5 Platoon on their way to their rendezvous point, Fly Half. The position fell silent and, for a few brief seconds, the barrage of gunfire was halted while the enemy switched attention to the higher ground to the south.

That was the chance 1 Section needed. They didn't need to think twice. They broke from

17: The death and life of Private Jason Burt

cover and hurried to the foot of the mountain and joined the rest of 4 Platoon.

If there's a point at which the Paras ceased to remember how the rest of the battle went, this could well have been it.

Tommy admits it could have been a few seconds, or a few minutes, between Brian Milne treading on the mine and this opportunity to rejoin 4 Platoon suddenly arrived. Time had already become uncertain. There was no watch ticking. Just a sequence of events that seemed to roll into each other; the unmistakable sound of a GPMG between the banshee screams and explosions of falling artillery shells that had been called on to the eastern end of the ridge, Fullback – and the continuing cries of their corporal.

The machinegun was 5 Platoon's GMPG. They'd started to get heavy too, higher up the rock face. An enemy position was holding up their advance. Huddled behind boulders, the men of 4 Platoon listened. It was all they could do for now.

Then they heard another familiar sound somewhere amid the din, a 66mm anti-tank missile.

Then another, an 84mm finishing off what 5 Platoon had started.

Then another, more distant. This time, it was the doof-doof-doof-doof of an Argentinian .50 calibre Heavy Machinegun sweeping across the high rocks, aiming to wipe out 5 Platoon, if it could.

Then the orchestra threw in another beat. Pte Ben Gough and Pte Dom Gray had pointed a 66mm at the Argies' HMG first, but twice it refused to fire. Under covering fire from L/Cpl Lenny Carver and Pte Gary Juliff, they charged the position instead, hurling grenades. Then they leapt in to the bunker, and only those with front-row seats heard the rest.

Until now, their training had told them the best way to use a bayonet. In reality, you just shoved it where you could. By the time they'd finished, only one Argentinian was left to surrender.

The turmoil above was what 4 Platoon needed. Lt Andy Bickerdike passed word through the huddle at the base of the mountain and led them off, still on the left, slightly to the rear of 5 Platoon and largely out of contact. As they edged towards a narrowing sheep track, however, that suddenly changed. They moved in to the night-sight view of snipers.

The crack of single shots, and the flinty smell of rounds spearing off rocks into the pitch black is something Tommy's never forgotten. Their instinct was to return the fire, but they couldn't. They didn't know whether the bullets were coming from 5 Platoon. So, terrified either way, while the men furthest forward opened up occasionally to clear the way, Jason and Tommy and the other Toms following in Bickerdike's bootprints held their fire.

They moved on until the track narrowed to a funnel between rocks and Sgt Ian McKay halted the advance.

Although the left forward section was in partial dead ground, the right section was pushing up behind 5 Platoon and had become intermingled. Both groups were forward of the Fly Half summit, where the rock ridges started to break up and the ground sloped away to the east, to an area known as The Bowl. For those advanced enough to see it, Fullback was clear, moonlit, in the distance.

Almost instantly, a wave of fire sliced the air to pieces and, just as quickly, McKay knew they had an immediate problem to deal with – a well-sited position up ahead, dug in for two months or more, containing 105mm RCL, at least two 7.62 GPMGs, one .50 HMG, and a number of snipers.

They crouched to shrink any silhouette they might show to the enemy. Jason and Tommy looked around for shelter and found it behind the shape of an Argentinian squaddie who'd dropped from 5 Platoon's position overhead. Even in the shadows, there were enough flashes of light to see he was in a hell of a state. He had a broken arm and leg. And one ear was missing. That's what it looked like, anyway.

But the body was warm. So, with no other choice, they sat on it and waited for Sgt McKay to give his next order from the head of the queue, where the rock-face turned and the track headed up towards the well-stocked enemy bunker.

Between every staccato or ratchet of gunfire, they could hear men shouting across the mountain. They were already aware of wounded men being snatched to safety, though they didn't know who'd been hit, how, or where.

Like the bunker that had hidden seven enemy in the rocks as 6 Platoon had swept at speed towards Fly Half.

Like the section 6 Platoon had hit from behind when the Argies emerged from their lair.

Like L/Cpl Doc Murdoch being killed – though some of them knew he'd gone down because, as he lay exposed on the mountainside, wounded in the head and trying to treat himself, they'd heard his voice on their headsets, moaning and talking to himself, "My eyes, my eyes!"

Everyone had a thing about eyes. Murdoch knew he was in trouble. He knew. They knew. But they didn't know about Pte Stew Laing, a 20-year-old who couldn't bear listening to his dying mate. He'd run out to rescue his stranded section leader. He covered only a few yards before three shots cracked and he was dead too.

The rest of it? They'd find out in snatched conversations, words passed in shadowy corners as they caught their breath, as the hours unfolded. For now, it was the doof-doof-doof of the .50 cal that mattered most.

"What's that, Sarge?" Tommy shouted, Jason just behind.

"That's a 50 cal, son," McKay answered.

In years to come, at the back door of his house, with me at his side, Tommy would replay

17: The death and life of Private Jason Burt

the next few seconds in his mind and try to give me an idea of how close the enemy was.

He'd ask me to imagine 4 Platoon lined up where we were standing, with our backs to the red Kent brick wall that represented the base of the rock face round which the sheep track twisted up towards the Bowl and Fly Half.

The majestic tree beyond a bench in Tommy's garden, 40 yards away, is where the Argentinians are, pouring endless fire at us. The space between? It's a killing zone. They've been staring at it, empty, since the day they turned Longdon in to a fortress. Now the Paras are coming. Forty yards. That close.

Tommy recalls McKay going round the corner to set his eyes on what lay ahead. It wasn't long before he was back in the line, a couple of men away from them, telling Lt Andy Bickerdike "there's a position here".

Bickerdike poked his head round the corner of the rock-face.

"Sir, you're going to silhouette yourself, you're going to be shot," McKay warned.

"They won't shoot me," the platoon commander joked. "I'm an officer."

Wrong. In less time than it takes to clap, he was down, clutching his thigh. He looked up at McKay, in pain and anxious with shock. His men looked at him. He'd come from another regiment to Para. You're Para Reg or nothing. The young Crows didn't think he was a bad bloke. Maybe he'd been trying to lead from the front, bravado. Maybe. But what he'd just done was mess about.

"Well done, sir!" someone shouted. Once a 'hat', always a 'hat'.

Bickerdike wasn't the only one to go down. Pte Mick Cullen, his radio operator, had been spun off his feet as a bullet ripped through his mouth, and 1 Section's machinegunner, the fearsome Pte Jeff Logan, had been hit in the hand. Taff Parry had received wounds to his right knee and foot, and Pte Dave Kempster had been shot in the left arm and right thigh.

Jason and Tommy glanced around. Tommy knew what they were both thinking. *If we were out in the open fields....*

But this wasn't open fields. This was Longdon. No one knew where anyone was, it was pitch dark. Tommy could barely hear. *There's sh*t going off everywhere!* It was a mess.

McKay didn't hesitate. He took command of the platoon and yelled for Cpl Scouse McLaughlin, high above on 5 Platoon's lofty perch.

Doc McAllister had been sitting feet away, listening to him grow more concerned, complaining "I just want to get this battle moving". Then McLaughlin moved forward to answer McKay's call and the rest stayed in their hollow, waiting for him to come back.

"We shouldn't be sitting here," Doc shouted to Pte Tony Kempster – the wounded Dave Kempster's brother – frustrated that he hadn't fired a shot yet. That wasn't the hardest part, though. With nothing to do until McLaughlin returned, he had time to hear what was going on below, and time to think. His mind was being pulled in three directions, *defend your mates, stay on the mission, no one can look after Tommy better than me.*

"This is what we must do," Kempster yelled. "That's why we're going to stay. We don't know what Scouse is doing."

The Argentinians didn't, either. They just knew something was going to happen. They could hear the two NCOs shouting.

"You've got a position down there with a 50 cal. We can see it," Tommy heard McLaughlin call down. "We can give you covering fire. You can get up there."

McKay quickly gathered a number of men from 4 and 5 Platoons, including Cpl Beetle Bailey's 5 Platoon section, and outlined the plan.

The .50 heavy machinegun had to be taken out.

It was hidden in a substantial sangar and protected by several riflemen, dominating all approaches.

The enemy's defensive position hinged on it.

It had to be checked out.

McKay pointed to Bailey and a handful of Toms.

Tommy watched them disappear round the corner to the short rise that would take them to the Bowl and into the full sight of the .50 cal. He was oblivious to whether Jason was with them or not. It would take more than 25 years for his memories to turn full circle.

Feet away, Tony Barlow had heard McKay and Cpl Ned Kelly swap brief words about one of the snipers, and he registered something that would convince him for years that Jason was one of the Toms heading out of sight.

Then all they could hear, on the sheltered side of the rock-face, or in their temporary hides, was McLaughlin in his box seat, 50 feet above, guiding McKay, shouting something like "they're ahead of you, there's two or three of them", and McKay's distinctive voice, "I've got two to my left….", then the jabber of Argentinians screaming orders of their own, then a burst of gunfire. Then a brief silence that was shattered by an explosion.

There was a pause before they heard McLaughlin call out to McKay again.

And again.

And again.

Nothing.

In the killing zone, Beetle Bailey could hear them. But he couldn't answer. He was dying, wounded in the right hip by a bullet fired from about 10 feet, wounded in the neck and shoulder too, listening to the rock-hard Liverpudlian's familiar twang as pain swamped his body.

"Sunray 21 down! Sunray Minor missing!"

Major Mike Argue listened to the radio report in Company HQ's new forward position, close to 5 Platoon on the ridge, and knew they were in trouble. Sunray 21 was Bickerdike,

17: The death and life of Private Jason Burt

Sunray Minor was McKay. Both of 4 Platoon's senior men were out of action. The tide had turned. The advance had been stopped in its tracks.

Argue called Sgt Des Fuller to his side and told him to find McKay, establish what was happening and then let him know by the fastest means.

Fuller didn't have a clue where to go. He wandered up and down the mountain, calling for Cpl John 'Ned' Kelly, the only 4 Platoon NCO he knew. Eventually, he found him. Kelly confirmed the worst. Then he took him to the wounded Bickerdike. The platoon commander couldn't add anything, except that 4 Platoon was in trouble.

They'd moved about 100 yards from the minefield. It had taken them maybe an hour, hour-and-a-half to do it. From the moment Brian Milne's leg had been shredded, there'd been constant firepower, a seemingly endless torrent of green tracer being cranked lower and lower towards them, nearer and nearer. Men had been dropping all round, and the enemy .50 cal was still drumming out its sickening beat.

Five Platoon was barely better off. They were under heavy fire from the east. After advancing eastwards through Fly Half, 6 Platoon was also pinned down under accurate sniper and automatic fire that had caused four casualties in little more than the blink of an eye. Platoon commander Jon Shaw had radioed Argue, anxious to 'go firm' – to stop the advance and consolidate the ground they'd won – so that he could reorganise, recover casualties and treat them.

Argue had agreed, but told him to be ready to support the other two platoons. That would be a tall order. Shaw's men had moved in to the face of the weapons firing on 5 Platoon. Most of his wounded lay among the rocks, and more were being wounded as repeated attempts were made to treat or rescue them, and destroy the source of enemy fire.

It didn't take Fuller long to decide what needed doing. After leaving Bickerdike, he asked Cpl Ned Kelly to fill him in on McKay.

Kelly was brief. The sergeant had gone forward with Beetle Bailey and three others, two of whom were stopgap guys, "mess stewards or something". That was the last they'd seen of him.

Fuller grabbed Des Landers and Scouse McLaughlin, the only section commanders he could find, and they hatched a plan to push on up the mountain again. Then he called to the remnants of 4 Platoon and detailed the plan.

"Right, we're going to do it, lads!"

The first time we met, Tommy told me that he remembered Jason was crouching to his right as Fuller spoke. I asked him whether Jason had gone with McKay, Bailey and Pte Roger James. But, because he had no recollection of him being in the line as they moved out of sight round the corner, he couldn't work out how Jason might have been on that attack.

The second time we met, he was less sure.

This is the first picture he painted of the minutes leading up to Jason's death.

Scrivs was to Tommy's left, with Grose to his left, as Sgt Fuller gave his orders in few words. They were moving round the corner of the rock face, out of shelter, and would form up by a small ridge of rocks and grass, 100ft or so from the main enemy bunker.

"Fix bayonets and prepare to move," Fuller finished.

Tommy's heart sank. 'Bayonets' flashed two thoughts through his mind. The eight-inch blade would drop the muzzle of his weapon. *I'm going to be firing low.* And, if they made it as far as the bunker, if, he'd have to plunge it into some other mother's son. *I don't know if I can.* He looked to his right.

"I'm not fixing my bayonet," Jason confessed. "Everyone who has so far's been shot."

It took Tommy almost 25 years to begin questioning what had made Jason say it. "Everyone who has so far's been shot." How did he know, unless he'd fixed bayonets for the McKay attack and seen for himself?

In that split second on the mountain, though, the thought didn't even register. In the freezing early-morning air, all he was thinking about was what was coming, once they were all in place – the order to charge, head on, towards the .50 cal bunker.

"Move round, move round," the order came quickly and, without hesitation, 4 Platoon ran low beyond the corner of the rock.

Six feet on, no more.

They dropped behind the ridge, anxious not to present a silhouette to the enemy hidden in their sangars 30 feet further on – 10 yards – across a patch of level ground.

Tony 'Frog' Barlow was probably the last man to hit the ground. As he'd passed Lt Andy Bickerdike, he spoke to the wounded platoon commander.

"D'you want me to stay with you?"

"If you must," was what he heard back. Frog looked at him.

If you must!

Well, you can f**k off! he thought. Instead, he left him lying on the icy mountain and joined the others round the corner.

Hours had passed like minutes until this point. Now the minutes felt like hours. Tommy glanced round. Scrivs and Grose were to his left, bayonets glinting. Jason was an arm's length away to his right. Tommy could feel his own apprehension rising. And theirs. The wait for Fuller went on.

On and on.

The wait for his call.

The Somme call.

Hot breath spiralled. Still they waited. Tommy's heart thumped and thumped.

Eight thousand miles away on this muggy June night, about this time, in the front bedroom of the Burts' welcoming home, Terry started screaming in her sleep.

17: The death and life of Private Jason Burt

"Charge!"

The Toms stood as one and legs began to pump. As they clambered over the damp rocks towards the .50 cal position, Jason slipped and stumbled to his knees. Cpl Ned Kelly was behind him, the first of those who hadn't broken cover yet.

"Get up!" he shouted a word of encouragement.

Tommy was clear of the ridge, running to the bunker, firing his weapon, by the time Jason was moving forward again. If Jason was like Tommy, and Tony, he was thinking of nothing. Not doubt, not fear, not anything. Robotic. Automatic. Adrenaline-fuelled.

Tommy's senses registered the rounds coming at him but locked the memory in the depths of his mind. They were razor sharp, shredding the air. The Paras crossed the ground in front of the enemy position, a couple of yards swallowed by every pounding step. Still the rounds came, still they charged, unstoppable, strangely unconcerned by the doof-doof-doof-doof of the Argentinian .50 cal they were nearing.

Tommy scrambled alone into cover at the forward edge of the enemy's gun position, vaguely aware that, on his right, Jason hadn't matched his progress.

He crawled through a gap in the rocks just short of the bunker's leading edge and pressed his body flat against the freezing, wet earth. He was so close, the man shooting at him couldn't crank the barrel of his weapon low enough to kill him. There was nothing Tommy could do but pray. Then he realised he couldn't return fire either from where he was. *Sh*t!* He'd have to crawl back to his first cover. In front of the .50 cal position.

He inched back, as low as he could, operating on survival instinct not training, until he felt the jab of a bayonet between his shoulder blades. He froze. Jason.

"F***ing move back!" he yelled. "This bloke's trying to kill me, for God's sake!" He was right, The Argentinian was. Tommy had moved back into his sights.

A second later, the pressure on his back released. He scrabbled the last few inches to the cover of the rocks and heard laughter. Laughter? He turned, but it wasn't the voice that had pulled blue-eyed blondes by the thousand, or urged him on through the months of Aldershot hell. Instead, it was Dave Wakelin, an attachment to the section from the Motor Transport Platoon, who looked at him and burst out laughing.

"F***ing hell!" Tommy shouted at him. "I thought you were gonna stab me!"

"So did I," Wakelin replied, with a huge grin.

Tommy twisted to open his ammunition pouch and changed his magazine. Better to have 20 fresh rounds than the so-called Dead Man's click half-way through the next charge. As he clipped the magazine in, he knew how close he'd come. He peered back through the dark, over the ground they'd crossed and, as the intensity of the fire dropped and his eyes regained their focus, he saw most of the Platoon, sheltering or lying motionless.

Then he started to hear the regulation calls across the battlefield.

"3 Section. What's your situation?"

"Twenty rounds left!" That kind of thing. But this time there was more, the kind of screams that hadn't echoed in the mountains of Wales.

This time, his mind was racing amid the chaos. Who's here and who isn't?

Then his thoughts flashed back to breaking cover, the first steps of the charge, and a vague memory of Jason, to his right, going down mid-charge.

Jase. I've got to look for Jase.

Tommy's heart sank. Maybe he'd just been shot. But he'd have shouted. It doesn't matter what situation you're in, you make a noise.

"Jase?" he called out.

"Tom, is that you?" a voice shouted back.

"Yeah, that you Scrivs?" Tommy returned.

"Yeah, I'm over here, with Grose. He's been shot. He's in a bad way."

Tommy's heart sank again. You never say anything like it. Never! The wounded man doesn't need to hear.

But Scrivs had said it, so Grose had to be bad. The last drop of adrenaline drained from Tommy's body. He was spent. Brief, sporadic bursts of automatic gunfire continued to spit from the enemy's position, and what was left of the Platoon returned fire in a desperate attempt to silence the guns.

Pte Taff Wynne-Jones crawled to where Wakelin and Tommy had taken cover. He was carrying the section's GPMG, but there was no sign of Jeff Logan.

"Jeff's been shot," he panted. "Looks like I'm the gunner now."

While Wynne-Jones settled the weapon into a firing position on the rocks, Tommy knew he had to look for Jason. He didn't have to go far.

Ten yards from where he'd taken cover, about a third of the way through the charge, Jason was lying face down. As he crawled nearer, he feared the worst.

"Jase!" he shouted as he went, but there was no answer.

"Jase!"

Nothing.

As he reached him, he grabbed his smock and turned him over. Jason's body slumped forwards and an arm fell to his side. A .50 cal round had hit his head. He'd died instantly.

In the darkness, the blood running down Jason's face took Tommy back to the Brecon Beacons. It reminded him of rivers in the night, trickling over rocks, glistening, running through the different colours of black. That's how it was. He didn't feel repulsed. He didn't feel sorrow. He knew Jason wouldn't have felt a thing.

They'd sworn that, if this happened to one of them, the other would remove their dog-tags and take them home. If they made it as well.

Tommy held his breath. But he couldn't do it. It was too much.

Silently, he apologised for breaking the promise and laid Jason gently back down.

17: The death and life of Private Jason Burt

(Top) Jason pictured on Canberra

(Above) The message the young 3 Para mates sent to Graham Collins

(Above) Steve Jelf (left), Stuart 'Doc' McAllister and Jason pose for Tommy's camera on Canberra

(Above) 4 Platoon – Jason, Tommy and Tony are fifth, fourth and second from the right on the back, with Duffy on the far left and Neil third left. Ian McKay is fourth from right in the middle. Scrivs is far left on the front

17: The death and life of Private Jason Burt

(Above) Jason on a beach at Ascension Island with Sgt Ian McKay sitting behind, a shot taken not long before the sinking of the Belgrano (below) changed expectations for good

17: The death and life of Private Jason Burt

3 Para head for the beach in San Carlos Water (above) while (below) Tommy's worst nightmare comes true – he's bashered up with Ron Duffy at Windy Gap!

17: The death and life of Private Jason Burt

(Top) Sunday, May 30, saw some of B Company's Milan anti-tank platoon leave Teal Inlet by trailer. This is how Jason left the settlement. He might be in this picture. Copyright unknown

(Bottom) On Monday, May 31, 1982, 3 Para snakes towards Estancia. This evocative picture is reproduced from Graham Colbeck's insightful book, With 3 Para to the Falklands. Copyright unknown

17: The death and life of Private Jason Burt

A snapshot from the family album of farmer Tony Heathman, showing 3 Para Toms sorting their kit out at Estancia House. Mount Estancia is in the background. (Below) Mount Longdon, a natural fortress for the Argentinian units defending Port Stanley

17: The death and life of Private Jason Burt

(Above) Longdon from the west, with the three routes taken from the left respectively by 4, 5 and 6 Platoons clearly distinguishable

(Above) Mark Churms' depiction of Sgt Ian McKay about to set off on the ill-fated attack of the Argentinian machinegun sangar. In reality, Jason would have been in this frame, or close by. Picture courtesy of Mark Churms

(Below) Sgt Ian McKay's helmet rests on top of his upturned rifle where he fell. In the follow-up attack on this same position, between here and the little dark line of rocks, was where Jason fell. Copyright unknown

CHAPTER 12
MINOR DETAILS

In Terry's dream, Jason was dressed in a white shirt and standing in their hall as Gurkhas tried to stab him. She yelled.

"They've killed him! They've killed him!"

The scream woke Syd and he shook her. It was about one o'clock, the early hours of a muggy, Walthamstow Saturday morning.

It was around nine on a bitterly cold night in the Falklands, eight thousand miles away, where B Company was nearing the foot of Longdon.

"Oh God! Jason's been killed," she told Syd. Within a couple of hours, the nightmare would come horribly true.

The next day, everything in the house was ice cold, even though it was mid-summer. On the Sunday, ice cold again.

Before he'd sailed, Jason had told everyone: "Don't drive mum mad with calls". That weekend, everyone called. One of them was Kerry, the girl he'd been seeing on his weekends home. It was the first time she'd called.

"I'm sorry, Mrs Burt," she explained. "Jason said he'd kill me if I phoned you up. But I woke up at two this morning and had this terrible dream. Is Jason all right?"

"Yes, he is," Terry reassured her, without believing – for one moment – what she said.

When no one answered the Burts' door around lunchtime on the Monday, the two uniformed Army officers went next door to Jean and Jim Court's house. Jean hadn't long come in from her night shift. As soon as she answered their knock, she knew why they'd come.

One of them asked if she knew how they could contact them.

"I know where they work," she said.

She doesn't remember how she asked the question, or whether she grabbed the book one of them was holding, with Jason's name on its open page, but they confirmed that Jason had been killed. She went cold.

"I'll quickly get something on," she told them.

Jim happened to be at home, so he stayed in case Jarvis arrived home. Jean composed herself, trying to take in the news and steel herself for what lay ahead. Then they drove to Petticoat Lane and parked their vehicle.

As they walked into the market, Jean saw that Terry was alone, and told the officers: "You're not telling her on her own. You've got to hide there until I come back."

She remembers leaving them mingling with the shoppers and then spending what seemed like an eternity walking up and saying something along the lines of: "All right, Tel?"

"Yes," she answered.

"Where's Syd?"

What's he done now? That was what Terry thought, so she said: "You look annoyed. Don't tell me he's hit your car."

"Where is he, Terry?"

"The toilet, but he talks to everyone down there."

"I want to talk to him."

Jean knew where the toilets were, so she returned to the two Army officers and walked round the back of the stall, so that Terry wouldn't see them.

As soon as Syd saw them, he knew.

"There's Syd," she told them, then walked up to him and said: "Syd, these gentlemen want to talk to you."

It was the way he heard them say "your son's been killed", then looked as if they were about to walk away, that made him start shouting at them.

Terry was wondering where he was and starting to think he'd said something else to offend Jean. Then she saw a car, maybe three-quarters of the way up the market, and heard what she thought was a row. The market came to a standstill.

"Go and tell Terry," Jean told Syd. "Don't let this crowd go up and tell her."

When she saw Syd coming back with his head down, Terry was even more convinced that he'd upset Jean.

"What have you done to Jean?" she asked. "She's been looking for you."

The crowd was gathering and Terry thought *Take no notice*.

Then Syd told her that Jason was dead.

Jean will never forget how she screamed and screamed.

"Would you like me to take you home?" She was shaking.

"No, we'll come on our own," Terry told her, eventually. So she went back to Garner Road with the officers.

Terry has few memories of their drive back to Walthamstow, but she does remember putting the radio in the bin. She hasn't had one in the house since.

One of the first things she did was call her sister-in-law Kay to break the terrible news. She remembers the phone ringing in the front room at about a quarter to one. For her, time froze. She didn't believe what she was hearing. It's a feeling that's stayed, and it still feels like yesterday, because she idolised the boys and knew how much Terry's loving, caring son meant to her.

Jim was working as a foreman out in Enfield, on a construction site. Kay phoned him.

"Jason isn't well," she told him, too shocked to say any more. "Come home."

He read between the lines. Minutes later, she told him what he'd already worked out.

Jackie was on the till in Sainsbury's when she saw Jim walking towards her, crying. Her mind flashed immediately to her mum or Paul, who was at school. Something had happened to one of them. Then Jim said: "Jason has died."

All she can remember now is leaving the till and a supervisor shouting at her to go back to it.

"No!" she shouted, and walked out of the shop.

For weeks afterwards, she refused to believe what her dad had told her about Jason being killed. She thought the cousin she'd fought and wrestled and played with in the park had simply gone missing, that he was hiding, scared.

They drove over to Garner Road straight away and remember the chaplain arriving soon after. I believe they stayed for a week or so, to give support.

At some point, one of the officers told the Burts that someone else from the Army would visit them that Monday afternoon with more details.

But Monday went, and no one came.

Tuesday went. Nothing.

By mid-day on the Wednesday, almost five days after Jason had been killed, Jim called Chelsea Barracks in disgust and threatened to phone the television and the papers.

That afternoon, just after lunch, two officers arrived.

"As a mother, I want to know how my son died," Terry told them. "How did Jason die? Did he live long?"

The answer echoed the "we don't give minor details" response of the Monday, the one that's haunted them since.

A minor detail? There's no way the information they wanted could have made its way back to Britain. The communication chain over 8,000 miles simply didn't allow that to happen. But how different their lives would have been if they'd explained the difficulties of the situation, and apologised for not being able to fill that space in their hearts and minds.

The detail they did mention was almost as devastating.

"When can we get Jason back?"

"Jason's been buried," came the reply. They didn't say where. They'd find that out later, from the television news. He'd been interred at Teal Inlet, alongside Neil, Scrivs, Ian McKay and the others.

"Was Jason's feet all right?" Terry asked, and the look they gave suggested that they thought she might be mad.

On the Wednesday, too, Kerry visited. The house was full but she came in waving the *Daily Mirror*. Her message to Jason had been printed, and she looked delighted.

Jim recalls the moment well. She didn't know what had happened. Someone told her and she broke down. Jim called her family to come and take her home.

What about Jason's other friends? It's perhaps unsurprising that Graham Collins had known before Syd and Terry. He'd received a call at about 10 on the Monday. A mate in Aldershot had seen the casualty list, read Jason's name and asked his dad to call Graham in Northern Ireland and tell him.

That Monday afternoon, Terry also walked down the road to the Laytons. Tony was at work, so she asked his sister Paula to pass on the tragic news. Paula rang Val, who was at work in the city. She was devastated. When Tony arrived home, she sat him down and stunned him as well.

"It was terrible," he recalls. "Absolutely terrible. The thing is, when you're 17 you don't expect it. As far as I was concerned, Jase is flying about over there like a lunatic and he'll be home. It's the way you think, isn't it? You never think someone's going to get killed. If you was another soldier, you might think that. As a civilian, you don't. I never, for one second, thought he would get killed."

Tony went straight down. Over the years, he'd hardly set foot in Number 18, but Syd invited him in. He doesn't recall much being said. Syd gave him a big glass of Scotch, and he sat down with Terry and Jarvis. Later on, Val and Dave called too. For years after, what Val saw if she closed her eyes was how utterly inconsolable Terry was.

"All Terry kept saying to me was 'Why did he have to die'."

At two on the Thursday morning, a reporter knocked the door, asking if he could have a picture of Jason. Jim had already warned them not to hand pictures out. Nineteen years or so in the Army had given him a healthy cynicism about the media. He was convinced the picture would be touted for cash.

The same day, a reporter from the *Mirror* called, claiming the MoD was insisting no 17-year-olds had died on Longdon.

"You just get back on to the Ministry of Defence or I'll show you his birth certificate," Terry told him.

Later that day, the *Walthamstow Guardian* appeared. From that point on, the phone rarely stopped ringing.

That was how Linda Jennings found out.

They lived on a corner house on the North Circular, so the local grapevine hadn't reached them. She was also in the middle of revising for college exams, so she hadn't seen anything of the friends she shared with Jason.

She'd followed the war on the TV – which meant there'd been little mention of 3 Para. Most of what she knew had come from Jason's letters, though the ones written closest to the battle were still undelivered, on their way north.

She was in bed when 15-year-old brother David burst in and showed her the *Guardian*. There was no subtlety involved.

All she remembers of the next few minutes is sitting in bed, crying "Jason's been killed".

Her mum, Norma, thought the Burts would be in no frame of mind to take visitors, so she left a few days before coming to see them.

Instead, because they'd be grieving so terribly, Norma suggested that Linda should write to them, in the hope that it would comfort them, to let them know that she and Jason had been swapping letters since he'd joined Junior Para.

On the Friday, the Burts' phone rang again. It was Neil Grose's dad, David. They'd heard about Neil at around 11 on the Monday morning. An Army officer had knocked their door while Ann was out shopping and her husband was sleeping after a night shift. She was putting the groceries away when a neighbour called over wall.

"There was someone looking for you earlier."

Seconds later, there was a fresh knock on the door. Ann saw a uniform through the glass.

"It was one person," she says. "I'd always been told it would be two if there was a death. But I think I knew then," she says. "He asked if I was Mrs Grose. I said 'yes'."

"Is your husband home?"

"He is."

"Would you call him?"

She asked the young officer in and felt sorry for him. Not the first time that's happened to a mother. Not the last, either.

"He didn't know how to deal with it. I called my husband. He was half-way down the stairs anyway. Then he asked us to sit down and said: 'Your son's been killed in action'."

"Are you sure?" she asked.

Then she wanted to know the hows, whys and wheres. But, like the Burts' two officers from Chelsea Barracks, he didn't know a thing. He couldn't give any answers about anything.

Once they'd seen Jason's name and Scrivs' in the paper, they went straight to Neil's room, where he had a noticeboard with a list of Para phone numbers. David called Syd and Terry straight away. Roy and Rosemary Scrivens phoned that afternoon, too.

On Saturday, June 19 – more than a week after Jason had fallen – Claire Acock sat down with her friend Julie in The Eagle, a pub not far from Brize Norton in Carterton, where she'd often gone with Jason. She remembers some whispering going on, then one of her friends taking a breath and plucking up the courage to say: "We've got something to tell you…."

That's how she found out what had happened.

She went into shock. Eventually, she was taken home – but she didn't tell her mum or dad until the next morning.

Her mum knew that Claire went to Brize and had had different boyfriends at different times, but she didn't know much about Jason. She hadn't met him.

And, though Jason had spoken often to her of Jarvis and life at home in Walthamstow, Claire hadn't met Syd and Terry. Nor had he given anything away to his mum and dad about the girl he'd met at Brize.

"Mum saw me as a typical moody teenager, but I was upset," she says. "There was no one I could talk to, no one I could ask questions. I didn't know a thing about what had happened. I had to keep this tragedy in my mind, to myself."

So, she was left with her thoughts and memories. The belief that he was too young to have been there in the first place.

The fact that someone older, someone who'd been in the Army 10 years longer, would have had a better chance.

The anger that he'd lost his life right at the end of the war.

If she'd known the Burts at the time, she'd have realised she wasn't alone in being haunted and angered by those thoughts. They would eventually meet by chance, many years later.

White flags flying in Stanley on Tuesday, June 15, passed the Burts by as they waited for the Army to turn up and explain how Jason had died.

While millions of us untouched by death or injury were rejoicing according to Mrs Thatcher's instructions – given the losses on both sides, 'sorry' might have been a better choice of words – they were about to embark on an apparently never-ending crusade to turn a minor detail into something they could understand, perhaps even accept.

As the remnants of B Company busied themselves 8,000 miles away in Stanley, finding somewhere to lay their battered bodies, they started their anxious search for information.

One morning, Terry picked up a paper and saw a picture of a 3 Para Tom being carried from Mt Longdon, with the caption 'Chris Dexter of London', so they started ringing all the Dexters in the London phonebook till they found his mum.

17: The death and life of Private Jason Burt

"Well, he's very upset," she told Syd, and promised to speak to him.

She wrote later to report what Chris had heard on the 3 Para grapevine – Jason had died with Sergeant Ian McKay.

The next trauma was Jason's final resting place.

They didn't know he'd made a will. Day and night, it worried them that he might have had a wish waiting. In short, what if he'd wanted to be buried where he fell?

"That was a nightmare because we wanted him back," Terry would reflect for family, friends and strangers – and herself – for years afterwards. "No matter what, we wanted him back."

A petition was quickly organised by friends, and she wrote to Mrs Thatcher. They weren't aware that Norman Tebbit was their MP, until neighbours started writing to him, too.

Until he saw Jason's name in the paper – he believes it was the *Walthamstow Guardian* – Mr Tebbit had assumed that his 60,000-odd constituents might include some involved in the war, and that, if there were casualties, "it might be one of mine". That was simply a question of statistics.

As a member of the Government – a close and valued advisor to the Prime Minister, but not a part of the War Cabinet – he'd been part of the decision-making process that had sent Jason, Scrivs, Neil, Tommy and the rest to war.

Once the Royal Navy had put the troops ashore safely, and the Task Force was inching its way to Stanley, he shared her conviction that – despite the inevitable setbacks that come with war – we would "take the islands back".

"In some ways," he recalled for me, years later, "what was more worrying was the international scene and the efforts being made to stop us doing so."

Until he discovered Jason had died, his focus was entirely on a war that he still believes had to be fought for bigger reasons than simply liberating the Falklands. Fundamentally, it was to show that a country like Argentina couldn't get away with resolving a diplomatic dispute by military force.

"The fact that it would be right to take back the Falklands was a very simple issue," he reminded me. "What was slightly different was the assessment of whether it could be done, and whether it could be done at an acceptable price."

By 'price', of course, he meant deaths and casualties. And he admitted that weighing up what would be gained against what Britain would lose was difficult. On balance, he believed the sacrifices of families like Jason's would be justifiable.

"At the end of the day, 256 lives were lost. The figure sticks in my mind. We were extremely thankful that there wasn't a great many more. We had some bits of bad luck and quite a few bits of good luck."

Although he's aware that one of the other basic facts of war is that many of the losses are young men – "after all, in 1940, we were chucking guys of 19 into the air against very much more experienced Germans when they'd scarcely finished their training" – he admits now that he probably hadn't appreciated how young some of the casualties would be.

"Jason was amongst them," he acknowledged.

As soon as he read the news in the *Guardian* about Jason's death, he ceased to be simply "one of the people that took the decision to retake the islands". Instead, he realised he had what he describes as "a relationship of responsibility and care" for one of the young men who'd been killed.

Hardly a week goes by now, 27 years on, when there isn't a reminder of that burden. He expects that, since Tony Blair took Britain into the wars in Iraq and Afghanistan, there'll be many in the current Government who sleep as badly as he did.

"That's what leadership is about," he reflects.

Because friends' and neighbours' letters asked him to lend weight to the fight for Jason to be brought home, he also found himself reconsidering other firmly held views.

"Traditionally, British servicemen are buried where they fall. I think, on the whole, that has always been a good principle. Apart from anything else, it means that, regardless of what family they have, or how far back it is, those soldiers are always looked after.

"But, in a curious way, in a war that's identifiable as a war rather than as a small military engagement, the smaller the casualty list, the more difficult it is (not to bring the bodies home). If Jason had been one of 10,000 casualties, it would have been easier for his parents."

In the end, although breaking the tradition didn't come easily, he realised it would be possible to bring them home.

"I came to the conclusion that, yes, we should do it."

On Friday, June 25, 1982, at 1115Z – 11.15am here in the UK, but around 7.15am in the Falklands – 3 Para left Stanley on the Norland, a converted car ferry. It would take them 10 days to reach Ascension Island through the wintry South Atlantic. From there, they'd fly home to Brize Norton. On the way, Tommy would 'celebrate' his 18th birthday.

By now, Keith Waterhouse's predictably direct *Daily Mail* column had informed millions of readers that the Burts had written to Number 10, asking Mrs Thatcher to direct that the lads who'd fallen should be brought home for the families who wished it:

Dear Mrs Thatcher,

We are writing to you as parents of Pte Jason Burt of the 3rd Paras who died in the Falklands, aged 17.

It is our desire to let you know that it is our dearest wish that our son be brought back to this

country for burial where we may visit his place of rest at any time we wish.
We also believe that other bereaved families feel the same way.
For the families who wish for their loved ones to remain where they are, we deeply respect their decision. Our hearts go out to the families of the men buried at sea who have no choice in the matter, but feel they would recognise the wishes of those families who do.
Hoping that you can let us know of your decision in the near future. Yours sincerely,

Mr and Mrs S Burt

In his column, Waterhouse criticised her for taking so long to decide. The question had been raised in the Commons three weeks before, when she'd promised the Government would be "considering the views of the relatives".

Behind the scenes, however, Mr Tebbit believes Mrs Thatcher's thoughts were already changing.

"I think she became aware of a good many of us who were moving to that view. And I think she was doing so too. After all, what would we have done if Prince Andrew had been killed? Yes, he would have been brought home."

While they waited for a response, life continued to unravel.

Four or five days after hearing about Jason, someone mentioned Christmas. Terry went upstairs, found the decorations, broke them into pieces and bagged them for the binman. Then she walked in the front room and said: "There'll never be a Christmas in this house again."

Jarvis busied himself writing a letter to the regiment's Colonel-in-Chief, Prince Charles, on Monday, June 21, asking for his brother's body to be brought home. As this was the day Prince William was born, he can perhaps be forgiven for taking so long to reply.

The family also received two letters from the MoD. One explained how Jason's personal effects would be returned, while the other envelope contained his death certificate with a photocopied covering letter. The certificate was dated Friday, July 2. Jason's name, rank and number were hand-written in ballpoint. Beneath were these scant details:

Place of death: Outside Port Stanley, Falkland Islands
Cause of death: Injuries sustained as a result of enemy action

That's it. All they ever had from the Army.

I remember clearly what Syd said, as I read the certificate in their front room, beneath a portrait of Jason on the wall: "If anybody had told me what silence is, I'd say there's more silence in that anything else."

It was another step backwards, and the arrival of Jason's last couple of letters home did nothing to slow the torment or the decline. The first was written on Friday, June 11 – the day they'd walked to Longdon:

Hi Mum + Dad
Hope things are ok, it's not here. Apart from the rain and cold, we have marched about 50 miles in the last week. I missed about 15 miles of it because I have 8 blisters and also called trench foot. Anyway, I'm in my sleeping bag at the moment, speaking to Tom. I haven't had a wash for 2 weeks now, and its great to think your not behind me telling me to wash behind my ears. That's the best thing about this, no washing.
Tom said to tell dad to send him some sandwiches and to tell him his a tyte bastard. And that he is going to treat him to a drink. We are now waiting for the Marines to catch up. We were told by the brigadier to slow down because we are going too fast for the Marines. They can't keep upso they are getting helicopters everywhere and they still can't keep up. Any I must go now, lots of love,
Jason xxxxx

His final, mud-stained letter arrived soon after.

Hi Mum + Dad + Jarvis
Just a short note to let you know I'm ok. We have marched 75 miles in the last week. We are 8 miles outside Stanley it has rained every other day and my –ucking feet –ucking sting. It is very cold. Anyway, must go love Jason xxx

When the phone went on the morning of Thursday, July 8, the effects of the bottle Syd increasingly turned to as a way of dealing with the strains of the previous month were quietly ravaging his body. It was Norman Tebbit's secretary.

"Can you stand by the phone because they're discussing bringing the bodies back?" she asked. At about five to one, the phone rang again. This time, it was Mr Tebbit's voice Terry heard. He had the news they wanted.

"You can have your son back," he said.

"Thank you very much."

"Don't ever thank me or any member of the Government," he replied. "We thank you."

On Friday, July 9, a letter to the *Walthamstow Guardian* headlined 'Young man we mustn't forget' suggested a permanent memorial to Jason. There was also a news story charting the flood of tributes to him and reporting the neighbours' efforts to amass signatures in support of the campaign to have his body returned home.

17: The death and life of Private Jason Burt

It also described Syd's bitterness at the way the MoD had sent his death certificate, and it concluded with brief details of the fund-raising for an orthopaedic bed at Whipps Cross Hospital, in Jason's name.

The same day, perhaps the last chance for them to start the slow, painful process of letting go had already dissolved. Syd opened *The Sun* and there, beneath the underscored headline FOR VALOUR and an image of the Victoria Cross, was a line-up of six pictures. On the bottom row, below a smiling Col H Jones, was Jason's face. The story's explanatory 'blurb' said this:

> *Britain's premier badge of courage, the Victoria Cross, is to be awarded to at least four of our Falklands heroes. Here The Sun lists the doughty deeds of the men most likely to win the coveted medal.*

James Lewthwaite's story started:

> *"Six valorous names have been recommended for Falklands VCs. And it's from these six that four or more will be chosen."*

'Doughty deeds' and 'valorous names'. The *Boy's Own* phrases might have rolled off the tongue, but the paper – the self-styled guardian of 'Our Lads' – was seriously lacking in evidence or detail. The article didn't indicate how the information had been obtained. There wasn't even the familiar catch-all 'inside sources' to which Lewthwaite attributed this careless talk. Neither was there an explanation as to why a story that trumpeted 'six valorous names' should include the stories of seven men – the additional hero being Scrivs.

"Among the others who may have been recommended", the article told its readers, were "Paratroops Ian Scrivens and Jason Burt, both 17, who died in the bloody hand-to-hand battle for Mount Longdon just hours before the ceasefire".

It went on to say:

> *"The two friends – they had been cadets together – had only been fully fledged members of the Third Battalion of the Parachute Regiment for four months, They were two of the 22 Red Devils killed in the fight to recapture Mount Longdon."*

The story would change their lives – though not in the way they imagined when they put it down again. Within days, Syd were admitted to Whipps Cross. The stress, kidney stones and the drink had finally taken their toll.

While he were being treated, a man and a woman from the MoD called at the house, to talk about financial assistance. One of them saw the photo Jason had given his mum on Mothering Sunday, and remarked how young he looked.

"How old is he?"

"Seventeen."

The man gathered his papers and apologised.

"You're not entitled to anything because your son was under age," he said.

After Syd was discharged from hospital, a council official knocked the door. He was delivering forms to add new voters to the electoral roll and asked for Jason.

"What d'you want him for?" Syd asked.

"To fill out his voting papers."

"Go away."

"Why?"

"Because my boy has died."

The man apologised and left.

On Monday, July 5, the returning men of 3 Para climbed on board an RAF jet at Ascension Island to start the final two-stage flight home, via a refuelling stop in Dakar.

As soon as they saw England through the clouds, a big cheer went up. But, within minutes, the elation had gone. The band struck up the regimental march, *Ride of the Valkyries*, and Tommy was meant to lead them off. But he stepped aside to gather his breath and his thoughts. For a moment, no one else wanted to be the first to go out either.

Why the reticence? Tommy's school friend, Stu 'Doc' McAllister, watched him back away from the door that day.

"It was just hard," he recalled, almost 25 years later. "The feeling on the aircraft was that we weren't the heroes. The people left back there, dead, were the heroes. We didn't want to claim any sort of valour from them. Everybody felt the same way. To jump out of the aircraft and say 'Here we are, the heroes' was not how they perceived themselves."

Stu recalled something he overheard CSM John Weeks saying about the youngsters just before they disembarked.

"I'm proud of the way the guys have shown an adult emotion towards death. They got on with the job," he said. "Now we've got time to reflect."

Time to reflect.

The reason the Burts didn't see Tom for a week or so after he'd returned – the reason his family didn't see much of him, either – was because he needed time away from the fuss, the parties, the pats on the back and the inevitable questions.

Put it another way, he needed to be with people who understood what he'd seen, what he'd done, what had been sacrificed.

People who knew what part the training and indoctrination had played in the battle being won.

People who knew that 3 Para had prevailed because the difference between taking Longdon and leaving it in Argentinian hands was something most of us haven't a clue about – the engrained determination not to let yourself, the Regiment and your family down. In other words, "completing the Mission".

"That's what it is," Doc says. "It's an unspoken promise you make. You make it to the guys next to you, you make it to the Regiment. You make it to the history of the Regiment, to the people who've gone before you. Everyone's had their turn, and now it's yours."

It wasn't long after leaving the transport, back at Tidworth, that Ron Duffy climbed aboard a London-bound train at Andover. From Waterloo, he took the Tube to Bank and then walked to the market at Petticoat Lane where, Jason had told him, Syd and Terry ran their stall. But they were nowhere to be found.

No one on the market could help, possibly because he was asking for the Burts. But Syd was known as Brooks, after his dad. It was only after visiting the *Walthamstow Guardian* offices, following a fruitless call at the police station and a trawl through the phonebook, that he was given their address and headed for it. They weren't in.

Instead of presenting them with the bottle of Scotch he'd bought in honour of their "bonny lad", and telling them what he knew and what he'd heard of Jason's heroic deeds on the mountain, he made his way back across London to Euston, and drowned his sorrows in malt on the Caledonian Express to Inverness. It would be five months before they became aware of Ron's pilgrimage that day, and the outcome.

Primed by the extremes of the Army's 'minor details' comment and *The Sun*'s VC story, they bombarded Tommy with questions about Jason when he finally visited in the middle of that July. That remained one of Syd's abiding regrets. He was right. It was too much, too soon for him.

Tommy knew how rocky Syd and Jason's relationship had been. A dad and son, both strong-minded individuals, both refusing to meet half way.

Even at 18, Tommy was streetwise enough to realise what was driving Syd's questions in the days that followed. The best he could do was keep the promise he'd made to himself – to tell them the truth as he knew it, and in a way he felt was most appropriate.

He was more bothered about making sure he'd seen them than he was about spending time with his own family, but the prospect of being their final link to Jason still prompted him to take his dad and Graham Collins the first day he visited.

He was oblivious to the anguish they'd suffered trying to pin down the pieces of Jason's jigsaw, and – in the years to come – he grew to realise that some the questions he asked might have sown seeds of contradiction and confusion in their minds. Those questions roll off his tongue like a well-worn list.

Did they receive the wedding ring back?
Did they receive Jason's last letter?
What about the insurance?

"I think I caused some of their problems," he says, "though not through anything that they didn't deserve to get. Jase had taken out insurance. Jase had written a last letter. And the wedding ring.... I was involved in all these personal things."

"It wasn't that Jase went off on his own to do insurance," he recalls. "It was me and him sent down by Ian McKay to take insurance out. No other reason. The wedding ring was because of me. I can remember the conversation. Me wearing my mum's (as a good luck charm). And the last letter," he referred to giving Jason his spare bluey not long before they tabbed out of Estancia towards Longdon. Perhaps that was the 'letter' found in Jason's battledress after he'd been killed.

"I was involved in all these things, so I said to Syd with genuine sincerity 'These things are coming to you'."

At first, he thinks, Syd and Terry weren't too bothered by the insurance – until the Army said Jason hadn't taken out a policy.

"The Army had that vagueness," Tommy told me. "I think that fuelled the fire. As I understand it, Grose wrote a letter with all his serial numbers on and his mum and dad got paid out. Scrivs? The family didn't know and they got paid out.

"My policy was there and Jase's weren't. Jase wouldn't have wrote (to his parents about) that because his mum would worry. And she would. You can see that.

"I never fabricated a story for Syd and Terry just because it's what I thought they wanted to hear. I saw the anguish from my mum's point of view so, if anything, I was telling them things that they didn't want to hear."

Slowly, he watched their hunger for answers start to grow. From that point on, he knew, there was only ever likely to be one result. They'd find out nothing.

"Syd got the Army with their closed-door attitude, and the Para Reg is secretive. Not just secretive, but unless you're a Para, you're no one.

"I think it was very difficult. And, like I say, (there were) good intentions here and there, with people saying what they thought the family should hear. Like the VC."

He worked with Syd on the markets during his leave, a routine that involved a daily visit to the steam baths, or Walthamstow dogs or to West Ham bars. Or all three.

Terry and Syd had already bought Jason's 18th birthday presents. He recalls a Ford Capri, an engraved Swiss Army knife and a Dupont cigarette lighter. They gave him the knife and lighter, which he still has.

With the benefit of hindsight, he believes they liked him around because he was like Jason.

"The market was a shrine to Syd. Everyone would nod. Everyone knew Syd. They showed him respect and they enjoyed him being there. If something cropped up that he couldn't answer about his boy, I could. And I think that gave him reassurance. I was in the Paras and, when we were down the market, he couldn't wait to introduce me – *Tom was with Jase!"*

Eventually, primed with Malibu and vodka in the pub one day, and with Graham Collins at his side, he felt he could talk about the things that had so far gone unsaid. Without realising it then, he nudged Syd further down the road to despair.

The picture he painted contradicted the one implied by the *Sun* story. Over the coming months, what he told them would be at odds with what emerged from the other 3 Para men they met who were prepared to speak.

When others were introduced to them and fled at the mention of Jason's name, they wondered why and began to fill in the own gaps. He recognises now what was happening.

"Para Reg blokes change. What was a very small point of the battle becomes the turning point. One man won the battle. Whatever. So Syd would get conflicting stories. Thinking back, to me, it was straightforward who did what and how. To other blokes…. It was difficult. It was difficult."

I chatted with Tommy for 10 hours or more over a couple of separate visits. What follows is how the story emerged about what happened on the mountain after he went back to Jason, saw that he was dead, and laid him down.

Describe how you felt when you realised Jason was dead.

I didn't feel repulsed or anything like that. And I didn't feel the sorrow at that time. They were still shooting at us, not from that position but other positions. Sniper fire.

How much of that is innate survival and how much is mission-orientated?

It's more complex. Survival instinct happens when you're running towards that kind of danger. You have an instinct inside that says you should take cover now. You have a natural instinct to think *That's going to be f***ing dangerous over there, I'm going this way!* And you had a training method that said if you went that way you'd keep low. Within seconds, you've assessed that. It's a natural thing that people have. Your training just polishes it off.

Dealing with death, you shut the feelings door. I had in my mind *I've got to go back and look for Jase.* I still had to get across to Grose, to see Scrivs and see what the situation was there. So I had something else to perform.

When Jase was killed, Neil Grose…

… he would have been hit seconds after. Same attack.

Scrivs is with Neil?

Yes. Everyone's…
    "Check your firing…!"

"We've got people moving to the left...."

"The position's clear...."

It's then that you get....

"Right, 1 Section, what state are you in?"

"What rounds have you got left?"

"Who's been hit?"

And that's when everyone shouts out. It's chaotic. Everyone wants to say their bit. And then blokes, involuntary or whatever, are screaming, and you realise all that as well.

Who's co-ordinating all this information?

The organiser of the whole thing was Scouse McLaughlin at the top. When we went forward in the sections, the bloke I remember shouting the most was a bloke called Alhaji. His section was in the cover of their rocks, and he was screaming and shouting that the grenades we were throwing were going over on them.

"You're going to end up killing your own men!"

Every time he talked, a sniper would fire. So you had "Shut the f*** up!" going on too.

You went to Ian to see....

I went to Jase first. I yelled out to Jase. Nothing.

Scrivs yelled "I've got Grose over here! He's been shot in the chest. He's in a bad way".

In training you never say anything like this because of shock. The patient doesn't need to hear it. But he said it, so you know the seriousness of the situation.

He'd been shot in the chest and one of his lungs had collapsed. The problem with that is that you have to get them on to their injured side so that you've still got the top of your body with the lung working.

I said to Scrivs I'd go and look at Jase in case he was in a bad way. I went back, saw Jase, then knew. Then I went back to Scrivs and said "Jason's dead".

Grose was in a hell of a state. He'd had a premonition that he'd take one in the chest.

You'd all carry your field dressings (in your) left-hand top pocket. It's waterproof. You'd use that over the sucking wound, where the lung's been punctured and air's being dragged in, to seal the wound.

He'd say "I've got the dressing in me top left-hand pocket. You do know how to put the seal on, don't you?"

He was always talking about a sucking wound.... Horrible, horrible. It's one of the worst wounds that you can get.

He was panicking. We'd been told that we'd be off to the (hospital ship) Uganda within 20 minutes, if you'd been shot. (But) They were sending the helicopters away because it was compromising and also the Marines were going to attack Mt Kent. So the helicopters

17: The death and life of Private Jason Burt

that were coming in to casevac couldn't land. They were being sent off, so there was no evacuation.

Neil's conscious through all of this?

Yes. And knows the seriousness of his wounds. If you know that, you know how long you've got before it's fatal. I think he was maybe working on an hour. That poor lad took about three hours to die.

For a while, we were talking. I'd say about 15 minutes. Just me and Scrivs. Talking about the situation.

Dave Kempster. He was in a very bad way. He'd been shot across the nose and in the shoulder by a tracer round that was still burning. He was in agony and was still screaming. All that going on, then the snipers opened up. They started picking off. They open up and you're just waiting for your turn.

Do you register these things?

Yeah, you do. It's horrible, because your survival instinct comes in. You want Dave Kempster to shut the f*** up, or someone to put him out of his misery. Because he's compromising your position. It's drawing attention. But you know they're in pain and this is for real.

It also affects you, the way you speak to your patient. Your voice trembles. You're not officious, but you are. You don't want to be. The situation requires more tender loving care.

When the sniper start picking people off, that's when you feel very vulnerable. But you're torn. Do you take cover and save yourself, or do you sort this out?

Scrivs is shot while you're trying to deal with Neil.

Basically, Grose is lying on the ground and they said they were going to start casevac people. People were starting to move back.

Grose is lying here, head towards the enemy position, and Scrivs is the other side. He's been talking to him, felt down his back for an exit wound, couldn't find one.

Scrivs is telling me all of that and I'm talking to Grose – "You're going to be fine. There's no problem. The helicopter's on the way" – and I put my hand on Scrivs' shoulder to say "We'll move him, you grab...."

As I did, he was shot. He fell over on me, so I'm on Grose. He's screaming and I pushed Scrivs off, and then... the realisation that everyone's dead.

*There's no f***er left!*

It was the start of the battle. It wasn't two days into it. It was 'wallop! There you go, everyone's gone!' That was terrifying.

Did you feel 17 then?

No, but it didn't matter. I thought I was going to die. There's only me and I'm going to be the next. I'm waiting for me death. It could come from anywhere.

Did that sharpen you up?

The realisation is terrifying. And I've still got Grose to deal with.

Was there a 'what am I doing here' moment?

It's too late. It's gone. There's nothing you can do. I don't like to use the word resigned, because there was a point in the battle where I *was* resigned to die. This was not it.

Is that a weight lifted off your shoulders, when it comes?

Yes. But here I was, still surviving. It was *He's gone, he's gone, he's gone – I'm the only one left. It'll be me next.* Then it was *Well, it's not going to be. I'm going to do this, I'm going to do that.* There was another point, where Grose actually died, where I thought *I'm never going to get through. I've had it. I've f***ing had it.*

> (Tommy's not clear on who helped him take Neil to the Regimental Aid Post (RAP). All he recalls with clarity is that it was an ordeal in every way imaginable.)

There were four of us who tried to move him. I think it was me, Johnny Weeks, Lieutenant Cox and a fella called.... Johnny Weeks came up to me and said: "Who've you got?"
Scrivs was dead, and I said: "I've got Grose, sir."
"What's his first name?"
"Neil."
"Neil, you're going to be fine. We're going to move you back." Reassuring him strongly.
"How you going to get him back?"
"I'm going to carry him."
"What have you got to carry him?"
At this point, I meant I was going to pick him up and walk with him, knowing that I was going to silhouette myself and that two of us would be a bigger target than one. So I wasn't over-confident in wanting to do that, but I didn't think I had any other choice and I wasn't going to leave him.
He said: "Okay, okay."
Then he went off and he came back and we've got ponchos.
"We'll put him on a poncho and we'll move him back."
So we laid this poncho out and we moved Grose on to it, which was very, very painful.
I put my weapon down. There was these four people, although I don't think Cox carried him in the end, and Binky Swain just knelt down and said "I've been shot in the rear!" And he had. He'd been shot in the arse.

17: The death and life of Private Jason Burt

Then I was just left, and I don't know whether... Johnny Weeks says it was him who carried Grose back. I don't believe it was. It was me and someone. But I carried Grose for part of the way on my own. It might have been Lieutenant Cox, and we bundled this poncho together like a makeshift stretcher and crouched back with it. But for the first part I think I dragged Grose on the poncho myself. Then Cox picked it up, because I was annoyed with him.

What I wanted him to do was put his arms around my neck and I'd carry him down, I think. And I couldn't do it with my weapon, so I put my weapon down.

In Para Reg you're so anti-sling. You don't have a sling on your weapon. That's a hat thing. You don't have it over your shoulder, you have it in your arms. I put it down and Cox was faffing about with it.

So you've got the sniper picking people off, you've got Grose screaming that he's in pain and wants to get the hell out of there. Scrivs has died and fallen on him. Binky's now been shot in the arse and gone down. Grose can see all these people getting hurt around him and he's still concerned about his own life.

"Sir, leave the f***ing weapon. We'll come back. Let's just get him out."

He didn't, and that's why I think I dragged him (Neil) first and then pulled him to an area and then Cox would sort it out.

What distance to the RAP (the Regimental Aid Post)?

(He looked from his kitchen and pointed to the tree that had marked the position of the machinegun post earlier in our talk) About that distance doubled. About 100 yards.

I'm with Grose, leaning over him, trying to get him on his injured side, saying that he's fine. He wouldn't go. I'd get him on his injured side and he'd push me off and lay back. I couldn't say to him "You're going to f*** both your lungs up if you can't do that."

It was very hard, but I felt for him because every time I moved him he was in pain.

I reckon I was with him for about 40 minutes, a long time, saying: "You're going to be all right. I've got you, mate. Nothing's going to happen. You're going to live."

Had he been seen by a medic at all?

No. They were all over the place. One per company. What a job to have that night. He believed me totally.

"It might be a bad wound, and it might be hurting, but you're not going to lose your life, son. I've got you."

Then there's a point where you've gone past that and you know you're going to die. And he knew. That's a really hard bit to do.

"I've got to be on my injured side, haven't I, Tom?"

But he couldn't.

Phil Proberts, who was the medic that night, was sitting in the RAP with his head in his hands. I'm not going against him. He was in a sh*t state. I didn't know Phil. He was an older lad, and I was still a Crow. Mentally, he'd gone.

He came over and shone a torch in his (Neil's) mouth. His throat was just clogged with blood. We couldn't get it out.... That's when he let go.

My thoughts wandered to Scrivs and Jase – dead is dead, if you know what I mean. You can't be half dead. But the full realisation of never seeing them again doesn't really sink in until you're doing things that you would have done with them. Then it hits home.

(After Neil died, Tommy and some others remained in the RAP for about 10 or 15 minutes. The Argentinians had counter-attacked through the ground taken when Jason was killed.)

Blokes who were up there covering for the evacuation were now coming back saying: "We need to do something!"

That was when Scouse McLaughlin took over again.

"Right, we're going to counter-attack."

But the only way to counter-attack was back up this poxy path. And I've got to say, I was (sighs).... I was sobbing, like Phil. Felt terrible.

Didn't have me weapon, and Scouse says: "We're going back up, and we're going back up now."

You'd been down there in the sh*t and there's only a few of you left, and he now wants you to go back up the same route that you know is a channelled (killing) zone.

"Right, you lead. Start getting everyone behind you and start going back up."

"Scouse, I haven't got a weapon."

I scouted around for one. I was given a 9mm pistol but thought better of trying to assault the enemy with a pistol, so I stayed with the wounded until they came back from the assault. The Argies pushed them back down the channel before they were able to secure the position.

Pete Hindmarsh was another guy who was shot in the bum. They were lined up with this cliff face behind them, with their backs next to that, looking towards the valley, where the snipers were firing. Even in the RAP, you could hear the hiss and zip of a round cutting through air. The speed. You sense everything. Then you could smell... it was like when flint goes. That was happening all the time in the RAP.

There's a will in you to get out of the situation and go back up, but you're not equipped. If I recall, where we'd come back down the channel, there was a big rock. I think it was a composite force of C Company or A Company that had now come in, fresh guys, that got up there. You'd got John Crow leading, who took a round in the middle of the forehead. And Kev Connery then gets involved.

And that was the decisive move?

Yes. We pushed them back... off the mountain. Then they start fleeing. And then used it as a bombing zone.

> (A group of them went back to the RAP and were detailed to move the wounded to the base of the mountain for casevac by BV, a half-track vehicle. Cpl Ian 'Beetle' Bailey had been seriously wounded in Ian McKay's attack. He'd been dragged to safety but left outside the RAP because, Tommy says bluntly, he didn't have long to live. As the wounded began to leave, though, someone moved Bailey and he moaned.)

"F***ing hell! He's still alive!"

So they took him.

Who did you help down to the BV for casevac?

I took Ned Kelly down. Ned was the full screw (corporal) who'd said to Jase (when he stumbled at the start of the attack) "C'mon, stop messing about, let's get up there!"

He'd been shot in the stomach on the left side. They think he was shot in the back and it had come out the side.

Ned wasn't a bloke I got on with. He was a feisty bastard with tattoos round his neck. He was Irish and aggressive, or Scottish and aggressive. I kept out of his way. He didn't like us because we were Southerners. He always took umbrage to the way you spoke, even if you said "Good morning!"

So he wasn't my choice, and it wouldn't have been. Someone must have said "You will take him down".

This is a very difficult thing, because this man was married – Jackie, I think his wife's name was – and he grabbed on to me. I was now his life. I'd just had three hours with Grose and I thought *If I cock this one up, he won't die, he'll beat me up.*

"You get me down there and you keep me awake. You keep me awake!"

I'd put Ned Kelly into the back of a BV. It had a light on inside, like a bulb, which again was unnatural. And the canvas that comes down to shield the light. You'd got the motors of the vehicle going. It wasn't a place you wanted to be.

Did you sense that you were out of danger?

No. I thought I was more in danger because of it. Lax. Not tactical. I remember sitting on the back of this thing. There's all this noise. Pete Hindmarsh is lying on his front with his arse shot, and Ned's looking at me going: "Don't let me go to sleep. If I fall asleep, I'll die."

Was that a reality or his fear?

It's a fear. (Long pause)

There's nothing you can do with stomach wounds. You lay them in a W position, the most comfortable for them. They can't have fluids. They can't have morphine because it relaxes the respiratory system. There's nothing you can do, so I think that there is a point that you can go unconscious and let go. If your respiratory system relaxes and doesn't want to fight any more, that's the end of it.

You also don't know with the (stomach) acids what they'll do, and I think he was terrified of that. And he gave me serious grief.

"Do not let me go to sleep!"

I don't know if I was in the BV 20 minutes or an hour.

He said: "Look at my wound and tell me how bad it is."

Now, from the battlefield, where it's pitch dark, I'm in a lit vehicle, very small, a closed environment, and I'm here (he places his hand down beside him) and Ned Kelly's there (moves his hand a foot) and I'm going to look at this wound.

It wasn't something I wanted to do. As I undid the smock, it's got bloodstains. Then he's got a jumper on that had laddered where it (the bullet) had come out.

*F***ing hell!*

Shirt split, open it and it's about that big (he makes a fist) and some of his stomach's sticking out.

I couldn't believe it. No blood! I could see the white skin and this rip. The relief to me... but I didn't say anything. Ned was obviously not looking, and he was saying "It's bad, isn't it?" He did get a bit loud with me.

"Ned, it's nothing!"

I put a dressing on it, held it on and held him.

(After the BV was emptied of the casualties, Tommy climbed back aboard and went back alone to the battlefield. It was about five in the morning. Then he walked to the RAP, at the base of the mountain. It wasn't there any more.)

I asked a black bloke – Chalky White, obviously – Steve Richardson, who was in 5 Platoon, whether he'd seen Stu. It was like a bowl area, and then it went up this narrow bit. This must have been the first crack of light.

"No, I haven't mate, I'm sorry" meaning that, if you hadn't heard about someone, they were dead. That's how it had been.

There was no one else I could relate to. Jelf (Steve, the youngest of the 17-year-olds) I didn't know. He was very quiet. Very, very quiet.

I thought Stuart was dead and, honestly, from that moment, I didn't give a sh*t. I walked back up the hill to where Grose was laid. I sat there. Grose had the poncho covering him, a boot was showing. I opened the poncho. I closed it and wished I'd never looked at him.

(Tommy sat down for a couple of minutes. He had no weapon. He'd put his rifle down when he'd picked Neil up.)

I thought the only thing I can do is move further up and find who's about. The back was full of support people. I couldn't go there. We were the leading people. So I walked back, and 100 yards further up was where 5 Platoon had dug in. As I walked up, Grant Grinham was on the highest point. I looked and Stu was there.

"I thought you'd…."

From that moment on, it changed again. I was back up.

At what point do you gather your thoughts about what's left of 4 Platoon?

Later that day. We took a lot of casualties during the day with the mortar fire. A lot of lads were casevacced out again. I think (Colonel) Huw Pike wanted to move on quickly, because we were sitting ducks.

I remember moving forward and seeing the green grass on the mountain. It was the greenest grass I've ever seen. They must have seen us, 'cos they were directing fire to the front of us.

Someone shouted out "Incoming!" and you could see these shells in the air, some of them. You could physically see them.

I took cover with Stuart. We went to ground. I had Northern Ireland gloves on and, when I put my hand down, it was just thick blood. Everywhere. Big thick blood. My glove was soaked. My mind had seen so much blood (but) now that you're seeing greenery, you focused on it.

I just said "Oh, f***!" 'Cos it's got a smell.

"Let's get the f*** out of here. We're right on it. We're souvenir-hunting now. There's no need for this."

(They returned to where they'd had the brew, but it was in the heart of the direct fire zone. Grant Grinham was hit, so Tommy and Stu thought there were better places to be. They went to the other side of the mountain and saw that 6 Platoon were back. He thinks that's where he met Duffy.)

Was he aware that Jason had been killed?

Yes.

What was his reaction?

Very sorrowful. I was with Stu and I said: "I'm going down to the morgue. I'm going to spend the night down that way."

Had Jason been moved back then?

Yes. This was the morning, up until about three or four o'clock in the afternoon. But later on, about five, Mike Argue got B Company together and was telling us about our next objective. The airfield, in Stanley. We would take the airfield in Stanley.

"4 Platoon?"

You had to put your hand up, whoever was left.

"Right, 4 Platoon will join with 6 Platoon…."

How many left?

Half-a-dozen from 30-odd. Not a lot. Then he read out the objective. Taking the airfield was one thing. But he said: "We know that the airfield has six 50-cals at the leading edge…."

Now, we'd just lost everyone taking out one 50-cal (machinegun). If you've got six, they won't be in a straight line. It'll be that one covering that one, that covering that….

I must admit, I thought (he laughs at the recollection) *What the f***! We've just…. You're losing it, sir!* Again, I resigned myself to the fact that I was going to die.

Stu must have felt the same, but I've never felt so alone in all my life, and there must have been 20 or 30 of us standing around, listening to the Sermon on the Mount and thinking (laughs with frustration) *Do you know what we've just done?*

So that was it. To be honest, I never thought I'd live on the airfield (attack).

Scouse McLaughlin, for example, was leagues ahead of me in relation to soldiering. What he considered to be strategically okay, Christ, they hadn't written the books on. He just had a brilliant mind. He was so calm.

Tommy stayed with the battalion to the night of the 13th, probably around 10, when he was casevacced with diarrhoea and vomiting. It meant he wasn't with B Company when the white flags went up in Stanley.

He was taken to a staging post in a sheep hangar and spent five or six hours on a drip until he felt well enough to go back.

"We'll get you back as soon as possible. A couple of hours."

Then the news came through. It was a radio transmission. Someone heard it and came into the room.

"The Argies have surrendered!"

After a scary chopper ride through murky weather to Stanley, they landed on the racecourse where the battalion was. They'd walked down the mountain and into the capital.

17: The death and life of Private Jason Burt

I seen Tony Kempster. He told me where everyone was. I went and found Stu. He was fine. Everyone was just... "Find a room in a house, doss, we're going home!" That was it.

On Wednesday, July 14, Major Mike Argue wrote to the Burts from Tidworth. His letter, speaks for itself. He had far more than one or two to write.

The same week, the *Walthamstow Guardian* reported that Waltham Forest Mayor Michael Fish was considering "various options" to commemorate Jason.

Nine days after that – on Monday, July 26, only days after *Daily Mirror* columnist Paul

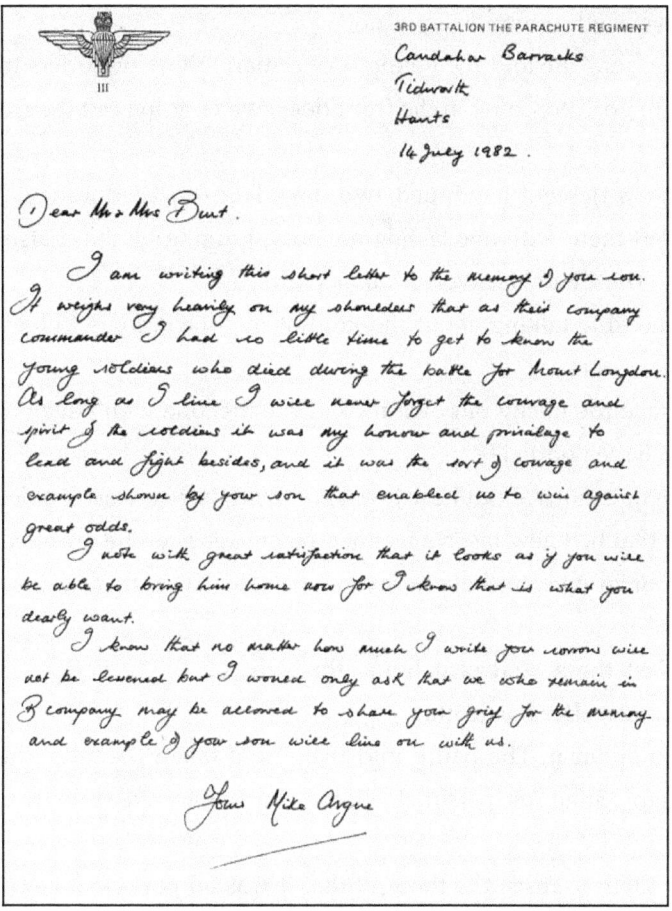

Foot had been moved to ask his readers whether 17 was too young for a boy to fight and die on Longdon – the Burts joined hundreds of families and friends at St Paul's Cathedral for a Falklands War Service of Thanksgiving.

Thanksgiving? Syd was already unhappy the Government had chosen to use that word, not 'memorial'. They had absolutely nothing to give thanks for.

They didn't like the fact that the service reflected on the suffering of the Argentinians.

They didn't like the way the despair and loss of British families, in their eyes, was remembered. Not enough was said.

Prayers for the enemy? They didn't care for them either. In later years, the feeling would change. But, then, they didn't feel like praying for anyone, let alone those who had killed their 17-year-old lad.

And they hated the way the families of the fallen were "herded" into an alcove afterwards. It added insult to injury.

The officials wanted the families to leave by a side door.

Terry long suspected it was because they didn't want them exposed to cameras and microphones.

It was Roy Scrivens who stood his ground.

"Out of my way, son," he told the young serviceman following orders to point the where they didn't want to go. "We come in the front door, we're going out the front door."

The Burts' relentless descent continued two days later on Wednesday, July 28 – Jason's 18th. If that day left them with one lasting memory, judging by the chats we've had, it was the visit of Derek 'The Cleric' Heaver, 3 Para's padre.

They spent some time talking about the kind of men he'd come to know. He said there were three types of Toms.

"One will just take the micky out of someone like me, one won't even look, and one will nod. Jason would have nodded."

They asked him questions about how Jason had died, but he wasn't able to give them any detail, other than that he knew Jason's feet had been bad. Then he dropped the bombshell.

"What stands out in my mind about Jason," he said, "was that, in his pocket, he had a comb and a letter."

A letter? The last three he'd sent home through the BFPO system had already been delivered in the weeks after his death.

They asked him about it. The padre told them he'd taken the letter. Jason should have handed it to Brian Milne, as personal effects were collected from B Company on the startline.

It was hard for them to resist the thought that it was all part of some conspiracy to keep information from them. It was the last thing they needed to hear and Terry phoned the MoD to tell them they wanted the letter. They couldn't say who had it.

If the edition date on the Burts' *Daily Mirror* cutting is a guide – Thursday, April 28, 1983 – Paul Foot took up the cause nine months later. He came and spoke to the Burts, then he phoned Derek Heaver and asked if he, indeed, had the letter.

"I wrote down 'A letter' on the list of personal effects I took from Jason's dead body soon after he died," Mr Heaver told him, according to the article. "The letter got back because it was noted in another place. There was no identification of it. It could have been a letter from a girlfriend or family or one of his own. I think it's one of those they received back."

For almost 30 years afterwards, Syd's recollections would shuttle backwards and forwards, across the years, the people and the rumours….

CSM John Weeks….

Star reporter Sue Crawford….

Whether or not Jason's 'final letter' was bloodstained….

Whether that suggested Jason had been killed by a chest wound, casting doubt on Tommy's explanation….

A torrent of recollections would tie him in knots.

Two days after Jason's birthday, the *Walthamstow Guardian* reported Syd's criticism of the St Paul's service being held in thanksgiving, not remembrance.

The helter-skelter of media interest in Jason's story, and their growing despair, had begun its long embrace. For the Burts, the relationship with the media was a way to vent anger, to let the world know that they'd been let down.

For the local media, every story that could include the words 'Falklands hero Jason Burt' was an opportunity to tell the community that they recognised their sacrifice.

The national media? Best not start me on that one! In the months and years to come, they would become a magnet to each other. And, in the absence of a physical commemoration of their gallant son's courage, every headline would be his memorial.

As July gave way to August, as Tommy went back to 3 Para, as the country became distracted by events like England's Test series against India, rather than the battles for Goose Green and Longdon, there was a knock on their door and a man in Army uniform asked them to sign a form. In exchange, he handed them a cardboard box that reeked of carbolic. It was Jason's possessions. The ones he'd left on Canberra on May 19.

When they opened it, they saw his photos, his fishing rod, his wallet and his provisional driving licence. There was also the letter that Ian McKay had suggested he write a few days before B Company cross-decked to HMS Intrepid. I'll never forget holding it.

Tuesday nite, 13/5/82
Dear Mum, Dad and Jarvis,

> *I hope you don't have to get this letter. I thought I write it just in case. It is now D-3, which means we are going in in 3 days. There are so many things going through my mind. I will end it hear. I not very good at writing letters. I will miss you all very much and I love you all. Your loving son, Jason xxxxx*

CHAPTER 13

THE LONG GOODBYE

The official listing of Falklands awards was made in *The London Gazette* of Friday, October 8, 1982. Nowhere in 30 pages of names, decorations and deeds does the word 'war' meet the reader's eyes. The first page declared:

The Queen has been graciously pleased to approve the posthumous award of the Victoria Cross to the undermentioned in recognition of valour during the operations in the South Atlantic.

The second entry, beneath that for Lt Col Herbert Jones OBE, was this:

24210031 Sergeant Ian John McKay, The Parachute Regiment

The citation contained a telling flaw:

"The assault was met by a hail of fire. The Corporal was seriously wounded, a Private killed and another wounded. Despite these losses Sergeant McKay, with complete disregard for his own safety, continued to charge the enemy position alone."

McKay's courage is unchallengeable, even if some of the citation's crucial details remain out of step with those recorded in the 3 Para battalion log, which formed the basis of the report published in *Pegasus* – the regimental magazine – that same month.

What hurt the Burts deeply, though, was that there was no mention of Jason, nor any medal for him listed elsewhere in *The London Gazette*. That was a knife through their hearts.

Waltham Forest Mayor Michael Fish told the *Walthamstow Guardian* that "lots of brave and deserving people miss out on medals. One of the terrible things about war is that many heroic deeds are done but, unless they are reported, they do not receive official recognition… A medal is often not a matter of heroics, but of luck."

The paper's *Comment* column went further in its attempt to ease the disappointment felt by the Burts and so many others.

"Let us also firmly reject and feeling that the lack of a medal is a slight; that it tarnishes the memory of a courageous youngster…. It does not."

The *Comment* writer added: "A striking feature of the Falklands conflict was the sheer guts and example set by a very large number of extremely young men, Jason among them."

"It's almost like the Government were saying they weren't there," Syd told the *Guardian*. "It's just funny nothing was mentioned about them. I was shattered when I heard."

On Saturday, October 2, a couple of weeks before the medals were made public, the family had met Jason's fellow 3 Para Toms at the battalion's own memorial service, which was held at Aldershot FC's Rec ground. As Tony Barlow walked to the car with them, Beetle Bailey appeared. They didn't know who he was.

"This is someone you'd like to meet," Tony told them.

Then he said to Beetle: "This is Jason Burt's parents."

They remember Bailey climbing into his car and driving off, Tony shouting in his wake.

Terry thought that was rude. Perhaps, though, it wasn't surprising. Still recovering from wounds that had seen him left for dead outside the RAP, to meet the parents of one of B Company's youngest Toms must have been a traumatic experience.

The 3 Para memorial service wasn't the only thing to test their frame of mind in the days either side of learning that Jason's name wasn't in the honours list.

Five days after – on Tuesday October 13 – 330,000 people lined the streets to watch 1,250 servicemen march in the Victory Parade. At the Mansion House reception, afterwards, Syd sloped away, determined to see Margaret Thatcher. He knew what he intended to say to her, if the Petticoat Lane charm had blagged a way through to her.

"I'm Jason's father," was how he'd decided to open the conversation. Then he planned to wait for her to respond.

"Oh, Jason Burt," is what Syd expected her to come back with, and he'd have gone from there, being a nuisance until he heard what he wanted to hear. He failed.

She swept past on the stairs before he had the chance to test her memory.

A fortnight later – on Thursday, October 26 – Ron Duffy sat down in Normandy Barracks and penned the letter he'd been meaning to write since his unsuccessful pilgrimage to Walthamstow on the day of 3 Para's return. On the next few pages is what he wrote.

Some time later, they showed the letter to Derek the Cleric, believing Duffy was deeply religious. Mr Heaver studied it and doubted it had been written by the man they described.

"It can't be him. He's a nutter. Only the other day, as I walked past the room," he held his hands a few inches apart, "the television missed me by that much."

Duffy hadn't been far behind Jason when Brian Milne stepped on the mine that, effectively, started the battle. Once Jason and Tommy had tended Milne, and Ian McKay had finally steered the section out of the minefield, Duffy was detailed to stay with the

17: The death and life of Private Jason Burt

gravely wounded, screaming corporal.

Tom's far from alone in believing that, had Duffy gone all the way with 4 Platoon, his presence on the battlefield during the hours that followed would have been mighty….

> Ronald Duffy
> 4 Platoon, B Coy,
> 3 Para
> Normandy Barracks
> Aldershot.
>
> Thurs. 26 October 1982.
>
> Dear Sir,
>
> I have just sat down and composed this here letter to you. Please forgive me for writing at a time which may seem to you rather belated.
>
> The truth of the matter is I know inside that I should have done this a long time ago.
>
> My conscience would never let me rest until I had set pen to paper and expressed my feelings to you.
>
> I am sorry for all of your troubles.
>
> Please accept my sincerest and profoundest sympathy at the loss of your beloved son Jason. Truly he was a Bonny lad.

17: The death and life of Private Jason Burt

Jason spoke to me moments just before he fell in his hour of glory and went to rest in the arms of the Lord till the Day of Resurrection comes.

May everlasting fame surround the name of Private Jason Burt.

Jason went out with flying colours and in a blaze of glory. He took on the enemy without a seconds hesitation of fear. If I were to live till the crack of Doomsday I will never forget your finest son.

Jason and I were comrades for a little time on that terrible onslaught across the worst place God ever made. East Falkland could only have risen from hell itself.

If there be any glory in war then it should belong to the fallen, of both sides. That war was ninety nine per cent sheer Bloody Misery, and one per cent glory. Oh, if I could turn the clock back I would of sacrificed myself in place of Jason.

17: The death and life of Private Jason Burt

On the path of duty and with great courage Jason passed in the sight of men.
You know he once told me Mr. Burt that you his father held a fruit stall down Petticoat Lane. Well beleive it or not sir I vowed to myself whilst journeying afloat onboard the Norland that soonest I was back in England that I would make a point to see you and comfort you in your grief and hour of Bereavement.
Well the first day of leave I arrived in London and I tried to find your stall in Petticoat Lane. I asked around the Fruit Stall Holders there in that busy bustling spot asking after you Sir, but alas to no avail it was. Everyone that I asked declared that they knew no one of by the name of Jason Burt at all.
The stallholders whom I spoke struck me as an insensitive bunch of individuals and totaly uncaring.

Before I took the trip to Petticoat Lane I made my way outto Walthamstow and sought to seek you at home first. Without the knowledge of where you lived at all I got the tube from Bank by the way of Waterloo after arriving from Andover. I came out the tube and walked out into the sunshine of the Bus Station. It was with feelings of complete desolation I then proceeded to try and track you down I was most unsuccesful. An old woman at the Bus Station directed me to Walthamstow Police Station where I made enquiry but they didn't have no knowledge whatsoever. Even after consulting the electoral rolls and the Telephone Directory, which all proved fruitless the local newspaper gave the address of your home sir. 18 Farmer Road. A woman Police Constable kindly offered to run me in her Patrol car along to your home I gratefully accepted. When at length I finnaly arrived at your doorstep I was deeply

17: The death and life of Private Jason Burt

thrown to find that you were not at home. Upon this discovery I wandered in a dreamt state of shock or maybe it was stern reality. So in the end I made my way back across London to Euston where I would board the Clansman locomotive bound for Inverness choking back bitter galls of sheer utter disappointment. There was a sad heart indeed onboard the Scottish train that day. On the journey northwards home over the Border I drank a bottle of Whisky which I purchase in Victoria Wines especially to give to you Sir. I sure needed something to drown my tears in. It didnt do a lot of good to me but it certainly helped me forget a bad past.

Aye well please believe me Joyce I realy did try to reach you and tell you personaly I failed in that direction so in the final analysis I took it upon me to write you this letter.

I am yours sincerly, Duffy.

17: The death and life of Private Jason Burt

According to the date typed on the top, the next document delivered to the Burts' home was signed on Sunday, October 29. The stark, functional form explained that "Probate has been granted to Mrs Theresa Mary Ellen Burt by the District probate Registry in Ipswich".

Terry had already had a dream that Jason was coming home. She'd woken up one morning and told Syd: "Jason's on his way back."

Nothing, so far, had appeared in the media about the bodies starting their journey so, unsurprisingly, Syd's response was to the point.

"Don't be silly!"

She phoned all their friends and described the dream in detail. A boat was moored on a riverbank, all the coffins were being lowered into it on chains, and Jason put his arm round her shoulder and said 'I'm in that one there, Mum. I'm coming home now'.

Syd spoke to Derek the Cleric to see if he knew any more.

"Are they on their way? Terry says they're on their way."

"No," the padre replied.

On Sunday, November 14, the family gathered at the civic centre in Walthamstow for the Service of Remembrance. Their wreath carried a small card that didn't survive the steady drizzle long before the ink began to run. It read:

"A silent thought, a silent year, for Jason we lost and loved so dear."

The two-minute silence was spoilt by a group of youths who thought it was acceptable to disrupt the reverend moment.

The Mayor's chaplain, Richard Marriott, didn't name Jason in his address, but he made an unmistakable reference when he said the borough had particular cause to remember "with gratitude and pride" what had been achieved in the Falklands.

But he did round on the youths who'd shouted during the silence.

Values had changed, he said. The "rot set in" when the nation chose Sunday as its principle day of remembrance, rather than the 11th hour of the 11th day of the 11th month.

The *Walthamstow Guardian* picked up the issue that week, but found words of praise for the "considerable number" of young people in the 300-plus crowd.

The newspaper also pictured Terry laying a Remembrance Day wreath at George Monoux School, and updated readers on matters like the wrangle over Jason's will, and the argument with the MoD about his final letters being returned opened.

It was a few days after when Syd started shouting from the front room.

"Terry, Terry, come in quick."

Terry rushed from the kitchen.

"They've just said that Sir Bedivere's on its way back with the bodies."

The Royal Fleet Auxiliary ship had left the Falklands on the day she'd had the dream.

17: The death and life of Private Jason Burt

At dawn on Tuesday, November 16, the RFA Sir Bedivere passed the jetty at Marchwood Army Port, Southampton, and a lone piper of the 2nd Bn Scots Guards played the regiment's traditional lament, *Flowers of the Forest*. Jason's coffin was among 64 men – 52 soldiers, 11 marines and one Chinese laundryman – brought home for burial.

As the coffins were carried ashore, the Army's Adjutant-General, Sir George Cooper, stood alone and saluted each one.

They'd have treasured the opportunity to go and talk to Jason, but it was never offered, even though Terry had asked where he was being taken.

They weren't at his inquest either. That was opened and adjourned the same day, at Southampton's Law Courts, so that the bodies could be released for burial.

The official record of the Coroner's Court states starkly that the cause of death as "gunshot wound to head", and adds "killed by injuries received as a result of enemy action".

Minor details? Those two short sentences might still have hidden a million facts, but they at least confirmed Tommy's testimony that Jason had been hit in the head, rather than the chest, which was the thought that had gnawed deeper and deeper since Derek the Cleric had visited on Jason's 18th and told them about the blood-stained letter found in the breast pocket of his battledress.

One detail the record has horribly wrong is Jason's age. It says he was 18 when he died.

The maths can't have been hard to do.

In their continuing grief, it's hard to resist the thought that the error would have stayed in their minds longer than coroner Roderick Maclean's tribute to the fallen.

"All of these – and nearly all of them young men – lost their lives during their duty, many of them, if not most, in heroic circumstances."

Ann Grose remembers the inquest. She was there. She recalls that Roy Scrivens was as well, but she says that it didn't tell them anything.

"It was a long list of names and 'Killed in action', 'Killed in action', 'Killed in action' 'Died from wounds', whatever," she told me. "It was entirely frustrating. Again, we were still without any real information regarding what had happened."

Evidence about 3 Para's losses was given by Lt Andrew Mills. He described the fighting to capture Mount Longdon and the extent of the artillery bombardment that followed.

Then he told the court how Jason had been shot dead when his company made a follow-up attack on an enemy dug-in position after an attack in which Sgt Ian McKay died from gunshot and shrapnel wounds.

> ... *a follow-up attack on an enemy dug-in position AFTER an attack in which Sgt Ian McKay died*....

17: The death and life of Private Jason Burt

It didn't answer the one question that had stalked them since 1982, whether or not Jason was part of McKay's attack party. But it did confirm that he survived and then fell alongside Scrivs and Neil in an equally heroic advance on the same dug-in. But the Burts weren't there to hear it.

They'd been involved in the arrangements for the memorial that was due to be held on Saturday, December 4, at Jason's old school. And they'd received a letter from Mrs Thatcher, timed to coincide with Jason's home-coming. She wrote:

"I know it has been a long wait, but I can assure you everything has been done as quickly as it possibly could. This must, I know, be a very upsetting time for you and I very much hope you will find some comfort in having Jason's body back in this country."

Tommy'd been struggling since he'd last met them. Struggling with the fact that he'd broken his pledge with Jason about bringing the other's dog-tags home, should one of them fall.

Struggling with how, in the hell fire of battle, he hadn't been able to keep his promise.

Five months on, he didn't want to talk about it any more, either, but he knew he had little choice. He knew the funerals would require him to revisit what he'd told Syd in the pub in July, even though he believed Syd didn't want to hear it.

Every time Syd asked, Tommy had told him: Jason hadn't been with Ian McKay when he died. Every time he repeated it, he felt he was staining Jason's memory.

He'd tried to convince himself it was the price he had to pay a grieving dad for coming home but, when he was alone, the relentless search for answers had left him consumed by guilt and in an increasingly dark frame of mind.

Then there were the nightmares. They'd come uninvited, as real and vivid as the sights, sounds and smells of Longdon that triggered them. Before long, he'd begun to fear turning the light off. Then he'd fought to stop closing his eyes, knowing that, within minutes, he'd be back there, deep in the battle.

When 3 Para returned to Tidworth after leave, they were told the battalion was moving back to Montgomery Lines, Aldershot. Once there, they'd begin preparing for the funerals of the lads who were being buried in their hometowns, and those who'd be laid to rest at Aldershot Military Cemetery.

Around the same time, Tommy was confronted with an agonising choice. Who would he carry to their grave?

The decision was almost impossible to make. He wrestled with it for hours and at first considered not carrying any of them. Finally, the decision almost made itself.

He'd been with both Scrivs and Neil when they'd died.

They'd all stood and charged on Des Fuller's call.

But Jason had fallen alone, so it was right that he should carry his happy-go-lucky mate.

Before leaving Tidworth, Tommy drove to Brize Norton to find Claire. It was a deliberate visit, though she's always believed their meeting was by chance, late one evening, when he walked in to the Spotlight Club during a course at the base.

The meeting was brief, and awkward. Tommy recalls they had a drink. She thinks it was briefer than that. He told her what had happened to Jason, and he gave her a photo of him.

Driving back to Tidworth, his head full of Longdon again, he missed a sharp right turn after a hump-back bridge and, after ploughing through a privet hedge, planted his car against the wall of a vicar's house. While the man of God ranted, Tommy told him his Christian duty was to help the two lads still in the wreck.

As autumn gave way to the first days of winter – their second in the space of six months – the battalion started practising funeral duties. Time and again, each burial party retrieved its coffin from a Land Rover and carried it to the Motor Transport yard. Every time they lowered it on strops into the inspection pit, the task became harder and harder.

Finally, they were told which burials they'd be attending.

At Tommy's first service, the family wanted their son's body taken to their home first, for a private farewell. The burial party met the hearse at the house and prepared to carry their companion into the front room, where his Union Flag-draped coffin would rest on two easels.

The family left their home to watch as the coffin was drawn from the hearse and placed on the shoulders of the six Paras. After a struggle down the garden path, which wasn't wide enough to take both flanks, they realised that the hall was too small to manoeuvre the coffin into the front room without a second struggle.

The family was asked to move into the kitchen while the pall-bearers lifted, twisted and tilted the coffin up the stairs until it could be squeezed through the door. As they stood to attention, heads bowed, the thought on every man's mind was the same – *can't we just pass him out a front window when the family's finished?* No one dared suggest it, though, so the reverse routine was followed when the time came to leave.

At another funeral, they lowered the coffin and came to the end of their burial strops with the bottom of the grave still four feet away. Lifting their eyes towards their colleague opposite, all they could do was let go in unison.

It wasn't a moment the workshop inspection pits had prepared them for, and everyone released their grip a fraction apart, bouncing their brave comrade off the sides of the grave to his final resting place.

There wasn't much else they could do, but neither experience sat well with him.

But there were lighter moments. The service at one funeral had been beautiful and the burial had gone well, until the bugler sounded *Last Post* and the firing party fired shots over the grave. The day was freezing, and the bugler couldn't hit the right notes. What came out was dreadful. At first, the pall-bearers cringed with every duff note. But it went from bad to worse until one of them couldn't take any more. Around the graveside, the family soon began to see Para shoulders going up and down in silent mirth. Then they started laughing too.

The night before the Aldershot funerals, the burial parties were in the NAAFI when a sergeant walked in and told them the hearses were arriving. As they hurried to pay their respects, Tommy realised it would be the first time he, Jason, Scrivs and Grose had been together since leaving Longdon.

The 15 hearses were immaculate. Inside each was a coffin draped with the Union Flag. They drove slowly through the main entrance to Normandy Barracks and stopped 100 yards short of the sports hall, the vehicles' dimmed lights and exhaust smoke casting an eerie spell on the cold night air.

The undertaker leading the cortege, dressed in a mourning suit, continued until he was outside the hall. Then he turned and, nodding solemnly, beckoned each forward in turn. As they pulled up, civvie officials stepped out and carried the coffin inside where, the next morning, the families would say farewell.

The lads who hadn't served in the Falklands moved to give those who had the easiest view, and Tommy watched in silence until all 15 coffins had gone. When the last hearse pulled away, he went to bed, knowing that, in the morning, he'd carry Jason to his final resting place. *Thank God*, he thought. *They're home at last.*

Friday, November 26. The Burts travelled to Aldershot with family and friends in a small fleet of minibuses. They'd ruled out going in a coach, Terry, because it would have felt like they were on an outing, not heading for a funeral.

Terry walked in to the sports hall with Syd and saw the coffins lined up in precise rows. Without being told, she knew which one was Jason.

Ann and Dave Grose were a few feet away from. Debbie, Neil's teenage sister, wasn't there, and neither was his brother Mark. He was on a Sally Line ferry, heading for Ascension on his way to the Falklands, where he'd be helicoptered to Teal Inlet and Longdon to pay his respects.

Though it had rained on the journey down, it had turned into a beautiful day. The late autumn sunshine bathed the Military Cemetery in a weak, warm glow. It was packed with families, friends and the media as the burial parties formed up by the main road, at the foot of the hill, waiting.

One by one, the hearses arrived. One by one, each party marched forward, retrieved their companion and slow-marched him along the narrow, winding pathways to his graveside. The final route was lined with men of 3 Para, evenly spaced, standing motionless.

As the first of the fallen came level with each man, he slowly went from 'present arms' to 'on reverse arms rest', turning his rifle so its muzzle rested on the ground. At the same time, he bowed his head, and rested his hands and chin on the rifle butt.

Graham Collins and Ray Ratcliffe had asked their 1 and 2 Para Commanding Officers, respectively, for permission to join Jason's burial party. Beneath his breath, Tommy greeted Jason as they lifted his coffin from the hearse.

As they carried him slowly past the honour guard, shiny South Atlantic medals glinting in the sunshine, Tommy gave Jason a running commentary.

He told him about the military precision that brought each guard to 'on reverse arms rest'.

He told him about the families, the friends, and the members of the public he could see.

He told him about the cars that had stopped in respect and curiosity on the main road.

Finally, they completed the slow march to meet Scrivs and Grose, who were to be buried beside him. Then, as they stood by the grave, with Jason's coffin resting on two planks, he explained what had been happening since he'd arrived home.

Rabbi John Rayner performed Jason's service. None of the Paras understood what he said, but the expression in his voice was sincere, and that was good enough for them.

In the thin winter sunshine, Tommy's thoughts wandered to happier days, to the trials of Recruit Company, to the pride they'd felt in themselves and each other in winning their wings, then reaching the Battalion.

He could hear Syd weeping a few feet away, but – for a moment – the picture he had of him was a moment of from their days in training, sitting in a café at Waterloo station one Sunday afternoon when Jason unscrewed a vinegar bottle top and, to Syd's horror, they'd all roared as some poor civvie drowned his food.

They'd laughed as loud on Canberra the day they'd stuck Graham Collins' Action Man flag up Jason's bum and taken pics to send to Graham's temporary Edinburgh home, where 1 Para were on ceremonial duties and missing the big adventure.

There hadn't been many laughs on the Falklands, though, just Jason's grim determination to stay with his platoon as his feet rotted on the tab to Longdon, then during the battle.

The minefield, Tommy thought.

His courage.

The first man to move forward to help Brian Milne, without care for his own safety.

Then that final charge.

Unwavering, worthy of the highest military award, even if they hadn't given him a brass button.

As his final words drifted across the cemetery, Tommy, Graham, Ray and their fellow pall-bearers raised Jason a few inches and the planks were removed. Then they took the strain on the burial strops and, as *Last Post* sounded, they lowered him slowly to his final resting place.

As the haunting lament drifted across the hillside, the burial parties moved back to allow the families and friends privacy.

Once they'd started to walk to the cemetery gates, Tommy wandered to the foot of Jason's grave and said goodbye. Then he moved to speak with Scrivs and Neil, and did the same. When he'd finished, he sat on the small grass mound that the families had occupied and surveyed the sad scene. What he saw were 15 holes. The headstones would follow, to tell generations to come who lay there and how old they were, but not how they'd come to be at rest.

Major Mike Argue, the OC B Company, talked to them after the burial. He'd written a few weeks before and had asked to meet. Almost immediately, he asked if he could attend the memorial service on Saturday, December 4.

And he'd remembered something else – the 'lost' last letter Derek Heaver had taken from Jason's tunic on the mountain. Before he left the hall, he said: "You'll never get that letter."

"Is it because my son criticised the Army?" Syd asked.

"No," he assured him. "Your son was too professional to criticise the Army. But you won't get it."

They never have.

Claire was at home in the Cotswolds that night, watching the news, when the pictures of the funerals came on the screen. As soon as she saw Rabbi John Rayner, she knew it was Jason being buried.

Within a matter of days, as the rest of the us gathered thoughts of Christmas, she drove from Oxfordshire to Aldershot. She slept in the car overnight then, at first light, climbed over the railings and began looking. As soon as she saw the Star of David, she knew.

After the visit, she did what she'd done for the previous six months. She kept her grief to herself. The Burts were oblivious to her visit, or the fact that she even existed. It would be some time before that changed.

CHAPTER 14

LETTING GO

George Monoux School was packed to the rafters for Jason's memorial service. The school had been swept by explosives experts with sniffer dogs, and roads leading to the building had come to a standstill as cars carrying Norman Tebbit and senior Army personnel arrived for the service, which was conducted by the Rev Alan Smith, one of the leading lights at Jason's old haunt, Highams Park Youth Centre.

Mr Tebbit was polite but to the point as the Burts met him.

"Before I go in, I must tell you I was one of the ministers who sent your son to the Falklands. We all feel responsible. All I can say is thank you for your son."

"I have a letter at home from Jason and it says 'If Maggie Thatcher never does another thing right in her life, they are British islands'."

That's what Syd told him. Inside, however, he was still bitter. His comment to the *Walthamstow Guardian* told a different story.

"I still think Jason was far too young to go to war. I brought up my sons to bury me. I never thought I'd have to bury one of my sons. He was so young."

Lt Col Hew Pike, 3 Para's commanding officer, addressed the congregation. He said Jason was extremely inexperienced.

"He probably didn't fully understand, let alone expect, what he was going into. It was far more arduous than anything he would have experienced during training. But he continued to march as if a soldier of huge experience.

"Every soldier expects and understands that he may have to go to war and lay down his life for his country. I believe that Jason's sacrifice was not in vain, and it is with great pride and great humility that we recall that sacrifice today."

A couple of weeks after the funerals, 16 temporary wooden crosses planted to mark the Paras' graves until headstones were ready were stolen. With them went Jason's Star of David. It was another setback that the Burts discovered by opening a newspaper. While all this was happening, they were also trying to resolve the question of Jason's life insurance policy.

17: The death and life of Private Jason Burt

Then, one Monday morning in February, 1983, the postman delivered another Jiffy bag. It was just as unexpected but, this time, it wasn't a joyous surprise.

The package contained Jason's Falklands Medal. And it was damaged.

Terry was in hospital at the time. Syd kept the delivery to himself until he went to pick her up on the Saturday.

"There's a shock when you get home," he said.

She couldn't believe it. It didn't take her long to reach for the writing pad to pen a letter to Prince Charles, accompanied by a clutch of newspaper cuttings that had already told the good folk of Walthamstow about this latest trauma. The letter went along these lines: "You're the Colonel in Chief. Are you aware how your men's medals have been sent out?"

He wrote back, apologising.

The following April, the MoD were good enough to write to the Burts, enquiring whether their recent visit to the Falklands had been "consoling and rewarding".

They might have. If they'd been invited.

It was another crass, insensitive and completely avoidable bungle. Given the Army's initial "minor details" blunder, it's unsurprising that the "how was the pilgrimage for you?" letter simply turned the screw a few more times.

At the same time, it's also understandable that – eventually – Roy, Rosemary, Ann and Dave would have found their apparently relentless campaigning difficult to deal with.

Roy recalled that they made almost a conscious decision to get on with their lives.

For the Groses, my feeling is it was a gradual acceptance that led to a realisation, one day, that they'd moved on.

As April gave way to May, and the anniversary points began to arrive – May 8 the departure, May 21 the landings, June 11 the final tab to Longdon, June 12 the battle and Jason's death – the intensity picked up again. This time for everyone.

Around the first anniversary, the man who tended the graves at Aldershot, Bob Brooks, noticed a young girl standing alone by Jason's grave. He walked up to her.

"What you doing?" he asked. He actually meant "Who are you?" but he still frightened the life out of her. It was Claire. Jason's Brize Norton girl.

She sat down and told him her story.

Not long afterwards, Terry picked up the phone one night and found herself talking to the mother of one of the other Paras who'd been killed in the Falklands.

"You're the third Burt family that I've phoned," she explained. "If I'm wrong I'm really sorry. But do you have a son who was in the Army?"

"Yes."

"Is he buried in Aldershot, in the Falklands graves?"

"Why?"

"There's a young girl. I've often seen her just sitting down in the cold weather, crying and lighting candles. She's in a dreadful state. I spoke to her today."

She gave Terry Claire's address. Soon she wrote.

Claire didn't know much of his home life, so she didn't know if he had a girlfriend in Walthamstow. She suspected, rightly, that he might. That's why she decided not to find his parents after she heard Jason had died, and why she'd taken to making graveside visits alone at odd times of the day and night.

Terry knew that Jason had been seeing a girl he'd met while the lads were at Brize doing their jump training. But that was about it. Typically, he hadn't given away too much information. The fact that she had a car, and that she was older than him, was about all they'd been allowed to find out.

When Terry's first letter arrived on Claire's doormat, it was such a relief.

The first time they met was a big day for her, too, even if Terry's initial scepticism did set the new relationship off with a question-and-answer session, just to make sure.

She knew Jason wouldn't have had the money to pay train and bus fares to go up to the Cotswolds and see Claire, so it didn't take her long to ask how they'd kept in touch.

"I used to drive down and pick him up," Claire said, and showed her where she parked the car in Aldershot. "I used to meet Jason in the week."

"Did he eat much chocolate?"

"Mars Bars and mints. He loved mints."

"How did he describe Jarvis?"

"He's overweight."

"Jason wouldn't have said that," Terry told her, and her suspicions grew a little. But they didn't last long.

"Not really," Claire agreed. "He'd have said he was a fat little sod."

Unsurprisingly, over two intense years, the Burts' phone number had found its way into the contacts books of countless journalists. They'd become a news commodity, a ready quote for a local line on a national story, an automatic target when an anniversary loomed.

If anyone urged caution at any point, they didn't urge loudly enough.

If anyone warned that such a close relationship with the media had the potential to slip out of their control, and badly so, they were deaf to that too.

In November, 1986, the media equivalent of a runaway train smashed through the Burts' lives. It started when Waltham Forest councillors were asked to name three streets in a new development off Queens Road. The Mayor was quoted in the *Guardian*, asking for suggestions from the public.

A street petition quickly grew to around 50 signatures to put Jason's name forward, but they didn't hear any more about it until a neighbour stopped Terry months afterwards.

"Oh, that was a shame about Jason," she said.

"What?"

"Well, they're not naming a street after him."

Alongside honouring Ghandi, one of the names chosen was that of Yunus Khan, a community leader who'd perished in an arson attack on his home.

A handful of people called Jarvis, who wrote a letter to the Mayor. It pointed out that none of the people who'd had streets named after them were buried in this country, and emphasised that Jason had been brought up in Walthamstow.

He sent a copy to the *Walthamstow Guardian*. Which printed it.

For some, it lit a blue touch-paper. Predictably, they were moved to write in. And, predictably, among those printed were a handful from readers who were anxious to hide behind the phrase Name and address supplied, rather than stand up to be counted publicly, as Jarvis had done.

"I believe it would be thoroughly immoral and irresponsible to name a road, or anything else, after Jason Burt, now that his name is linked with such an attitude which shows such insensitivity to the Asian community," one anonymous correspondent wrote.

"Such discrimination against a true native of England," wrote another reader, "can only cause bitterness and not create any feelings of harmony or peace."

On Thursday, December 23, the *Guardian* was back on the case. 'Road signs vanish in protest' was the headline of a story that told of police hunting a bogus workman, dressed in white overalls, who'd leaned a ladder up against a house in Yunus Khan Close, taken down the road name and replaced it with a notice saying *In remembrance of Jason Burt*.

Embarrassed council officials quickly replaced it with a spare Yunus Khan Close sign they'd had made up, just in case. And *Guardian* journalists had been called by a man representing the group claiming to have made the switch as a "peaceful protest" against the road-naming.

The next day, they returned from the market stall and found Jarvis in a state.

"You've got to go to Leyton Police Station," he said. "It's urgent."

"We're not going anywhere Christmas Eve, and tomorrow we're going to Jason's," they responded.

They went on Boxing Day but the officer in question wasn't there. About a week later, he phoned.

"Do you know who's changing the street names?" he asked.

Not only didn't they know who was responsible, it was something they didn't want.

Years later, the family was off somewhere and phoned for a cab.

"Lived here long?" the driver asked as they climbed in.

"Yes. Quite a while."

"Well, you'd have known Jason Burt, then."

Fearing what might follow, Terry turned to Syd.

"Tell him we're his parents, because I don't know what he's going to come out with."

He didn't come out with anything. Not until they'd reached their destination and stepped out of the cab.

"By the way," he said after Syd had handed him the fare, "if ever you want to get streets named after Jason, you won't have to make the signs. We've got them all at the cab office."

The penny dropped. The men in council workers' overalls, who'd taken the Yunus Khan Close signs down and substituted ones commemorating Jason, were the cabbies.

The expanding pile of cuttings had become the substitute for the thing the Burts craved most, a permanent memorial for Jason.

The first plea I've found was July 9, 1982, in a letter by James Penrice to the *Guardian*. This is what he wrote.

> *"Modern youth are much maligned because of the malignant minority among them who steal, rob and molest the elderly. Those of us who care about and are associated with young people know that the vast majority are good and so worthwhile."*

That plea went unheeded, if not unheard. Over the next three or four years, the appearance of Jason's name in the papers ebbed and flowed, but it never left completely and two more years would pass before their greatest wish in Jason's memory came true.

On Thursday, April 8, 1992, the *Daily Star* repeated its decision to pay for the school plaque memorial. The day after, the unveiling took place.

It was a perfect spring day, by all accounts, in the starkest possible contrast to what Jason had faced almost 10 years before on that final slog up Mount Longdon.

"This is the first time the sun has shone for Jason," Terry told the *Walthamstow Guardian* just before the simple stone plaque was dedicated in his memory in the grassy quadrangle of what had become, by then, Sir George Monoux Sixth Form College.

Though the paper perpetuated the error that Jason had died from a single shot in the chest – the fog of war creeping into an otherwise beautiful day, it stated for posterity the other details of their day.

The Monoux Brass Group played three quiet pieces – *Mohrentauz*, by Susato, Arbeau's *Pavane*, and *Volte* by Prateorius – while the remembrance was led by the Mayor's Chaplain, the Rev Peter Trendall.

Captain David Rowntree, of 3 Para, read from the Gospel of St John. It was fitting that he should be there. It was he who had interred Jason's body at Teal Inlet and had overseen the

17: The death and life of Private Jason Burt

first stages of Jason's final journey home. He had also given them the dog tags that are so cherished by the family to this day.

After the dedication – to the sound of more music from the students – Capt Rowntree led the wreath-laying, accompanied by Colour Sergeant Graham Heaton. As a 5 Platoon corporal, he'd been about 50 yards from Jason on Longdon at the fateful moment that night, and had later lost a leg during the battle.

If there's one cutting that stands as a beacon to Jason's death, and its almost ceaseless torment, it's the *Walthamstow Guardian Comment* column of Friday, April 16, 1992, following the dedication of Jason's memorial stone. Beneath the headline 'Never forgotten', this is what it said:

> *While most people were caught up in the polling day excitement and speculation over Thursday's General Election, there was one spot in Walthamstow where there were quiet thoughts and reflections, not of the future but of the past.*
>
> *Had there been an election 10 years ago, 17-year-old Walthamstow boy Jason Burt would not have been old enough to vote.*
>
> *Instead, there was a war in the faraway Falklands. Young Jason WAS old enough to fight for his country. And he died for it, shot on a wet, freezing night on Mount Longdon during the final assault on Port Stanley.*
>
> *Thursday saw a stone plaque dedicated to his memory at a moving ceremony in the quadrangle of Sir George Monoux Sixth Form College.*
>
> *For Jason's family the shock of his death has not been eased over the intervening years by the sad lack of a permanent memorial in his home town. They had come to believe that the young hero's death would remain unrecorded in the borough where he grew up.*
>
> *But last Thursday's spring sunshine and simple dedication service must have at last brought some solace to grief and bitterness. And in the final event there was probably no more appropriate place than his old school.*
>
> *There is no point now in chiding anyone that last week's tribute could and should – somewhere in Walthamstow – have been made earlier. For such arguments would simply serve to unfairly tarnish the memory of a brave young man.*
>
> *Waltham Forest won't forget Jason, and it remains important that his sacrifice and example, together with that of others like him, should endure.*
>
> *But our final thought is that perhaps the new Government might find the time to look back at the Falklands, and more recently at the Gulf War, and decide that our teenagers, however willing to don uniform and volunteer, should not be put out in the front line.*
>
> *Ironically, much closer to home, you have to be over 17 before you can be sent to Northern Ireland. And after last week's events in London, can there be many left who will still argue that's not a 'war'?*

By "last week's events in London", the newspaper meant the IRA's truck-bomb attack outside 30 St Mary Axe in the City of London. It killed three people, including a 15-year old girl, and caused £800m of damage.

For all its simplicity and frequent truths, the column was lacking. If the *Guardian* believed whole-heartedly in what it was saying about 17-year-olds, why did it leave the matter to a couple of paragraphs? Why not expand on the topic in the form of a feature? Why not do a little fact-finding?

Yes, Jason would have needed to be 18 to be in Northern Ireland with 1 Para, but that wasn't law or Government policy – I understand – it was a question of maths.

By the time he'd slogged his way through Recruit Company and Junior Para, then claimed his wings and joined his battalion, he would be nearing his 18th birthday. Add the thick layer of specialist training that was vital to preparing a Crow to survive a tour there – streets one day, open countryside the next, a threat on every corner or behind every hedge – and he'd have turned 18 by the time he stepped off the ferry.

Jarvis Burt was 14 when Jason sailed for the Falklands. The two had grown closer in the couple of years he'd been in the Regiment. It's not hard to understand why.

Jarvis was the little brother, the lad to whom mishaps seemed to happen naturally. The willing opponent across the card table, regardless of where Jason's remorseless sense of humour might lead him.

Jason was the big brother Para, the hero figure no one would mess with, Jarvis's protector, the scheming opponent across the card table when he needed to win the pound in his pocket to pay for the taxi-fare.

Syd and Terry were robbed of many things by Jason's death. One of the greatest is was their boys grow as brothers. Instead, they saw Jarvis become their rock, a son who – by his own admission – was often pushed away in the years after Jason's death. Starting with his mother's decision to cancel Christmas in favour of an annual pilgrimage to Jason's grave, instead, on December 25.

Until Syd's health made it too arduous, and the cost of fuel made it too expensive, they used to go down to Aldershot every week. Then the trips became once a month. Then Jarvis started going to the cemetery on his own, leaving at maybe four in the morning, climbing over the railings and tending to the duties.

In 1994, Jarvis went to pieces. He'd rise, head off for work, catch the train and wherever he looked he saw Jason's face. One night, he went downstairs, upset again.

"Why is Jason in my room haunting me? Why is he haunting me after all these years?"

None of his friends could cope with him.

"He was the tough guy, the explosive guy and, all of a sudden, he was in tears," Terry recalls. "They'd booked to go away on holiday, about 10 of them, in the September. The day they got there he phoned up and said 'I'm cracking up'.

"I said 'You're going to spoil it for everyone else out there. Pull yourself together. Don't phone back again unless you can speak to me properly'."

Eventually, Kay and Jim took him to a priest. They asked friends to say mass for Jarvis' peace of mind and for Jason to rest in peace.

Jarvis wasn't alone in suffering turmoil. Neil Grose's sister, Debbie, struggled on through what their mother, Ann, describes as her "diabolical" teenage years, blaming Neil's death for whatever went wrong.

Debbie doesn't remember her school being supportive. Then again, she doesn't think Neil's death sank in for nine years. She pushed her grief away until she hit her early 20s and the shooting started again, this time in the 1991 Gulf War. It was the 3 Para's commanding officer, Col Huw Pike, who produced a Para for her to talk to. I don't know what thoughts they shared. I do know, however, that only then did she start the slow journey to acceptance.

Combat Stress is a charity that looks after service veterans with a wide range of mental health issues. The organisation isn't just concerned with the care of those suffering from Post Traumatic Stress Disorder, though many veterans do, whether that happens in the immediate aftermath of action, or they fall through some emotional trapdoor that's waiting for them years afterwards.

The charity's doctors deal with a host of conditions like clinical depression, raised anxiety states, phobic disorders, manic depression, and drug and alcohol abuse, among others.

Dr Morgan O'Connell is a genial Irishman to whom many Falklands veterans and their families owe an incalculable debt. He knows hundreds veterans of all kinds of conflicts. He knows they often suffer from more than one of these conditions. He knows their problems are often complicated by difficulties in relationships or strife at home.

Jason's story, and the ones that Syd, Terry and Jarvis could have told him over the year, is familiar ground. Like their obsession with 'the truth'. Like Syd's insinuation that he was responsible for Jason's death by virtue of signing his joining-up papers. Like their accusation that the Army abandoned them the moment the words "minor details" were spoken that grim Monday lunchtime.

When we spoke, Morgan didn't ask why I'd chosen those examples to describe the way they'd dwelt on their loss for two decades and more. He understood. Instead, he described meeting a Second World War veteran the previous day. It amounted to saying that there was no reason for Syd to bear responsibility.

"Stephen went over the beaches of Normandy, was posted as missing in action for three months, fought with the French Resistance and won the Legion d'honneur. Yesterday, he ended up talking about his son, saying that, if he'd approached him (about joining up) at the same age, he'd have done anything to dissuade him, including breaking his leg.

"I challenged him, because many young men of 17 and 18 want to win their spurs. That's been the nature of society. It's the difference, generally, between boys and girls. Boys are trained to go out there and hunt and kill and bring it home.

"Military communities, over the years, have survived on that basic instinct. The ethical question of whether or not we should allow young men of 17 to join?

"In the Second World War, they deliberately chose to send in inexperienced troops when they had the opportunity to send in experienced troops over the beaches of Normandy, because they recognised the attrition rate was going to be very high.

"And they recognised that the old salts were probably likely to go for cover, instead of running up the beach. That was a command decision. I'm not saying it was a command decision to send 17-year-olds to the Falklands.

"The Falklands happened overnight. The Task Force was on its way by the Monday morning.

"Okay, it hovered around Ascension Island for a week or so, so there was perhaps a good opportunity to take the young men away. But why should a 17-and-a-half-year-old be taken away and an 18-year-old be left?

"At the end of the day, you go to war because (as a nation) you've been conned, or you've allowed yourself to be attacked, or you've volunteered to serve and you've gone through basic training with your mates. Then, in something like the Parachute Regiment, the cohesion that they seek to achieve by getting the maroon beret and jumping out of the hole in the side of the aircraft is all about 'I'm not doing it for Maggie Thatcher or the Queen. I'm doing it for my mates, so the last thing I want to do is to be seen to be a shirker in the eyes of my mates'.

"That's why 17-and-a-half-year-olds do it. Because it's so important for them to be part of this young bonding group, Band of Brothers, whatever you like to call them.

"For a father to sign the documents," he paused…. "If you asked the parents 'What was it like to go to his passing out parade?' you could be sure they will say 'It was the proudest day in our lives'. You ask the young lad 'What was it like when you were passing out?' 'Best day of my life'. Because it is. It's very special. But part of the price for having that sense of achievement is that the person who's paying calls in the debt.

"To lose a son, to lose a daughter, is painful. Guilt is a normal feature of bereavement. Some families, after a period of time, say 'Right, okay, it's time to go on. We can't turn the clock back. He's dead. We're going to think about him in a positive sense, rather than a negative sense'.

"That's what pathological grief is about. Queen Victoria is the arch example of pathological grief. She never let go. You can't move on unless you let go, however painful that is. But, of course, we never completely let go, because we have anniversary reactions."

He paused, then went on.

"They're on their own," he said about the Burts. "It reflects how relatively few people in the country were intimately involved with people deployed in 1982. Even fewer, because we only lost 257. The families of the dead are scattered across the country. It's not surprising that there should be people who are isolated in their grief."

CHAPTER 15

SEVENTEEN

At 17, Private Jason Burt couldn't vote for the Government that sent him to war.

At 17, Private Jason Burt wasn't able take a drink legally in a pub in his final night in England.

At 17, Private Jason Burt couldn't give blood. Or see a film that depicted the kind of X-rated violence he witnessed, first hand, on Longdon.

But he was old enough to go to die for Queen and Country.

On Thursday, October 21, 1999, the *Walthamstow Guardian* picked up the baton where it had, effectively, dropped it seven years before. Its front page lead trumpeted the unsurprising fact that "the parents of a soldier killed in the Falklands at 17 years old have thrown their weight behind a national campaign to raise the minimum age of recruits".

'Thrown their weight' neatly covers the fact that reporter Danny McCord had phoned to ask Jason's parents what they thought of the campaign, which had been launched in Berlin.

"To be sending people into a war zone at the age of 17 is ridiculous," Syd told the paper. "They are really just kids and they have an awful lot to go through. The age must be raised. There must not be any more loss of young life."

Thirteen months later, as part of the Coalition to Stop the Use of Child Soldiers' campaign, Amnesty International published its own 19-page report on the issue of what those aged under 18 who were at risk in the UK. The first paragraph of the report's introduction said:

In the United Kingdom (UK), members of the armed forces under the age of 18 (under-18s) are not merely recruited and trained: they are also sent into the battlefield. The UK has the lowest deployment age in Europe and it is the only European country to routinely send under-18s into armed conflict situations.

The second paragraph put Jason's name in lights once more:

Jason Burt was 17 when he died in 1982 in the battle of Mt Longdon, in the Falklands. Not long before being deployed to the South Atlantic, he was told that he was too young to donate blood.

17: The death and life of Private Jason Burt

He was too young to vote. Yet, he was not too young to be sent to war and to die.

His mother said: "He wrote to us from the South Atlantic saying he had wanted to join up and potentially to go to war, but had not expected he would be going to war quite so soon". His father added: "I kept saying he was just a boy, but they kept saying he was a professional soldier." (Daily Telegraph, 19 October 1999)

It went on:

Amnesty International opposes the recruitment and participation of under-18s in hostilities. The United Nations Convention on the Rights of the Child (CRC) states that a child is "every human being below the age of eighteen years unless under the law applicable to the child, majority is attained earlier".

In the UK the age of majority is 18. Amnesty International considers that the participation of children in hostilities amounts to a grave violation of their rights to life and to their physical and mental integrity.

The voluntary or compulsory recruitment and participation in hostilities, whether on the part of governments or armed groups, are all activities that ultimately jeopardize the mental and physical integrity of anyone below the age of 18. Amnesty International believes that the government is obliged to take special measures to ensure the protection of children's physical and mental integrity and urges the government to increase the minimum age of recruitment and deployment to 18.

By June 2003, Amnesty had won important concessions from the British Government, which had signed what's described as an Optional Protocol, in which it declared that the minimum recruitment age of 16 reflected the minimum school-leaving age. While the Protocol stated that no one under 18 should take part in hostilities, it fell short of the minimum recruitment age of 18 that Amnesty wanted.

The Government had also stated that safeguards for children were maintained by the practice of informing the potential recruit about the nature of military duties, ensuring the decision to enlist was voluntary, and obtaining free and informed consent from the parents.

It's worth dwelling on each of those safeguards and wondering whether the Government truly believed they were as robust as, perhaps, they would have us accept. Let's change the order slightly.

Ensuring that the decision to enlist was voluntary?

Jason came home that fateful day with two copies of his joining up papers for Syd to sign – the first to put in front of him, the second to replace the first set if his father tore them up.

Obtaining free and informed parental consent?

As far as he was concerned, Jason had given Syd a chance to provide his free and informed consent by bringing those two sets of documents. Syd's first choice was to sign or tear up the papers. His second choice was the same. The third choice, I remember Syd once telling me, was to accept that he'd lose his son anyway if he didn't sign.

Informing the potential recruit about the nature of military duties?

Jason, of course, was still 15 when he walked into the recruitment office. He was also headstrong, wilful, his own person. He knew his own mind. Would he have listened to the uniformed words of warning from the other side of the desk?

Unlikely. He was ripe for what followed – Junior Para. If we consider the words of the military psychiatrist Dr Morgan O'Connell, once Jason, Tommy, Scrivs, Neil and all the others climbed off the train at Aldershot, the likes of Des Fuller, Tom Camp and Ossie Howells continued to inform them about the "nature of military duties" in words of one syllable and in every colour from white to black.

Given the 'Band of Brothers' spirit they eagerly wrapped around themselves, the recruitment officer might as well have told the lads that they were heading for a Girl Guides jamboree. The promise of the jump training school's motto – 'Knowledge dispels fear' – dealt with the rest, until Brian Milne stepped on that mine. That's when fear took over. By then, it was too late.

"Amnesty's view is that for recruitment and participation in hostilities there should be a minimum age of 18," Amnesty's Martin MacPherson told me. "The fact that a minority of 16 to17-year-olds or even 15-year-olds may complete the training or even consent to the training is not the issue. The issue is that, just like in some civilian occupations, 'children' – persons under 18 – are prohibited from such employment, and that same protection should be extended to military service. I realise that this standard of 18 may, at times, seem arbitrary. But, in law, you have to set a standard somewhere and, by universal consensus, states have agreed to use the international bench mark of 18 for transition from child to adult."

He agreed that, although progress towards the objective was slow, it was moving in the right direction.

"During the drafting of the CRC (the United Nations Convention on the Rights of the Child) the UK was very difficult about raising the age above 15. That changed with the Optional Protocol, and practice seems to be that under-18s do not participate directly in conflicts.

"However, I think it will be many years before the recruitment age is raised to 18 years, given recruitment shortfalls for the armed forces."

And what about the wars in Iraq and Afghanistan?

"The MoD seems to be reluctant to give any guarantees that might cause it operational difficulties. However, in practice, the MoD does seem to have taken measures to keep under-18s out of hostilities. As far as we know, there are no under-18 UK troops in conflict areas."

Lord Tebbit's view about whether 17 was too young, morally, physically and mentally, to be sending a lad to war is somewhat different. Perhaps that's not surprising for a man who was a commissioned Royal Air Force officer at 19, leading other aircraft in flight and anticipating fighting in Korea.

He describes it as a process of "enforced growing up".

"If you go back a bit further, 200 years ago, you'll find that Nelson, at the age of 11, was taking command of a sloop. A lot of them at 17 are like that. You put stress on, some will collapse, the great mass will cope. And I think that's true of young soldiers.

"I don't think that's a total defence to the charge that they're too young in the society we live in. But I think it's a very good defence and, on balance, I think it carries.

"It's just that, in society, we're getting rather soft. If you legalise alcohol (for 17-year-olds) you legalise all sorts of peculiar social conduct. If you allow them to marry, then you're treating them as adults. As to voting, there I think you have to carry the fact that voting and fighting are different. They just are. And after all, if Jason had been 18 instead of 17-and-a-half, he wouldn't have had the occasion to vote. How many voters actually had a say whether we went into Iraq?"

Jason's name on those war memorials is a testimony to his courage, service and sacrifice, as well as to his parents' spirit and determination, of course. But there's another legacy that they might have cherished equally.

Brief though the reference to Jason was in all the Amnesty and Coalition campaigning, his story played its vital part in the fact that no under-18s have been killed in Iraq and Afghanistan since 2001.

It's scant consolation, perhaps. But we'll never know how many families have been spared their fate as a result, or the experiences crystallised by this brief passage from a conversation between Tommy and Doc McAllister, which sees them back together not long after dawn on June 12, after the Argentinians had fled Longdon towards Stanley and the enemy resistance had begun raining artillery shells down on the mountain instead. They're talking about a wounded Argentinian whose cries interrupted their brief moment of rest after the battle. I've left my questions in.

What happened with the Argentinian?

Tom: We were in the crevice and he was below and round, by the Bowl. Slightly more forward than the Bowl. He was just screaming out for water. It was constant. It had gone on for, I don't know…

Stu: … an hour, two hours.

Tom: We just ignored him. There were still gunshots going off where blokes would find an

Argentinian, or whatever. There was still that happening, so you just ignored things. You thought everyone was just dealing with it, because the majority of B Company were all in that Bowl area taking cover.

Was there ever an instruction about taking prisoners?

Stu: A message had come through (a few days earlier) that the Argentinians had pretended to surrender (at Goose Green), and as the guys walked forward to take the surrender, they'd put the machinegun back up and killed the guys. So we adopted a policy, unofficially, that, basically, we were going to shoot.

So when you (Stu) went back to deal with the Argentinian who was moaning…

Stu: I was going to shoot, 'cos I was fed up. It was bad for morale for all of us. It was giving our position away, it was hitting our morale and I was going to go and put a bullet in him. It was f***ing annoying.

Was he a threat to you?

Stu: He wasn't a threat. It was just that he was giving our position away and bringing our morale down. We'd got a couple of hours to cook a meal and he was yelling at us. He had a head wound. I think he'd been shot in the head.
Tom: I think he was the guy who'd been thrown down the mountain. When you relate to the head wound, I think Stu's being kind. I think he'd had an ear cut off.
Stu: Yeah, you're right. 'Cos he was thrown down.
Tom: I think he was the guy we (Tom and Jason) sat on (during the battle) and had kept quiet. Think of the terror that man must have been through. Now it's early morning, but it's daylight.
Stu: That guy dressed him. The guy with the moustache in that picture (he showed me a picture). He went over to him and dressed it with a field dressing. Dressed his ear. I think he saw Tony Kempster and was asking for water. He gave him a field dressing to suck on and then he was moved off. It was a really sad, sad situation.
Tom: We'd had enough.
Stu: I'd had enough. I was just going to go round and put a bullet in his head.

What stopped you?

Stu: When I saw his eyes, I couldn't… I couldn't shoot him.

Is that brother-in-arms? (Stu goes quiet. Tom steps in)

Tom: It's not that. It's more than that. You know you're still fighting the enemy. You still know there's more to find.

You become a human being.

Tom: He'd been through enough. He was no threat. I think we knew this bloke was the one that they'd done. He'd lay there for hours crying. It must have been terrifying. He'd obviously crawled from that position to ask for help. I just think you get to a point where you're like, F***ing hell....

You step over a line then, at some point, you step back?

Stu: You're driven by something, aren't you? You've got adrenaline, you've got hatred. You could see what they'd done to us. I couldn't do this.
Tom: This is like killing a lame duck.
Stu: It takes a lot to stare someone in the face and shoot them. When you put a gun... I had my SLR (rifle). When I put it to his forehead, and I was going to pull the trigger.... You see the eyes recognise what's happening, and they realise it's their fate. I thought *This is not good*. So I gave him some water, propped him up.
 "Just shut up!"
Just shut up! Know what I mean? That was all I could do. You was giving him water. These people had been killing us. I didn't feel good about that. I didn't feel good about that at all.
Tom: I remember Stu coming back.... and sitting there. And even when Stu said "I've had enough, I'm going to put him out" and he just went off, you didn't give a shit. It didn't matter to me. Just shut him up!

The nation expects people to pull battledress on, and to put themselves into the state to walk into battle with a bayonet fixed. In effect, we've asked them to step beyond a line. Should we be surprised when some don't conform to rules?

Tom: But I still think you've got a line. I don't think there's any worry about pulling the trigger when the bloke's trying to kill you and you understand the situation. That's an instant reaction. But this guy was just in a mess, and the basic fact was I was close to going down there and shutting him up. Stu just did that (gave him water) and came back. And there was no noise.

Is he sitting in Buenos Aires now, do you think?

Stu: I don't think he made it.

It's when you listen to the men who were there, on Longdon, feeling tracer fry the air above their heads, that it becomes the hardest to agree that sending 17-year-olds to the front line was right. The phrase 'stepping over the line' figured a lot in that part of our conversation. It's a reference to something crucially important to Jason's story, and the

Burts' pursuit of the truth.

Here's another sample, this time from Pte Mike 'Babycakes' Southall – the second youngest on Longdon – and Pte Tony 'Frog' Barlow. Their memories, of course, could easily have been Jason's.

Babycakes first. He was in 5 Platoon, so had that elevated view of 4 Platoon – Jason's unit – moving towards the enemy positions, including the machinegun post. His night had been eventful by the time Sgt McKay gathered that ad-hoc attack section together and moved forward:

There was an eruption of noise as an attack was obviously taking place, there was the noise of grenades and automatic fire and the screams of men charging. I fired into the rocky areas to my front, firing at the flashes of the enemy weapons and what I thought were enemy positions. The noise was horrendous, as everyone seemed to be firing all sorts of weapons at the same time.

I didn't hear a command to stop – it just, all of a sudden, went quiet. We could hear the cries for help coming from both sides. This was very upsetting. No matter what side they were from, they all wanted the same thing, their mothers. Very sad. I remember someone grabbing me and pulling me to follow them. It was L/Cpl Lewis, from 4 Platoon. We were going to find our injured and treat them.

As we got round the rocks, we could hear moaning from our left. We moved to the noise and found Beetle Bailey. He'd been shot three times, in the hip, hand and neck. We treated him as best we could. I was given the task of reassurance, just talking to him, basically. We left a man called Alhaji with him and went to find any others. It was at this stage that L/Cpl Lewis found Sgt McKay. He told me he was dead.

Sgt McKay was my platoon sergeant in training and had been really good to his platoon. I was very upset. I looked at the body and couldn't believe he was dead. He'd treated his recruits firm but fair, and was always the father figure in the platoon. Now, there I was on a mountain, 8000 miles from home, looking down on the body of a man I'd grown to like and respect very much. I really couldn't believe this was happening.

Within what seems minutes, Mick and the others were given the order to move back and help the wounded:

At some stage, somebody – I believe it was Jason Thomas or Steve Jelf, who both joined the Army with me and were only 17 themselves – told me the true horror of what had happened to our friends.

He told me Baz Barrett had been shot. He told me Jason was dead and that Scrivs was out in the open, wounded. He told me Ian had been wounded treating Neil and that they were both still out in the open. I heard, later, that CSM Weeks had tried to help them, but couldn't get them both

17: The death and life of Private Jason Burt

back. We were all told to get our ponchos out and start gathering in the casualties.

Myself, possibly Tommo, Dave Wakelin and Steve Jelf took all our heavy kit off. I think this was as a result of CSM Weeks telling everybody they would need to move very quickly.

We set off in search of our friends. We found them very quickly as Neil was screaming very loudly. The enemy were still firing at us but, fortunately, they were missing. We looked at Scrivs and assessed his condition. He was obviously dead. This was hard to take. We didn't have time to grieve. We had to help Neil, who was obviously very seriously injured.... The medic did all he could but, eventually, he lay there silent. I thought Thank God for that. He's going to be okay. But the Medic said: "That's it, he's gone."

It took a moment for this to register. Then it hit me and my heart sank. We'd all risked a lot to save Neil and now it was all in vain. I felt so sorry for Neil, and I felt cheated and angry that we'd done all we could. I asked the medic if he was sure there wasn't anything else we could do.

"Of course I'm f***ing sure!" he shouted.

I really was having difficulty coping. I'd lost three young friends and my recruit platoon sergeant. I felt very angry and sad at the same time. It was as if our young group of men were cursed or something. To this day, the events of those few minutes haunt me and I still feel very guilty and sad about not being able to help my friend any more than I did.

At some point in our conversation, Tony Barlow showed me the battered Instamatic 92 he'd carried with him across the Falklands, the smallest camera he could fit in his pocket. He found some of the pictures he'd taken with it, too:

I was on the front line, and my experience is you freeze, and you don't want to take another step further. You get to the part – and if anybody tells you different, they're lying – when it first kicks off you can't move. You're scared. You're a coward, to all intents and purposes.

Then, once you get over that barrier.... We was on this ridge and, when we went over that ridge, all hell let loose. It absolutely was bullets after bullets after bullets. To go over that ridge takes more balls than to walk off the Empire State Building. It was incredible. But, once you go over that line, you become fearless.

The only thing I can bring to mind in the whole thing I've seen in the years since is this. There's a scene in a film called Platoon, and Charlie Sheen's getting off the plane, and there's an old bloke walking past him going on the plane, and they cross. One is old and haggard and has a stare. The other is fresh and young. That's the only thing I can relate to.

Once you go over that line, you don't care. You'd walk through a screen of bullets. You'll walk through bombs going off. And that's how it happened. The longer the battle took place, the more

17: The death and life of Private Jason Burt

risks you took. Well, you didn't give a shit. You just got up and walked around. Snipers were still firing at you. It's just one of them things.

There's one sentence that – for all his uncertainty at Teal Inlet – could just as easily reflect Jason Burt's frame of mind when Sgt Des Fuller gave the command to 'advance' towards the Argentinians.

Once you go over that line, you become fearless.

Jason's instinct to tend Cpl Brian Milne in the minefield, and his part in the ill-fated McKay attack, might have scared him rigid, but he didn't flinch when Fuller yelled that order and they sprang towards the enemy, the four youngsters with Cpl Ned Kelly behind.

CHAPTER 16

THE FOG OF WAR

The fog of war. And the fog of dementia.

The first never cleared for Syd Burt before the second took its cruel grip as the 30th anniversary of the war approached.

All of the previous 29 had remained shaped by the conversation that had felt more bewildering with the frequent telling, the one that happened in the days after two Army officers had visited Petticoat Lane Market to break the news of Jason's death – 60 hours after he'd fallen on Mount Longdon – and Syd asked how he'd been killed. The information was a "minor detail". A clumsy response to a difficult question that, at that very minute, had no answer. The fog of Longdon had smothered the Burts' lives ever since.

Minor details.

Eyewitness stories.

Second-hand tales.

Contradictions.

Grief.

Anger.

Frustration.

Hope.

Pride.

Irresistibly cheap, easy headlines sign-posting ill-chosen words….

They knew all these things intimately.

Eventually, like a thief in the night, dementia robbed Syd even of the twists and turns that had made it so very hard to arrive at a reliable version of Jason's story, the claims and counter-claims that had marked his and Terry's search for something they could believe in about Jason.

The Sun: Three days after 3 Para's arrival home, *The Sun*'s misinformed *For Valour* story of Friday, July 9, 1982, was negligently short on detail as to why Jason's or Scrivs's actions on the mountain warranted a Victoria Cross to mark their gallantry. Ian McKay's name was missing from *The Sun*'s list. Nevertheless, the Burts' expectations had been raised.

3 Para: On their return, word filtered through that Jason had been with Sgt Ian McKay on what amounted to a suicidal charge on that Argentinian machinegun post. In the background was the presence of Cpl Ian 'Beetle' Bailey, a 5 Platoon NCO who'd been wounded in the attack. We can't be sure how his recollections about Jason reached the Burts, or whether he even played a part in the story coming out, but they believed it.

Tommy: A couple of weeks later, Tommy kept his promise to see the Burts and provide some details about how Jason had died. With his dad and Graham Collins by his side, he sat in Syd's Wentworth Street local and explained.

Jason hadn't been killed on a recce with Ian McKay. This story had come about by someone telling Syd an embellished version of events, "best intentions in mind and all that".

Tommy could see Syd listening to him but, from the outset, he knew it didn't fit what the Burts had already been told, and that it wasn't what Syd wanted to hear.

Derek Heaver: On Jason's 18th birthday, 3 Para's padre visited the Burts in Walthamstow and revealed that a letter home had been found in a chest pocket on Jason's body. He explained that they couldn't have that letter because it was blood-stained. The inference was that Jason had been shot in the chest, not – as Tom insisted – the head.

3 Para: Still desperate to know who was telling the truth, the Burts were bewildered by the number of 3 Para men at the various post-Falklands ceremonials who – it appeared – went out of their way not to meet them, including Beetle Bailey. Meanwhile, men like Tony Barlow, Ron Duffy and Major Argue unwittingly bolstered their mistaken belief that Jason would be awarded the VC by speaking in admiration of Jason's heroism on Longdon. None had witnessed him in action, however.

The London Gazette: The Falklands awards edition of Friday, October 8, 1982, told the story of Ian McKay's gallantry. In his citation, it said: "He was in no doubt of the strength and deployment of the enemy as he undertook this attack. He issued orders and taking three men with him broke cover and charged the enemy position:

> "The assault was met by a hail of fire. The Corporal was seriously wounded, a Private killed and another wounded. Despite these losses Sergeant McKay, with complete disregard for his own safety, continued to charge the enemy position alone."

So, a four-man party was involved, and a private was killed. No names given. And Beetle Bailey's Military Medal citation was even shorter on detail.

3 Para: If they'd had access to it, the battalion log would have offered the Burts more of an insight, but it contradicts Tommy's claim about where Jason was killed. It was written a few hours after the battle. It says that, after Lt Bickerdike was wounded:

> "Sgt Ian McKay at once took command of the platoon.... After quickly gathering a number of 4 Platoon and using Cpl Bailey's section, Sgt McKay determined to take out the .50 HMG, around

17: The death and life of Private Jason Burt

which the defensive position seemed to be organised. This weapon was in a substantial sangar and protected by several riflemen who dominated all approaches.

"In this attack, Sgt McKay and Pte Burt were killed and Cpl Bailey seriously wounded. Sgt McKay's body was found later in an enemy sangar. All displayed great gallantry under Sgt McKay's leadership, and enemy resistance was greatly reduced in this area, although the .50 HMG continued to make progress difficult."

The B Company log differs again. It says that Jason was killed by the same hail of fire that wounded Lt Bickerdike, before Sgt McKay launched his attack. Which is right?

Inquest: On Tuesday, November 16, hours after his coffin was brought ashore from the Sir Bedivere, Jason's inquest was opened and adjourned at Southampton's Law Courts. The official record stated the cause of death was "gunshot wound to head", and added "killed by injuries received as a result of enemy action". The Burts weren't there to hear or read the verdict. However, it underlined Tommy's testimony, not what they'd inferred from Derek Heaver's visit on Jason's birthday.

Had they been in the coroner's court, or read to the end of the *Walthamstow Gazette* report, they'd have been struck Lt Andrew Mills's evidence. He described the fighting to capture Longdon and the extent of the artillery bombardment that followed. Then he told the court how Jason had been shot dead when his company made a follow-up attack on an enemy dug-in after an attack in which Sgt Ian McKay died from gunshot and shrapnel wounds.

A follow-up attack on an enemy position AFTER an attack in which Ian McKay died? Maybe Tommy was right, after all.

The raft of books written about Longdon had also proved to be unreliable witnesses to Jason's last minutes. That's not a criticism of the storytellers. It's an observation of the reality that a battle is no place for the ordered, consistent and accurate recording of events. Men four feet apart will argue about the same incident. Look, it's what happens:

***Two Sides of Hell*:** Vince Bramley's second book, the follow-up to his controversial *Excursion to Hell*, states firmly that Jason was killed with Ian McKay, though he doesn't back up the claim by naming a source. Vince himself was in the machinegun platoon and didn't reach the position where McKay had fallen till some hours later. He has told me that his inclusion of Jason's name was based on a well-established B Company anecdote.

***With 3 Para to the Falklands*:** Graham Colbeck reveals that he came upon the body of a Para in the aftermath of the battle, and considered taking a picture of it, but thought better. He describes it as "kneeling against a rock with head bowed, rifle with fixed bayonet pointing across the ridge and an unpinned grenade clutched in his right hand". I'm not sure who this is, except that it doesn't come close to tallying with Tommy's description of how he left Jason.

Green-Eyed Boys: Adrian Weale includes a similar passage to Colbeck's. He describes Jason's body being found "nearby" to McKay's, propped up in a kneeling position because his bayonet had dug in the ground. The passage says Jason had "followed his platoon sergeant into the enemy trenches", and he'd been hit several times.

In a phone conversation with Weale, he identified his source. It was Vince Bramley – whose account was based on anecdote.

Beetle Bailey's also quoted as saying he was hit as he and *three* privates made their way across open ground.

Three privates? Two were killed, he says, while one made cover. He doesn't name them, but the other written accounts don't tally so far as the deaths of two privates are concerned.

3 Para Mount Longdon: The Bloodiest Battle: Finally, Jon Cooksey's book, which was published long after all the others. It muddies the picture even more.

He maintains that Ian McKay took Beetle Bailey and three privates with him – Jason, a Pte Jones and a Pte McLarnon. He says Jason was killed almost immediately, and Jones was wounded. McKay, Bailey and McLarnon charged the sangar, grenading and firing, until Bailey was hit. McLarnon, the account suggests, was the only man left standing.

Tony Barlow says it's possible McLarnon was with them, but he'd never heard that. He was part of Supply Company, not a rifleman. They used to travel to Manchester together on leave.

Can we trust that the account is true in any case?

I spoke with Jon Cooksey. He told me he'd gleaned the 'facts' from authors of books already published, and from Beetle Bailey. He'd taken them to be true. Those facts, of course, were based on second and third-hand information.

Put all those accounts together, and they do speak eloquently of one thing, however – the bloody slopes of Longdon were no place to record clinically and accurately the history of the battle. No one took notes. So what were Syd and Terry left with before dementia stole his life?

This. A history of Longdon that emerged from the word-of-mouth testimony of men who saw the same things happen, but from different angles, or who'd heard stories and passed them on. Men probably still base the story they tell on the one they settled on in the months after June, 1982, rather than the things they actually witnessed and heard that night. Well-meant. Sincere. But unreliable. Unintentionally, the cruellest game of Chinese whispers.

Then there's this.

Thousands of Falklands veterans boxed up their memories soon after the war. In went the sound of men screaming for their mothers, the squeal of incoming shells, the stench of cordite, shit-lined sewer-pits and congealed blood, silhouettes shifting in the shadows,

17: The death and life of Private Jason Burt

shattered limbs, and the frozen look of terror on a dead man's face.

The day those veterans walked on the green grass of home again, most closed the lid and slid the box into a dim corner of their minds. For many, that's where it will stay.

Not for everyone, however.

For some, darkness falls when rooms echo to sounds that have survived the years deep in that corner. Others stride on, blissfully unaware that there's a moment lurking when a noise, a movement, a smell, a death in the family, ill health, or even retirement will plunge them into a black hole. This trapdoor can open any time, on any of them.

I'm not sure Doc and Tommy have been to the blackest of black places since 1982, but they haven't always found life easy. In Estancia, a couple of days before the battle, Derek the Cleric had bored them rigid by sitting down to chat for half-an-hour as he delivered socks to 5 Platoon.

"How can you be a good Christian and go and kill people?" Doc enquired of him.

"We're like the Crusaders," is the answer Doc remembers. "We're on the right side... They believe in God, we believe in God. But we've got God on our side."

God? On a battlefield? If so, it's not just interesting but right to ask which way He was looking, that same night, as Cpl Stewart 'Scouse' McLaughlin wrote a remarkable, if grim, chapter in Para Reg history. Spending too long wondering what part the Almighty played in his actions, though, would be a diversion from the effect they had on the Burts' lives.

Sgt Ian McKay's storming of that .50 cal machinegun post might have been unsuccessful in its own right, but it was the turning point in the battle and – justifiably – earned a posthumous Victoria Cross.

However, by common consent, from the moment Cpl Brian Milne stood on that mine and unleashed a hellfire response from the woken Argentinians, it was McLaughlin who turned the tide, again and again and again.

I'm sure not many on the mountain that night would deny that, it if there were just one VC to be won – and there's rarely more than one awarded, such is the way the system works – it was McLaughlin, not McKay, who merited it.

What equips a man to act as he did?

Instinct?

Training?

A psychopathic death-wish?

A belief in invincibility?

Maybe all those things. I don't know. Never will.

Insanely heroic though McLaughlin was, there was no VC. For, after he'd been killed, padre Derek Heaver found 12 pairs of Argentinian ears in his webbing. To many in 3 Para, it's the only explanation for his name being absent from the very top of the awards made four months after the fighting ended. It isn't hard to grasp why.

I'm not sure where the majority will stand on the subject, but I'm in no rush to judge.

Wars draw extraordinary deeds from extraordinary men. We celebrate and honour them. We're prepared to accept one of ours bayoneting one of theirs, in our name, in the indescribable depth of battle.

So, when the savage heart beats stronger and longer in some than others, and the raw, animal killing instinct blinds him to a moral line scratched randomly across a snowy mountainside, can we condemn him without first condemning ourselves?

I know the answer I should give. But I know the one that nags in the back of my mind, and it's based on the truth that war isn't cricket. Perhaps, however, it's only those who've faced nights like Longdon who have the right to judge.

As it was, the story did the rounds of private Para conversations for years, until Vince Bramley's *Excursion to Hell* finally made it public in 1991. The book triggered a police investigation and unleashed on Bramley the hostility of many former comrades for tearing apart what they treasured most, the very thing that had dragged them up the mountain – the trust, the love and loyalty of their fellow Para.

Ask Tony Barlow about the ears, and he reflects on Bramley's book and reserves his scorn for the guys who made the Para rumour public, not for Cpl McLaughlin.

He bounced my question back at me when I visited him at his home near the Lancashire coast, the afternoon of a genteel Captain's golf tournament at his local golf club.

"Where do you draw the line? Guys trained to put a bayonet through someone need to be in a frame of mind where they'll follow orders to do what's necessary.

"This is the way I defend it. You're 16, 17, 18, 19 – all you do is train in an aggressive atmosphere to kill, to save life, your mates' lives. For your country. That's it. I'd have died for my country at 19. I wouldn't now. But first and foremost was my mate next to me. I'd die for him now. If they called me now, *I need you*, I'd come. I might not have spoken to him for 15 years. I'd be there. That's the comradeship you build.

"Where do you draw the line? You don't draw the line. What you don't do is go and tell your story afterwards and make some money on the back of them people who have fell. On the back of Jason, who got nothing for it.

"To me, Jason was a war hero. A hero that people should look up to, be proud of. Go to the cenotaph and lay a wreath. Go to his grave and clean it. Not just Jason's, Sgt McKay. Not just Sgt McKay, Crow, Westie, all them that died.

"They were only pub rumours. He (Vince Bramley) hasn't shown me a bloke who said 'I cut the ears off an Argie'. No one would, whether it happened or not. Not in the right mind."

But Tony wasn't on that part of the mountain, unlike Pte Mike 'Babycakes' Southall, one of Jason's other 17-year-old mates. He was in 5 Platoon. Scouse McLaughlin was his

17: The death and life of Private Jason Burt

corporal. The last time he saw him in one piece was in the Bowl, some time after Neil Grose died.

McLaughlin and Sgt John Ross were in an enemy bunker, chatting, watching the steam from a brew spiral into the freezing half-light of dawn. Without warning, an explosion shook the ground as a Mamba anti-aircraft missile struck their position. Southall hit the deck and heard the instant screams of yet more casualties. Pte Grant Grinham had lost most of his lower leg, Pte Andy Steadman had been hit by shrapnel, and McLaughlin had sustained serious back wounds. While he was walking down the mountain to be casevacced out, another artillery strike killed him.

"Scouse wasn't a man you argued with," Mick remembers. "He was a hard man who insisted on his men doing exactly what he wanted. He was a very well-respected soldier. I liked him. He was your typical Para. He'd get knocked down again and again but get up and into the fight.

"The stories of him having ears in his webbing are true. I saw him take at least two. He was familiar with the Gurkha technique of taking a trophy from your enemy dead. Unless you're there, you couldn't possibly understand how men behave when an enemy threatens your life. It's a brutal and a dirty business. To an outsider, it will look savage. That's because it is.

"Scouse inspired me throughout the battle. He was an amazing leader," he adds. "He saved many lives with his calming influence. I know he'd done wrong in regards to the ears, but I believe his actions far outweighed his crimes and he should have been honoured, in some way."

The significance of Scouse McLaughlin's story to Jason's 'truth' is worth recording.

If the men of 3 Para who were on the Longdon front line feel scarred, exposed and even betrayed by one of their own – and many do – why would they trust anyone else – a stranger, a parent, a journalist – asking questions about another comrade, namely Jason?

It was Cpl Ned Kelly who swapped thoughts with Ian McKay shortly before the sergeant's impromptu attack party made its suicidal dash towards the machinegun post.

It was also Kelly, a 4 Platoon corporal, who urged Jason back to his feet, after his ragged feet slipped on the icy ground a step into that final charge, a second or two before he was shot.

And it was Kelly who asked Tommy to examine his horrible stomach wound in the half-track medivac vehicle an hour or two later, before the Argentinians fled in the face of B Company's final push up the mountain.

But, for nudging 30 years, he maintained a silence.

It took the best part of two or three more years after interviews for this book began for Tommy to gradually draw the missing pieces of Longdon from the depths of his mind. As is often the case, a meeting or a phone call would sow seeds rather than prompt an immediate memory. In the weeks that followed, more would come back to him.

The first time I met Tommy, after his initial e-mail explaining Jason hadn't been with Ian McKay, we sat in the dining room of his beautiful Kent farmhouse and he agreed that there would have been time for Jason to join McKay on the machinegun post attack, and for him to return when it failed.

But he didn't believe that's what had happened.

We stood at his back door and he used the distance from there to a tree to measure the run into the killing zone that faced them when Des Fuller yelled "Fix bayonets and prepare to move!" down the line, and told them they'd be charging the .50 cal position that had ended McKay's one-way run.

Fix bayonets?

Five Platoon had done so on the startline, because they'd be fighting in close quarters. But 4 Platoon hadn't. Their route up the mountain was different.

Tommy admitted he was troubled by Des Fuller's command. First, the bayonet's weight would drop the muzzle of his weapon, and this wasn't the time to be firing low. Second, if they made it as far as the machinegun sangar, he'd be plunging his bayonet into some other mother's son. He didn't know if he could. He looked at Jason, lying close to his right.

"I'm not fixing my bayonet," Jason said. "Everyone who has so far's been shot."

A few minutes before I packed for the long journey home, Tommy had a hunch about one of the privates in McKay's attack party. It was an HQ Company messman called Pte Roger James, who'd been sent forward to find a rifle and help plug a big hole in 4 and 5 Platoons' ranks.

One other recollection would haunt Tommy a few days later. The bayonets. He hadn't had the time on the mountain to take in what Jason had meant. But, 22 years on, in the absence of red tracer ripping past his head, that changed.

The next time I sat in Tommy's dining room, chatting with him and Doc, he explained.

"After I'd spoken to you," he said, "I was down here, early one morning, and I realised the part I couldn't understand was the 'fix bayonets' bit. The conversation was seconds before we're moving round. Jase said to me: 'The people that have fixed bayonets have been killed or injured', or words to that effect. The only injury I'd been involved with was Brian Milne in the minefield. I just wonder whether Jase had been round first with Sgt McKay and come back."

The questions lined up to be asked, one after the other.

It would be logical for McKay to take Jason, wouldn't it?

Yes. He was Jason's platoon sergeant, and they'd been standing only a few feet apart when the decision was taken.

Who else would know? Cpl Bailey?

Unlikely, said Tommy. He was 5 Platoon. No reason to believe he'd recognise a young 4 Platoon Crow who'd been pulled from the shelter of the rock to move up into the killing field. And Bailey had been wounded. Left for dead.

Pte Roger James?

Because James had been wounded several times in his right leg, Tommy understood the Liverpudlian had been in McKay's hastily assembled attack party. It had always struck him that, if they were pulling a messman into the front line, things must have been bad.

"You don't shout 'Waiter!' and expect a man with a rifle to turn up, or vice-versa," he suggested.

But James couldn't be found.

Would Jason have had time to follow McKay on the attack and come back, un-noticed?

Once again glancing at his back garden as a yardstick, Tommy agreed he would. If Jason had been grabbed by McKay, he could have been at the back of the section that advanced up that single-file sheep-track, face on to the .50 cal. And he could have been forced back before he'd gone more than a short distance – though not before he'd seen the outcome, Bailey and James wounded, McKay killed.

"If so, why didn't he come back and tell me?" Tommy asked the next question before I could, and answered it.

"He was still in a state from Brian Milne," he suggested. "I'm sure he'd have still been shaking, in shock."

It wasn't hard to understand why, later, Tommy told me that he'd been troubled by thoughts of Longdon until recent months. But I wasn't expecting what followed.

He admitted tagging along with a mate on a visit to a medium. He can't remember why it had been arranged, but he soon found himself talking through her to Ian Scrivens, Neil Grose and Jason. It was like they'd never been parted, he told me. Grosey was fretting about his family. Scrivs was the calm, reassuring voice. Jason said they were having a great time. *Typical*, Tommy thought.

The bare statistics of Longdon tell a story of their own, even if they hide a million minor details. Twenty-two men were killed in the battle that, by common consent, wiped out the Argentinians' final resistance. Forty-three men were wounded, and 21 were recorded as trench-foot casualties.

However, there's one particular consequence of places like Longdon that I'd never considered in relation to the lads who made it through that night. Many, like Tony Barlow, closed the lid on his box of Falklands memories soon after 1982 and slid it into his own dim corner. In reality, Tony's box is a suitcase that's kept in his garage. It comes out rarely but, when it does, there isn't a photo or piece of paper that fails to drop him into the middle of

1982. Then he can step in any direction.

He admits that, after he overcame the fear of dying on the mountain, he lost the plot.

"I'd have killed anything. You get your paralysed fear, and you're so scared of dying. Then, all of a sudden, you accept it. You think *F*** it!* It's a massive weight off your shoulders, but what you can't live with is the burden that you survived. How d'you get back to having that fear of dying again?"

He went through a stage of doing extreme sports, base-jumping off cliffs, bridge jumping, thinking *I'm going to die here!*, grateful that he wasn't married and didn't have kids, and clueless as to how the lads who did were coping.

"How do you do it? I'm still lost," he asked. It was an important question for a man who now fights fires.

"People have survived because I've had that lack of fear. I've done stupid, stupid things to save lives. I've sat back afterwards and thought *What the flipping hell did I do there?*"

Dr Morgan O'Connell has lost count of the Falkland veterans who've asked themselves that question. Over the years, they formed a constant trickle of men and women who walked through the door of his study at Tyrwhitt House, Leatherhead. It's one of three centres run by Combat Stress, the Ex-Services Mental Welfare Society that treats about 600 veterans each year – the youngest in their early 20s, the oldest in their 70s – including Paras for whom Longdon isn't over.

"The first engagement with the enemy is the most frightening," Morgan told me. "After that, you almost get that *Well, I should be dead already, so what the hell!*

"What's the difference between careless and courageous? The result may be the same, that you get an award, and that you die in the process of getting the award. Or you survive and you think *How did I survive? I don't want to do that again.*"

There's a greater motivating force in such situations than living, however. Remember that Terry Burt's instinct, as a mother, was to write begging Jason to run if his life was in danger.

"The key point is *I don't want to be seen to be a wimp*. Every instinct is to run away. His mother was right. When you're in danger, run away. But that's where training comes in, and particularly when you're with your mates."

Jackie O'Meara – Jason's cousin – knows what it's like to be confronted, out of the blue, by a veteran in the grip of his Falklands demons. She was 19 when she met a guy in the Royal Oak.

"He really was not on this planet," she said. "Another bloke came in with him and said: 'Sorry, he's been like this ever since coming back from the Falklands'. He was still young, about 20, 21. He'd totally lost it. He couldn't look you in the eye. He was shaking. He'd get up, he'd wander round. He'd get drunk just like that. He was shouting at people.

17: The death and life of Private Jason Burt

"It was all because... as soon as I said I knew someone there, he said: 'I lost a friend as well'. He told me who he lost. It was Jason. I never knew his name. Everyone at that time knew Jason Burt. All I remember is that, for a young fella, he had a very big moustache. That's what I kept looking at."

The Burts' attitude to Mrs Thatcher has been conditioned by Jason's attitude towards the Task Force being sent to reclaim stolen property, as well as her response – one mother to another – to their plea for her to allow Jason to come home.

But Jackie has no doubt where she stands on the Iron Lady.

"My two children have been brought up knowing that she was the reason Jason died," she says. "My girl's 13. They don't have much to do with Thatcher, 13-year-old girls. But she knows who she is and that's the murderer of Jason."

Jackie might not speak for everyone where Mrs Thatcher's concerned. But, to my ears, she does when it comes to Jarvis.

"This focus was on Jason. It was on big brother. I felt for Jarvis, 'cos I thought if it was my brother that wasn't coming home.... He did struggle. Very bad. A lot more than everyone knew. He's a big man, but he's a soft man. He hurts easy."

Among all the people closest to Jason's family, at any point since the war, it's Tommy who best understands what drove Syd and Terry to seek their 'truth'. He struggled with the anguish of not being able to provide them with the crucial item of evidence.

In the years before Syd slowly succumbed to dementia, Tommy always maintained that, if someone admitted they'd seen Jason go with McKay, Syd would have gone straight on to the Army, insisting he should be given a medal. It would have been confirmation that his son was a hero.

"But look what he did," Tommy says. "He went to Brian Milne's aid and he was shaking. He was the first one there. He offered him his own morphine. He ran through that minefield without thinking. It was what he saw when he got there that did for him.

"And he moved the second that Des Fuller yelled 'Charge!' He slipped and got back up. I don't know whether he fired a round. He might have got one or two off. But he was advancing, head on towards a machinegun, when he was killed.

"If that's not a hero, I don't know what is."

17: The death and life of Private Jason Burt

An Inquisition taken for our Sovereign Lady the Queen at Law Courts, Civic Centre, in the Parish of Southampton in the said County on the Sixteenth day of November 19 82 adjourned to Tues day the 14th day of December 1982 at in the noon before me, RODERICK NEILL MACKEAN one of the Coroners of our Lady the Queen for the said County on view by me of the body of

JASON STUART BURT

as to his death; and I, the said RODERICK NEILL MACKEAN do say: That the said JASON STUART BURT died on the Twelfth day of June 19 82 at Mount Longdon area outside Port Stanley, Falkland Islands

~~in the said County~~ and that the cause of his death was: GUNSHOT WOUND TO HEAD KILLED BY INJURIES RECEIVED AS A RESULT OF ENEMY ACTION.

IN WITNESS whereof I the said RODERICK NEILL MACKEAN have hereunto subscribed my hand and seal the day and year first above written.

AND I, the said RODERICK NEILL MACKEAN do further say that the said JASON STUART BURT at the time of his death was a male person of the age of 18 years and a Private in the 3rd Battalion of the Parachute Regiment.

17: The death and life of Private Jason Burt

(Above) The 3 Para graves at Teal Inlet, where the fallen were initially laid to rest and (below) a national newspaper story published after the Argentinian surrender telling of Neil and Jason's deaths

17: The death and life of Private Jason Burt

Four of the Falkland Heroes will get VC

By JAMES LEWTHWAITE

SIX valorous names have been recommended for Falklands VCs. And it is from these six that the final four or more will be chosen.

Dozens of names have already gone forward for other bravery awards, especially the Distinguished Service Order.

But for Britain's fighting forces it is the VC that holds pride of place wherever servicemen meet to talk of war.

The Sun has already revealed that LT-COL H. JONES—the commander of the Second Paras—will definitely become a posthumous VC.

The heroic 42-year-old officer was killed leading a successful raid on two machine-gun nests in the victorious assault on Goose Green.

Chosen

Another candidate for the medal died with him in the death-or-glory charge — 18-year-old STEPHEN DIXON, of Basildon, Essex.

Stephen was one of 17 paratroops who volunteered for the raid—although they knew it was suicidal.

His mum Linda said: "My son stepped forward and was chosen. He died a hero."

Risks

Among the others who may have been recommended are:

Bomb disposal expert JIM PRESCOTT, who was blown to pieces trying to defuse a 1,000lb bomb which failed to explode after hitting HMS Antelope.

Staff Sgt. Prescott of the Royal Engineers was working partly under water when the bomb suddenly exploded—sinking the ship.

His father said at home in Hindley, near Wigan, Lancs: "He wanted to serve his country, and do his duty. He knew the risks."

CAPT. JAMES "SAM" SALT of HMS Sheffield, the destroyer sunk by a deadly Exocet missile.

Friends

For five hours Capt Salt and his men struggled in appalling heat and smoke to try to save the ship.

The modest sea-dog from Birdham, Sussex, said later:

"We are no heroes. How can you be a hero when you come home without a ship?"

LT NICHOLAS TAYLOR, 22, killed attacking Goose Green in his Sea Harrier.

Paratroops IAN SCRIVENS and JASON BURT, both 17, who died in the bloody hand-to-hand battle for Mount Longdon just hours before the ceasefire.

Killed

The two friends—they had been cadets together—had only been fully-fledged members of the Third Battalion of the Parachute Regiment for four months.

They were two of the 22 Red Devils killed in the fight to recapture Mount Longdon.

The Sun Says—Page 6

Colonel H. Jones, led "suicide" raid

Capt Sam Salt, fought to save ship

Pilot Nicholas Taylor—died in jet

Jason Burt... died at Mount Longdon

Stephen Dixon... a proud volunteer

Sgt James Prescott... bomb victim

'He knew the risks but did his duty'
JAMES PRESCOTT'S FATHER YESTERDAY

The Sun's ill-informed story that sparked decades of despair for the Burts, a story so well-informed that Sgt Ian McKay isn't even mentioned!

17: The death and life of Private Jason Burt

(Above) Para burial parties await the start of the funerals at the Regiment's Aldershot cemetery, as families move towards their hillside position. (Below) One of the many cuttings that the Burts saved in the wake of Jason's death

Hero's medal sent in plain brown box

THE ANGRY mother of a Walthamstow Falklands hero has written to the Prime Minister about the way she received her son's medal.

Mrs Terry Burt said her son Jason's campaign medal had been sent in an envelope in a plain brown cardboard box.

"I am terribly upset," she said this week. "There was no covering letter and the medal wasn't properly inscribed. The people who sent it didn't even wrap it in wadding for protection."

Jason Burt of the 3rd Paras was only 17 when he died in one of final battles for the Falklands.

Said Mrs Burt of Garner Road: "I think it is an insult to my son's memory. At least they could have put it in a proper presentation box. And the fact they didn't even put his battalion down in even more upsetting. All it says is Jason Burt, Paras."

Mrs Burt has also written to Prince Charles who is honorary Colonel in Chief of the Parachute Regiment.

She added: "I wanted to take it from his coffin after Jason was buried at Aldershot. But I was told I couldn't because it had to be registered by the army. An officer told me it would be specially mounted because Jason had died in battle. Now it has arrived like this and I find it heartbreaking that they couldn't have shown more consideration."

A Ministry of Defence spokesman said: "We have been looking into the type of boxes medals are sent out in and have ordered better ones for the future. However, these have not arrived yet and we thought it best to despatch Jason's without delay."

The spokesman added: "The medal was properly inscribed. We don't put down men's battalions because they belong to the regiment and can be moved around.

"If Mr Burt wants the medal mounted I'm sure the Parachute Regiment would be only too willing to help."

Heartbroken: Mrs Terry Burt with Jason's medal.

17: The death and life of Private Jason Burt

(Above) Claire pictured with Terry and Syd Burt during a visit with the author. (Below) Jason's lovingly tended grave, alongside that of Sgt Ian McKay, at the Parachute Regiment's Aldershot military cemetery

CHAPTER 17

EPILOGUE

The truth that Syd and Terry Burt had been hunting, for almost 30 years, began to emerge one cold and frosty morning in 2012.

I'd been swapping emails with Tommy's daughter, Cher, over the New Year. What she wrote in the one that dropped into my Inbox on January 22 was unexpected. Totally.

"I have some information that may interest you," she said. "I was over mum's and dad's last night. Out of the blue, dad was contacted by a Jim Kelly on Facebook, who turns out to be Ned Kelly's son."

Tommy, remember, was known as Jason by his family, Mark by his acquaintances, and Tommy by his Para mates.

Jim Kelly 05 January at 21:55

Hi Mark

I have recently come on to facebook, I have read your book and briefly met you at a service in Aldershot a couple of years ago. My Dad is Ned Kelly. Over the years I have read as much as I can find about the Falklands campaign. Particularly 3 Para's involvement naturally.

I was wondering if you had any photo's, literature that talks or shows my Dad. As you probably know more than me my Dad is a man of few words and seems to have been camera shy in his Army days. Sod that was a great read and thanks for attending to my Dad on Mount Longdon. Kind regards Jim Kelly

Mark Eyles-Thomas 08 January at 11:49

Great to hear from you Jim and I remember meeting you at the 'dumhead service' at Aldershot cemetery, trust you and your family are well.

With regards to photos and the like - it wasn't that Dad was particularly camera shy or anything like that but technology back then wasn't what it is today. We only had the old style plastic kodak instamatics which required film and they were a pain in the arse to carry round and the picture quality wasnt very good.

There was also the concerns of security so you were limited as to what was considered okay/appropriate to take a picture of. Now add the fact that you are a crow (new boy) in the battalion - if I was to take a picture of your Dad he would have been more than likely to rip my head off and shove the camera up my backside.

There may be one or two older lads that may be able to help you with your quest - Brian Milne is an obvious choice (he is on facebook) and John 'Taff' Hedges is another (on facebook as well), Kev Capon was another NCO who was a keen photographer but I havent a contact for him (sorry) maybe Brian or Taff has. Im sure they may have some photos of Dad and may also have some suggestions and/or contacts with other older lads that may also be able to help.

Thanks for commenting on the book, much appreciated, with regards to helping Dad no probs it was what was required at that time and we can only thank our lucky stars that the outcome for Dad was a good one.

Jim Im sure many people have told you in the past but for the record your Dad was a very special bloke - very strong and an exceptional NCO - I know in the book I refer to Ned as a fella that you didn't want to mess with but to us youngsters he was inspirational, everything a paratrooper should be. I trust life is being kind to him.

Actually there is one small point you may be able to help me with - most recently an author called Mark Higgitt wrote a book for Jason Burts family - the book is not in the public domain just for family and close friends.

In the book they are trying to resolve an issue of whether Jason was killed with Ian McKay VC or on the assault that followed Ians recce/attack. I have on numerous occasions told the family that Jason was killed on the follow up attack but haven't been able to substantiate this in any way.

This is where you could help. When we went to assault the position after Ian was killed we had to charge the guns. On the charge Jason Burt slipped on the rocks and your Dad spurred him on (helped him regain his feet).

Although this seems a trival action or minor detail it substantiates what I have told the family and proves without any doubt that Jason was on the follow up assault. I know you have said Dad is a man of few words but if Dad could say to you that he remembers helping Jason to regain his footing and you could pass this on to me I will ensure that the family receive this info.

I cannot tell you how much this would help them with their personal closure. Both are now getting frail and this small piece of information will without doubt assist them with the loss of their son.

If Dad doesn't want to talk to you about it I understand and the matter is best left. If Dad doesn't remember I also understand as we were the new boys and Dad was an NCO so I'm

17: The death and life of Private Jason Burt

unsure whether he will recall this event.

Anyway all the very best and I trust that are paths will cross again in the future. Perhaps next time we'll have a pint or two!

Remember me to Dad and pass my regards on to him. I trust 2011 is kind to him and his family. All the very best for now. Please feel free to contact at any time. Tom (Mark Eyles-Thomas)

Mark Eyles-Thomas *09 January at 16:11*

Did you get the photos Jim?

Jim Kelly *09 January at 19:08*

Yes thanks Tom, much appreciated.
Just been round Dad's for dinner and dug out a few old photo's but none from the Falklands.

I asked him about Jason Burt, he confirmed that Jason was with him on the assault after Ian McKay's assault.

Mark Eyles-Thomas *09 January at 19:18*

Thanks for that Jim. I'll pass it on.
Regards as always

One Sunday, a couple of weeks later, Tommy and I finally managed to find an hour or so to chat on the phone. He was anxious that I was able to write to the Burts and provide one of the two remaining missing pieces of Jason's puzzle. For him, of course, it marked the end of 29 years of anxiety – attached the fact that it was he, and he alone, who had contradicted the initial claim that Jason had died alongside Ian McKay.

So that left just one piece of the puzzle – did Jason go with Ian McKay and fall back when his platoon sergeant, Beetle Bailey and Roger James were all hit?

Tommy felt he had a lead there, too. He'd been in conversations with another Longdon veteran, Jimmy 'Scouse' O'Connell, who'd laid his hands on transcripts of 3 Para's radio transmissions that dreadful night. I dropped Scouse an email, asking if the fruits of his research meant he'd be able – and willing – to close the door for Syd, Terry and Jarvis. His answer was the one I expected, though not the one I hoped for:

Hi Mark, I am sorry but I am trying to write a book my self and spent hours and a lot of money

traveling up and down the UK meeting and chatting with these blokes, so I am afraid all the stuff that I have researched I will keep to myself as I am sure you will understand, that this sort of stuff has been hard done I myself lost the right side of my face that night,
So I am sorry but I cannot help, bye for now Jimmy

Three years on, the wait was over. Scouse had finished his account, a book called *Three Days in June*, a remarkable work shaped by the names that had echoed around the Burts' living room since 1982 that confirmed what Jason had been doing in his final minutes.

How fitting for that piece to be slid into place by a man who fought alongside Jason.

And how sad that Syd was never able to share its secrets. He died just months before Scouse finally delivered his truth:

Corporal Ian 'Beetle' Bailey
As we prepared to move out, I heard Sgt McKay shout up to Cpl McLaughlin: "Scouse! Prepare to give covering fire." As we moved out, we went into extended line. On the left was Pte Tony McLarnon, L/Cpl Roger James, myself and then Sgt McKay.
We'd only gone a short distance when we came under fire from multiple positions. We had no choice but to attack them.
We grenaded the first position and went past it without stopping – just firing into it.
I'd lost sight of Roger James and Tony McLarnon. I thought they'd been wounded or were dead. That's when I got shot from another position, which was about three metres away.
At first, I thought I'd tripped, but a round had struck me square in the right hip. It spun me around and I fell to the floor.
Sgt McKay was still charging on to the next position, but there was no one else with him.
I then heard a grenade explode. I noticed that the firing had stopped as suddenly as it had started and it was now very quiet. I was lying on my back, looking up at the starry Falklands night sky. I then heard voices shouting "Are you all right, lads?"
I was lying on my back and in great pain and decided to roll over on to my stomach. I heard someone shout something. Then, suddenly, there was another burst of fire. One round hit me across the back of my neck and a green tracer round (Argentinian) struck me in the middle finger of my right hand.

Roger James and Tony McLarnon had run to the left when Beetle Bailey was hit and continued firing at the position. Then they, too, heard the grenade explosion, followed by a burst of automatic fire.

Then it went quiet. Ian McKay had just been killed.

In my search for both, I'd drawn blanks. In the McKay attack, James was wounded in the foot. He always seemed to be one address ahead of me. Eventually, I ran out of leads.

The closest I came to finding McLarnon was the name of a solicitor who'd represented him when – I understand – he'd fought to gain compensation for the Post Traumatic Stress Disorder he'd suffered. Sadly, according to Scouse O'Connell, Tony died in 2009.

The final word goes to Ned Kelly, the last man to speak with Jason. Tommy paints a fearsome picture of him, a fiery character to the eyes of a 17-year-old. I suspect that's simply because he was a fearsome, fiery character. Nothing less. A Para.

In the wake of Ian McKay going missing, he and Sgt Des Fuller hastily hatched a plan to push on up the mountain, through the killing field, to take B Company's objective. Ned had Jason next to him as his section led out, with Fuller's men next and Cpl John Lewis's section to the rear.

In extended line, they'd advanced about 20 yards and round to the right towards the main rock face when a wall of fire erupted in their faces.

"We came under intensive fire," Ned told Scouse O'Connell. "It seemed to be coming from everywhere. Jason Burt was shot next to me, and then I was shot. I fell to the ground. The machinegun carried on firing, but they didn't seem to be able to hit us once we were lying on the ground.

"Eventually, when the firing subsided, I saw the dark shape of a body lying by me, and I said to someone: "It's young Jason."

3 PARA ROLL OF HONOUR

The following comes from a variety of sources. I'm not in a position to claim all of it is accurate....

- Pte Richard Absolon 19 (D Co) Killed on June 13 by mortar fire

- Pte Gerald Bull 19 (A Co 2P) Killed by shell in June 12 daylight bombardment from Port Stanley

- Pte Jason Burt 17 (B Co 4P) Shot during June 12 advance

- Pte John Crow 21 (B Co 5P) Shot in chest on sheep track as part of mixed 4Pn and 5Pn section on June 12, after Jason died

- Pte Mark Dodsworth 24 (B Co 6P) Wounded before Jason on June 12. Died from chest and thigh wounds

- Pte Anthony Greenwood 22 (B Co 6Pn) Shot in firefight alongside L/Cpl David Scott on June 12

- Pte Neil Grose 18 (B Co 4Pn) Died in RAP on June 12 from lung wound sustained during advance in which Jason fell

- Pte Pete Hedicker 22 (Milan Section) Killed on June 12 alongside Pte Phil West and Cpl Keith McCarthy by 106mm fire

- L/Cpl Peter Higgs 23 (Patrol Co) Killed on June 12 by a mortar round walking with wounded Cpl Scouse McLaughlin to RAP

- Cpl Stephen Hope 27 (A Co) Shot on June 12 by sniper as A Co approached their objective

- Pte Timothy Jenkins 19 (A Co 2P) Shot by sniper on June 12

- Pte Craig Jones 20 (9 Sqdn REME) Killed on June 12 (daylight) by shell blast that killed Alex Shaw

- Pte Stewart Laing 20 (Support Co) Shot on June 12 by sniper while trying to save Cpl James Murdoch

17: The death and life of Private Jason Burt

- L/Cpl Chris Lovett 24 (B Co medic) Killed by mortar fire
- Cpl Keith McCarthy 27 (Milan Section) Killed on June 12 by the 106mm fire that also killed Pte Phil West and Pte Pete Hedicker
- Sgt Ian McKay 29 (B Co 4P) Killed on June 12 attacking machinegun post
- Cpl Stewart McLaughlin 27 (B Co 5P) Killed on June 12 by mortar round walking with L/Cpl Peter Higgs to RAP after being wounded
- L/Cpl James Murdoch 25 (B Co 6P) Shot by sniper on June 12, before Jason. Pte Stewart Laing killed trying to save him
- L/Cpl David Scott 24 (9 Sqdn) Shot in firefight alongside Pte Tony Greenwood on June 12
- Pte Ian Scrivens 17 (B Co 4P) Shot by sniper while tending wounded Neil Grose with Pte Jason Thomas
- Cpl Alex Shaw 25 (REME) Killed on June 12 by mortar in attack that fatally wounded Pte Craig Jones
- Pte Phillip West 19 (Milan Section) Killed on June 12 by same 106mm fire that killed Pte Pete Hedicker and Cpl Keith McCarthy
- Cpl Scott Wilson (9 Sqdn REME) Killed on June 12 by explosion, shortly after death of L/Cpl Chris Lovett

RIP

Printed by CreateSpace, an Amazon.com company
Available from Amazon.com

www.ingramcontent.com/pod-product-compliance
Lightning Source LLC
Chambersburg PA
CBHW081327090426

42737CB00017B/3050